W9-AKC-967

In These Girls,
Hope Is a
Muscle

Also by the author:

The Heart Is an Instrument: Portraits in Journalism

In These Girls, Hope Is a Muscle

Madeleine Blais

THE ATLANTIC MONTHLY PRESS
NEW YORK

Copyright © 1995 by Madeleine Blais

All rights reserved. No part of this book may be reproduced in any form or by any electronic or mechanical means, including information storage and retrieval systems, without permission in writing from the publisher, except by a reviewer, who may quote brief passages in a review.

Grateful acknowledgment is made to the following for permission to reprint previously published material:
The Boston Globe: for an article by Bruce Schecter. Reprinted courtesy of The Boston Globe.
The Daily Hampshire Gazette: for passages from various Gazette articles. Reprinted courtesy of the Daily Hampshire Gazette.
A portion of this book originally appeared as an article in The New York Times Magazine. Reprinted by permission.

Published simultaneously in Canada
Printed in the United States of America

FIRST EDITION

Library of Congress Cataloging-in-Publication Data

Blais, Madeleine.
    In these girls, hope is a muscle / Madeleine Blais.—1st ed.
    ISBN 0-87113-572-8
    1. Basketball for girls—Massachusetts—Case studies.
2. Amherst Regional High School (Amherst, Mass.)—Basketball.
I. Title.
GV886.B53   1995   796.323'62'09744—dc20   94-30394

Design by Laura Hammond Hough

The Atlantic Monthly Press
841 Broadway
New York, NY 10003

10 9 8 7 6 5 4 3 2

For John

Acknowledgments

The Hurricanes and their extended families all deserve a special debt of gratitude for allowing me into their lives. For their support of this project, I would also like to express my gratitude to several students and former students at the University of Massachusetts: Lisa Curtis, Luke Erickson, Michele Fanzo, Sam Kennedy, Sarah Levesque, Amy Richards, and especially Julia Richardson. Thanks are also due to Howard Ziff, the chairman of the journalism department, and Lee Edwards, dean of the College of Humanities and Fine Arts, who offered nurturance during a crucial point in the composition of this work. Nick Grabbe of the Amherst Bulletin and E. Douglas Banks and Marty Dobrow of the Daily Hampshire Gazette were most generous about providing files from their papers. The students in Janet Kaye's fall 1993 writing class at Hampshire College shared insights about their campus, as did Diana Wetherall about her alma mater, Smith College, and Kim Townsend about the Amherst College campus, where he teaches. Susan Snively, also of Amherst College, shared her expertise on the life and work of Emily Dickinson. David Kaplan was an invaluable source of information about the entire coaching scene in Amherst. Others who provided assistance are Sara Eckert and Tom

Barr at Cravath, Swaine and Moore. This book grew out of a piece that was originally published in the *New York Times Magazine*, and I would like to especially thank my editors there, Jack Rosenthal and Margaret Loke, for their initial encouragement.

Prologue

The first member of the Amherst Lady Hurricanes that I met in person was Kristin Marvin, the team's starting center. Our regular sitter couldn't make it one day, and Kristin was the sub from the bench. We were living in a contemporary house surrounded by our contemporaries on a hill in the northern end of Amherst, Massachusetts, a combination college town and farming community. Kristin lumbered into the house in her big confident way. The confidence came in part from her memory of visiting the site when the house was under construction. Her stepfather is a contractor, and she sometimes accompanied him on the job. She was sure she knew which nails were hers.

Unlike some of our sitters, who were content concocting homemade Play-Doh or teaching the children how to make bracelets out of yarn or the words to old songs like "If You Wanna Be Happy," Kristin had a different style. She was tall and ranging, drawn to action and to the outdoors, especially to the communal hoop at the end of our driveway shared by the other five houses in the neighborhood.

"Hey," she said to our son, who was about ten at the time, "let's go shoot some baskets."

He gave Kristin the same skeptical look he'd given his pal

Timmy's mother, Kacey Schmitt, who teaches gymnastics and whom we'd begged to do a handstand in our yard one day. After she'd executed the move with perfection, he'd exclaimed with puzzlement, "But moms can't do that!"

"What do you mean, moms can't? I'm a mom, aren't I?" Kacey shot back.

But my son, using me as the standard, was, of course, right.

I grew up pretty much a sports virgin. I did play outdoors, skating on ponds and sledding in the winter, building forts in the nicer weather, but I was never on a team. I was so completely removed from the world of organized competition that to this day there are strange gaps in my vocabulary. When someone says, "Maybe we should just punt" or "You gotta keep your eye on the guy on third," I often nod and only pretend to understand.

I used to think my case was extreme because my father had died when I was five and my childhood home was Irish Catholic and woman-heavy. I did not know how to throw or catch a ball, but I did learn women's lore, knew arcane trivia, such as that the way to revive a stale baguette is to sprinkle it with water and then heat it in an oven, or that a self button is one covered in the same fabric as the garment it adorns. But there was little of the musk of men, nor of that drone of games on the radio that infiltrate one's consciousness so that after a while, without realizing it, you find yourself knowing about the day in 1951 when Bobby Thompson's home run was heard around the world or when Alan Ameche scored from the three to win the greatest football game ever played for the Baltimore Colts or how in 1961 Roger Maris hit sixty-one to break Babe Ruth's single-season home-run record. That whole roiling sweat-filled world of streaks and fabulous finishes, triple plays and incredible shots and touchdown runs, was as unknown to me as the moon plus China.

2

But now I recognize that something larger than my individual circumstances was the reason for my sports ignorance. During the fifties gender division was practiced as a kind of apartheid, and the older I got the more I realized my experience was more typical than not. Leaving aside for the moment the question of whether I possessed any native athletic talent, which is doubtful, I acknowledge that there was nothing in my life of a team nature that supported even the free expression of brute energy, of which I have plenty.

At some Catholic girls' high schools, you could find nuns who believed in sports, if only as a tonic against hormones. But my parochial school had only one athletic goal: that we, the girls of Ursuline on Plumtree Road in Springfield, would retain our title as the best marchers in the Saint Patrick's Day parade held in Holyoke. Starting on a gray lug of a January day, we would spend our gym time outdoors in the parking lot, marching in formation through the slush, so that on the day of the parade we would shine with militaristic precision. In our green gabardine block-pleat skirts, white camp shirts with the collars always outside the gray blazers, nylons, and loafers—and especially with our white gloves and green berets bobby-pinned to our skulls— we would proceed to once again win the very award that no one else seemed to even want.

Taking huge groups of girls and coordinating their physical movements was also the goal of the athletic program at the College of New Rochelle, which for a certain period of time in the sixties competed favorably with other schools in the somewhat soggy arena of synchronized swimming. We coordinated our frog kicks and our underwater arabesques to themes: the Trojan War when I was a sophomore, the Roaring Twenties during my senior year.

This recital was known as Swimphony.

A little marching, a touch of immersion. That was about it.

If I felt pained by the absence of a certain kind of opportunity in this regard, I was less aware of it than, say, a woman like Kacey, who had enormous natural prowess and finesse. After her acrobatics, Kacey told the admiring children:

"You don't know what it was like back when your mom and I were girls."

Of course they didn't; one of the great burdens of childhood is to be held responsible for the felonies of one's forebears.

For whatever reason, most likely the fact of that perfect flip of hers distinguishing an otherwise sorry lawn in early spring, the children's eyes did not glaze over at the prospect of yet another diatribe about the olden days.

"We didn't get the encouragement we give you boys. If you were a girl and you liked sports, you could be a cheerleader. If you did play a team sport, it was intramural, and you got to practice only during those times when for whatever reason the boys didn't need the gym. No one went to your games. Even if you wanted to play hard, you were discouraged by the rules. In basketball you were allowed to dribble only three times. Only one girl, the rover, could play the whole court. That was always me because I had so much excess energy. Our uniforms were—get this—skirts."

As for myself, I was a bookish sort and built up my reading muscles, perhaps as a compensation, like the blind person with great hearing.

For reasons still a bit murky, I determined early in life that I wanted a career in journalism. When I graduated from college in 1969, I was happily oblivious to the fact that most papers still had on staff only a token woman or two, whose job was to write about brides, female criminals, and kitchen news. The women's departments were often referred to (unofficially, of course) as

"Bras and Girdles," in a tone similar to the one used for calling out an elevator stop.

The most frequent question I was asked during job interviews was "What does your father do?"

At first the question threw me off; the hidden meaning was lost on me.

"Is your father in the business?" the inquisitors would persist.

I remember the man in personnel at the *Boston Globe*, where I got my first real job (as opposed to what the college kids I teach today call a "McJob"), who had described the prospects at the paper mostly in sports metaphors.

"We're looking for team players," he said.

"Oh," I rushed to assure him, "that's me." Having never been a member of a team, I certainly had no evidence to the contrary.

"We want determination, spunk, the kind of person who's still there even if the game lasts fifteen innings."

Even I knew fifteen was a lot.

"Someone who writes like a man, the way, what's her name, Sara Something did before she married that guy and moved to New York."

I tried, after I got a part-time assignment in the suburbs, to write mannish sorts of things about the nightly meetings I covered, which are, of course, the bane, the training ground, and often the Waterloo of most young reporters.

One Friday afternoon in 1972, there was more than the usual commotion at the city desk, in those days an all-male enclave, except for Gwen, a nineteen-year-old news aide known for her dishy eyes.

The men were poring over the day's assignment sheet, asking for Gwen's help, shouting the names of several women reporters, trying to figure out who was where. Gender integration had come to the paper, mostly at the lowest level, my level.

I could hear them mumbling: Chris, Otile, Cindy, Maria, and then expressing disappointment.

Everyone was either out on an assignment or off for the day. They were looking for a female reporter to go to Fenway Park and cover the evening's Red Sox game.

Was I interested?

Interested? Of course. Anything was better than covering the bond issue for new sewer pipes in Quincy.

The editor explained that Diane Shah, a reporter from the *National Observer*, a since-defunct weekly paper based in Washington, famous for the excellence of its features, had sought a press pass from the management of the Red Sox to cover the game that night. She had not asked for access to the locker room. Her request was merely to walk onto the field, chat with the players who were willing to chat during the pregame warmups, and then sit in the press box with the two dozen or so male reporters who were there with their portable Olivettis in tow to record the evening's proceedings.

At first the Red Sox said no, changing their mind only after the lawyers from the *National Observer* threatened to sue. Someone had tipped off the sports department at the *Globe* about Fenway's impending "liberation," which was what we called all acts of precipitous change back in the late sixties and early seventies. My charge that night was to write about Diane Shah writing about the Sox.

It was almost a quarter of a century ago, a late September day, sunny, lacking the humidity and the bugs of high summer. Having been forewarned of our presence, the Sox, to their credit, treated us pretty much the way they treated the male reporters. Reggie Smith, who preferred to be left alone by all reporters, said it was a matter of utter indifference whether the people he did not speak to were men or women. Yaz (Carl Yastrzemski), a left fielder and local hero, was a little more out-going, admitting to a couple of pregame rituals, like wearing the same socks on the outside if they'd been worn during a previous winning game. In the clubhouse there was some kind of recep-tion planned for after the game, and I remember seeing lobsters and oysters and shrimp in big bowls filled with chipped ice. The press box was nearby, and during the game it was filled with a lot of men and with Diane and me. I remember one of the guys, a rotund fellow wearing the kind of squashed hat I always as-sociated with robbers in cartoons, a cigar protruding from his mouth, sighing at the sight of us:

"You girls are ruining our racket."

My report ran on page 1 the next day. At first I read it flushed with bravura—*page 1!!!*—a sensation that quickly gave way to queasiness when I realized that the real story of the game, written by a man, was on the sports page and that my piece was a perfect example of what is known in the newspaper business as "breaking fluff."

There was one element missing that was so crucial its ab-sence called into question the integrity of the entire enterprise. For some reason, surely the euphoria of the moment, I had for-gotten to include the score.

Years later, decades really, when I tried to summon this an-ecdote to impress my son and his pals with my one tenuous brush with sports glory, any prideful emotion was gone from the telling, and all I was left with was the silly accolade of being the first woman to cover the first woman who covered the Bos-ton Red Sox.

"Mom," my son would say, "you're stretching."

Looking that day out of the living room window at Kristin, watching her face twist in anticipation of the next shot, the sweat matting down the hair that had fallen out of her ponytail at the back of her neck, the determined set of her lips, and especially watching my son record her every move with a kind of shy worship, I realized that progress had been made.

"She's good, don't you think?" I said to my husband.

"Her shooting needs work, but she's clearly a terror on the boards."

They came into the house, mopping the sweat off their faces, clanking glasses onto the counter and filling them with Paul Newman's lemonade. My daughter, who was then six, looked up at Kristin, way up, and said, "Will you teach me how to play?"

"Sure. I bet you'll be great." And then Kristin leaned down and said just to her, "Good enough to beat your brother."

The little girl looked up at the older one, her eyes shining with conspiracy.

In her book *In a Different Voice*, Carol Gilligan of Harvard University writes about how being the mother of anyone is a tricky business, but the nature of the trickiness varies depending on whether you have sons or daughters. Gilligan and many others have identified the final years of latency as the time when some girls will turn in on themselves, lose the drive that earlier made them excel in math and cartwheels and storytelling as if none of that stuff ever really counted, not logarithms, not leaps, not a heroine who saves the day atop her trusty steed. Their grades go down, they stop eating, they welcome nicknames like "Skeleton" and "Toothpick," hate their hair, legs, teeth, nose, ears, freckles, pinkie finger, mole at the bottom of their back, baby toenail, whatever, define their value in terms of what other people, especially boys, think of them. By the time they get to high school they have, some of them, become pale versions of their former colorful selves.

Even those who stay strong and outspoken worry that it won't matter. I recently attended the Bat Mitzvah of a young woman named Ariana Zukas. As part of the ceremony she was called upon to compose an original prayer. The prayer was precisely what one would expect of a young woman of conscience in her somewhat privileged circumstances.

She wished, she said, for a world in which everyone could enjoy the peace and goodwill that her family and their friends had been blessed with.

A world without war.

A world free of homelessness, poverty, debilitating or un-treated disease.

It was the final sentence of her prayer that leapt out and embodied, at least to my way of thinking, a wish that could only belong to a girl her age, a girl on the outer edge of childhood.

"Grant me, as I grow older, the confidence to raise my voice that I might be heard."

A voice that she might be heard . . .

Why is this an issue for her, for any of our daughters?

Girls are not born mute.

Most teachers of children in very young grades will tell you that girls are not only as loquacious as boys, but probably more so. While boys are making their motor and airplane noises, rac-ing around in their reckless yet endearing way, turning every-thing, even croissants and cotton candy, into weapons, girls are telling stories, long-winded accounts of who had play dates with whom else, who just got her ears pierced and who else might, who's taking skating or clay or tap, what baby-sitter is back in town for the summer, and on and on and on. They knit with words, an endless quilt of talk. Girls know a ton, know above all how capable they are.

Gilligan says that during adolescence girls suffer not a loss of innocence but a loss of knowledge, knowledge in most cases

about how good they are, not in the moral sense of kind or be-
nevolent, but about how good they are at things: adept.

We stood around in the kitchen while Kristin told us
about the team she was on at the high school in Amherst.

"You know about Jenny and Jamila, right?"

I worried I would seem as ignorant as my University of
Massachusetts journalism students must feel when I ask them if
they know who Woodward and Bernstein are: *We've heard the
expression,* they say. *Are they the guys who wrote all those musicals?*

We rushed to assure Kristin. Yes, we had heard of the famous Jenny and Jamila.

Our regular sitter had spoken of them and how great they
were on the court and off it.

"Awesome," that all-purpose term of approval, was the
most frequently applied adjective.

"Who else is on the team?" I asked. "Anyone else we've
heard of?" In a small town there are always lots of connec-
tions, a genealogy of who knows who based on car pools and
day care and Little League, shared moments as simple and
faithless as sitting next to each other at the all-town band concert at the high school or as profound and wrenching as waiting with sick children to see the doctor at Kaiser Permanente
over on Route 9.

"Have you heard of Kathleen Poe? Her mom's at the uni-
versity, and her dad teaches at one of the colleges; I think at
Hampshire. Maybe you've seen her running a lot around town.
She's training pretty hard."

No, I had never heard of Kathleen.

"Kim Warner is another senior. She works at Hastings . . ."

"I'll keep my eye out for her." Hastings in the center of
town was the place to pick up the papers, gum, and gossip.
"What's she look like?"

"Tall, ponytail." Kristin paused. "Actually that's what most of us look like."

Kristin, Kathleen, Kim. Three kids whose names begin with K. How would I keep them straight?

"There's two Emilys."

"Two?" Emily is a popular name, especially in Amherst, not just for its music but also its pedigree. The poet Emily Dickinson was born in Amherst.

"They go by their nicknames. Emily Jones—her father's pretty well known, he's a pediatrician at Kaiser, Emlen Jones—is called Jonesbones." I knew Emily's father. He had prescribed Ventolin to my son one cold December morning years ago. "Everyone calls Emily Shore 'Gumby.' "

"Gumby?"

"Yeah, she's real flexible."

"Bones and Gumby." I repeated the words slowly.

They sounded like a pair of undertakers in a Dickens novel.

"There's Jade Sharpe."

"Nkosi and Maia's sister?" We didn't know Jade, but her younger siblings played with my children.

"Yup. And then there's Lucia."

"Loo-sha who?" I asked, echoing Kristin's pronunciation.

"Maraniss."

"Oh. Maraniss. We know them." Years ago I had worked on a paper in New Jersey with her uncle. He ended up, as I recall, at the *Washington Post*. During our days at the *Trenton Times* he played on the paper's softball team (no women allowed), where he was known as a fierce competitor and given the nickname of Maddog.

Kristin continued, "Sophie King, Jan Klenowski, Rita Powell, Carrie Tharp, Jessi Denis. Some of them will probably play junior varsity until the postseason."

They were all unfamiliar. A blur of names, a blur of girls.

"Will you come watch us?" she asked, turning to the children.

They looked as if they'd happily go off that minute in her dilapidated brown VW Rabbit if she wanted them to, but it would be months before the next season commenced. The Hurricanes had just recently ended the 1992 season with a wretched game against Northampton.

"I'll make sure you get a schedule. This year we lost," said Kristin, holding up the lemonade cloudy with pulp, then taking a clean puckery sip.

"But next season . . ."

The look on her face was not winking or apologetic, not crazed or predatory, but something much more calm and pure and certain. ". . . will be different."

I

Losing

Everything went wrong.

Early in the second half, the girls on the bench began to weep.

It was a game that made everyone connected to the Hurricanes wince to relive.

On the court of Cathedral High School in Springfield, Massachusetts, on the night of March 3, 1992, the Amherst Hurricanes had disintegrated into four players standing around as if waiting in line in the cold for tickets, stomping their feet to no avail. They appeared distracted and out of it while their point guard, Jamila Wideman, lunged about, contorting her body in any number of ways. She was everywhere and she was nowhere. Although she was dazzling, she was also doomed. For every effort she made as an individual, the Blue Devils from Northampton replied with a chorus of five passes, ending, with frustrating inevitability, in an open shot and an easy deuce. When Amherst wasn't frantic, it was comatose. The message the Hurricanes had heard from their coach all season, those rousing talks studded with terms like *team* and *unity* and *DYB* (for *do your best*), seemed to have fled, scattered leaves lost to a gargantuan gust.

Coach Ron Moyer sat on the sidelines, watching the carnage.

He shook his head back and forth and thought: Einstein was right. Time is relative. When you're winning, the game can't end soon enough, and every second on the clock moves forward as slowly as traffic caught behind a farmer on a tractor towing a corn planter. When you're losing, like tonight, it's over in seconds, a sudden skid on glare ice.

Tonight's loss fit an old pattern.

As usual the Hurricanes had had a distinguished regular season, winning twenty games and losing only once, yet for the fifth year in a row, when it came to the crunch of the play-offs Amherst lacked that final hardscrabble ingredient that would take them over the top. A scrappiness was missing, that hard-driving desire to be the best.

At times even Coach Moyer was tempted to believe that their reputation as players was doomed to mirror the college town they represented: kindly, ruminative, ineffectual; more adept at eating sprouts and quoting Emily Dickinson and singing nature songs like "I Love Seeds" than throwing elbows going for a rebound or hitting the floor for a loose ball. They came from a town that prized tofu, not toughness. You think something's not fair? Stand on a street corner holding up a placard. Still not fair? Write a letter to the editor.

A finesse team: the *Lady* Hurricanes, *nice* girls from a *nice* town. The eleven-point loss didn't begin to describe how badly they'd been beaten. Amherst never found a rhythm, and Northampton was able to penetrate at will.

The fans from Amherst were entertaining the same misgivings, wondering further why Coach Moyer didn't make an adjustment. Hamp was using a two–three zone. Look at Jen, buried on the weak side. Why was Coach Moyer keeping Kathleen Poe, a junior forward, on Lauren Demski, who was eating her alive?

When the game was over, Kathleen couldn't even walk off the floor to the locker room without first collapsing in a corridor outside Cathedral's gym, the neutral site, which at this moment engendered feelings that were anything but neutral.

Immobilized, she placed her head in her arms.

Then her strong broad shoulders convulsed as the victorious opponents trooped by, muttering the usual sportsmanlike phrases, "Good game" and "Nice try."

The well-intentioned comments only made it worse.

Out-and-out trash talk would have been easier to take.

The weeping continued as their tin can of a school bus, nicknamed the Yellow Cadillac precisely because it lacked both comfort and style, headed out of Springfield on a journey that would last an hour through a cold dark maze of small towns, Ludlow and Granby and Belchertown, past what Dickinson once called "lonely Houses off the Road a Robber'd like the look of."

Some players kept to themselves; others played music quietly and spoke in subdued tones.

Defeat creates orphaned thoughts.

Jen Pariseau felt as if she had spent the whole night running up and down on the perimeter, a helpless stick figure unable to join the action.

She felt torn, a disloyal unsettling mix of disappointment and relief. It had not been a good year. There'd been tension with Coach Moyer; why did he persist on singling her out during practice?

Jen, don't give up the baseline.

Jen, square up on the shot.

Jen, put your feet on the darn line.

It was as if (this was not a thought she would ever voice out loud) her longtime friend Jamila could do no wrong and she could do no right. Outside the bus, the night air was frigid and still. As the Hurricanes rolled past bare trees and dirty dispiriting patches of snow, Jen wanted spring and she wanted softball.

Jamila's analysis had a different cast. The more driven she was, the more her teammates faltered, yet the more she pushed ahead, all the time processing what was going wrong while it happened:

The rest of the Hurricanes have bought into relying on Jenny and me far too often. Everyone is waiting for someone else to do it. Even if they keep messing up, I'm going to play the way I can. Whoever wants to come with me can. It's my right and my responsibility to take from the game what I can. I'm not giving up just because my team has.

On the way home, Jamila glanced over at Jen. At times during the game Jen's bushy eyebrows had dwarfed her big eyes: It was what Coach Moyer always called her scared look, the look of a squirrel desperate for a tree. You could see it at the foul line the way she shot from her shoulders; it was as if the rest of her body didn't even exist.

Sometimes during the previous season, Jen and Brenda Sepanek, the lone senior on the team who had just played her final game for the Hurricanes, would catch each other's attention for a moment on the bus or a quick exchange in the school corridors and make remarks about Scottie Pippen and Michael Jordan, the dynamic between the two Bulls players.

Jamila would hear one girl say, "Pippen's doing a lot of the work that makes Jordan look so good."

And the other might respond, "You'd think Jordan might give him some of the credit."

Jamila assumed her teammates were speaking allegorically about their relationship to her. This was code with a razor's edge. She knew that Jen sometimes felt overshadowed, but lately Jamila's sympathy for what Jen was feeling had changed to anger:

She should have respect for my situation too.

When Jamila's eyes swept the bus, eyes filled with a piercing elderly knowledge, she could see that Jen wasn't the only person on the bus who looked at last unburdened.

Everyone looks relieved, as if all along they wanted the pressure gone more than they wanted to win.

When at last the bus made the final heaving, laborious turn off Triangle Street into the parking lot at Amherst Regional High School, Coach Ron Moyer arose from his traditional place in the first seat opposite the driver on the right-hand side. He unfolded his six-foot, six-inch frame as best he could, cramped from having stuffed himself into a seat intended for someone half his size. If he ever retired from coaching, it would be to escape this one torment.

There was the usual ripple of nudges and commands: "Quiet, quiet, Coach Moyer wants to give one of his parking-lot talks" and "Listen up, everybody, it's the last speech of the season."

The respectful silence that greeted the coach was not just for him. Everybody was feeling bad for Brenda. All season there had been a secret chant, a hidden motivation: *Win it, not just for ourselves, but for Brenda.* Tonight she sat in a quiet huddle with Jen and Jamila in the prized backseat of the bus, the place of honor reserved for captains and seniors by unspoken assent. The disappointment they radiated was as unmistakable as the cloying odor from the fertilizer in the fields surrounding Amherst during the growing season.

Lucia Maraniss, one of the youngest players, a freshman who just that night had moved up from the junior varsity, experienced the defeat as a thing of shame, not because they lost but because they played so poorly. Yet she also felt an inner glow; the opportunity to play alongside Jen and Jamila and the others as if she were their equal made her feel beatific, anointed, touched on the shoulders by a sword. She gazed down the length of the shadowy bus at Coach Moyer.

"This won't be long.

"First of all, I want to tell Brenda how much I admired her

spunk, her consistency, the way she came to practice every day, ready to play. I'm sorry we couldn't win it for her. At the same time we owe it to Brenda to start thinking about next season. We need to be tough, we need to learn from this defeat. Look at yourself; think about what you didn't do in this game. Did you take the ball all the way to the basket? Did you finish the play?

"I hope you'll dedicate some time during the summer to getting yourself ready for the challenges next year."

He paused. He likes to let the team own the victories, and he believes it is his job to take on most of the defeat. If tonight they needed to blame evil spirits, he was willing to be the designated evil spirit.

"I know you gave it everything you had."

He looked at their upturned faces, big-eyed, tremulous, sincere.

"Maybe you just didn't have the right preparation."

It wasn't maybe.

Something had gone wrong, not just wrong, but spectacularly awry.

He knew he would be revisiting tonight's game compulsively to figure out why his kids, over and over, had failed to finish the play. They were dutiful, they worked hard. Several of them, not just Jamila, had the potential to be great. They would not easily forgive themselves tonight's failure; that was his job.

"Look, you kids couldn't screw up bad enough for me not to love you. I have two great daughters, and if I could have fifteen more, I know I could get them right here on this bus in the Amherst uniforms."

Up until now, there had been a few sniffles but no raging displays. The mention of "daughters," however, inflamed them. *Daughters*: the word reverberated, hung in the trapped air like a ball wavering on the rim of a basket. First from one, then another, a wail arose, so that soon the entire bus, already overstuffed with gym bags and the bureaucracy of outerwear needed to endure winter, was further overtaken by full-scale sobs, a luxurious unstoppable lamentation. It was a stampede of tears.

This, he thought, is not the note on which to end an entire season.

This, he thought, could be a disaster.

If Ron Moyer has a streak of hubris, it's his pride in his sense of humor. He always says that if someone wrote a book about him, the title would be *Ron*, and the sequel would be *Moron*.

And so on this night, lunging about for a lighter tone with the same ferocious hope Jamila had shown on the court earlier in the evening, he remembered with gratitude Schwarzenegger's famous words in *The Terminator*; and so he said, in Arnold's authoritative Austrian accent, pluralizing the original promise, "We'll be back" (pronounced "We-al-be-bach").

One or two deeply dutiful daughters managed a weak grin.

And then, the final ritual of the season, the descent from the bus.

There was none of the usual backslapping and snippets of song, shouted plans about meeting at Friendly's for ice cream (or, if you have strange tastes, like Jen, for plain whipped cream in a cone). It was a sullen solitary exodus marked by lowered faces and red swollen eyes.

As always, Coach Moyer went inside and waited in the Amherst gym until the final girl had left the locker room and was on her way home.

His plans were vague, and they mostly had to do with taking it easy for a while and then shining up his extra-long Striker golf clubs.

Most New Englanders think there are four seasons, but to him there are only two: basketball and summer.

On this evening when the temperature hovered at freezing, basketball was over, and summer had begun.

Later that night, teenage insomnia was rampant in the Amherst area, a wild vine of twisting thoughts and knotted associations.

Her face stiff with unwashed tears, Lucia lay awake on the low narrow bed in her small room on the second floor of her family's sprawling old white wooden house near the center of town.

She reached into the bookshelf, pushing aside the tools for her artwork, passing over the stamp collection that embarrassed her a little because practically everyone she ever met thinks stamps are nerdy. But she still treasured them for their artistry, all that intense miniaturization and tidy perfection. She had a lot of normal stamps, with the usual themes of flowers and founding fathers, but her all-time favorite came from Indochina, showing in little more than a square inch that region's history as one of the most-bombed places in the world: explosives flying over a tropical landscape as if they were delicate birds. What she applauded was the instinct, the courage really, that it took to find beauty in something that terrible.

Her strong hands, muscled from all the years of piano practice, lighted at last upon a small journal, which she opened to a blank page.

In tiny, perfectly rendered capital letters, she recorded her feelings about the evening:

Today I realized how much I love basketball. We lost the Western Mass semifinals to Hamp. The game was a blur. All I remember was how we were in a constant struggle to come back. We started off well, but after the refs gave Hamp a boost, they ran with the ball. No one played exceptionally

well besides Jamila, who was the high scorer with thirty
points. Jenny wasn't having a good night and the forwards
couldn't get the ball to sink either. I felt as if everything that
the team had worked for so long just left our grasp.

It's not fair. It's not fair. The team has some of the
finest athletes in the world, not to mention the most funny,
smart, beautiful, incredibly awesome people ever to walk the
earth. Just seeing anyone on the team makes my day. Jamila
has got to be the sweetest person. She is funny, beautiful,
amazingly athletic, and to top that off she is nice to everyone.
Jenny is the one person who I respect and love the most. She
seems to know everything and whenever she speaks to me
I'm speechless because I look up to her so much. I love it
when she slaps my hand, or hugs me. It makes me feel like
I'm worth something.

And then she wrote, in what could only be interpreted as
pure boosterism, given the facts of the night:

Northampton is not a team like Amherst. Amherst is a team
of unselfish, incredibly talented, team players who love their
teammates. Northampton is a bunch of good basketball
players put together who do not feel or look like a team.
Kuzmeski, Demski, Frost, Stiles—they're all good, but they
don't deserve to have won. On the bus on the way home
everyone was shocked and miserable.

A couple of miles away, on a tree-lined side street in a suburban development, Jamila could not sleep either.

She had been a member of the girls' varsity basketball team
since seventh grade, and this was the second year in a row that
they had won the Valley Wheel league title and gone to the
Western Mass tournament, only to lose in the semifinals.

In five years Jamila had never missed a game.

In five years she'd never missed a practice.

Tonight's defeat was unacceptable.

She tossed in her bed: Even before the game, she'd had a bad feeling. The Hurricanes came out flat, without any fire. They were waiting to see what was going to happen. They worried about reacting, not acting. Hamp came out excited and ready. They put their famous press on, and after six steals it was obvious they'd won the game. The Hurricanes had everything, on paper. Good players, good seeding in the tournament, no injuries. Everything was there, except for what really mattered. There wasn't the trust in each other, the confidence in themselves, the sense of team that makes you play beyond your individual abilities.

If it is possible, mentally and physically, to be more yourself on a certain occasion than on another, to be yourself squared, then that is one way to interpret Jamila's performance during that game against Northampton that clinched the 1992 season; as her father, John Edgar Wideman, once wrote in *Philadelphia Fire*, "Leg and heart and mind and breath working hard together. You forget everything you know and play." Shooting, he maintained, is all in the mind:

> You must believe the ball's going in. Confidence and the amen wrist flick of the follow-through. You reach for the sky, launch the ball so it rotates off your fingertips and let it fall through the rim. When you hold on too long, when you don't relax and extend your arm and let nature take its course, you shoot short. Because you don't believe. Because you're trying too hard to maintain control, you choke the ball and it comes up short.

Jamila was one to keep her own counsel, but it was obvious to anyone who saw her play, the fury and the heroism, that, as is true of every great athlete, the game was more than just a game.

Next year she would be a senior: her last chance to go the distance as a member of the Hurricanes.

In her neighborhood, built during the eighties in boom times, each dwelling was different, so that a Cape might be next door to a contemporary with a stucco exterior next to a Dutch Colonial with a gambrel roof alongside a neo-Victorian. The one feature that unites many of the houses, the common "quote," as architects like to call characteristics that are shared or echoed, are the basketball hoops found in driveway after driveway, as American as a flagpole, and like one in their tall rectitude.

Her father, who had played college ball at the University of Pennsylvania in the early sixties (including one season against Bill Bradley of Princeton) and who could still be observed, in pickup games at local parks like Mill River, holding his own with men half his age, promised that the next day they would be at their hoop, working on shooting drills.

Jen Pariseau also lay awake, in her room with the sloping ceiling in the house she shared with her older brother, her father, and her stepmother in the town of Pelham, just east of Amherst.

Her head rested on a pillow, behind which was her "strong women" wall, filled with taped-up magazine images of women whom she admired.

She was racked by the thought that basketball was no longer fun. She felt shunned by the spotlight. *We weren't the Amherst Hurricanes; we were "Jamila's team."*

She used to love it. She had joined the team in the eighth grade, a year after Jamila. But now; now, she had to wonder. Jen admitted to herself she'd been angry a lot of the preceding season. Coach acted as if the only person on the team was Jamila. So did the media, for that matter. It was as if in the eyes of the world they were Jamila's team, not the Amherst Hurricanes. It made her angry. It frustrated her. It wasn't right. There had to be room for both at the top.

She missed the old inseparability between herself and Jamila, grieved the loss of the way it used to be, that easiness that comes from spending every weekend, all weekend together. Now their exchanges as they passed in the hallways at school were brusque, a quick hi-hi. Some of the disenchantment went beyond basketball, belonged to that universal sixteen-year-old trading in and testing of loyalties and friendship. Jen perhaps felt a special vulnerability. Her parents had split up when she was only two. Maybe that was the problem, maybe change, even the natural evolution of a friendship, its ebb and flow, could easily be confused with loss.

But what if next season was more of the same?

What if it was just more averted glances, more coded talk, more snubs?

Unlike Lucia, Jen could be clear-eyed about Hamp that night.

The Blue Devils knew what they wanted and they didn't choke.

The Blue Devils had shown themselves under pressure as capable of that smooth interlocking series of quick-lived gestures that occurs when teammates sense not only where another player is but also where she will be, one second, two seconds, three seconds from now, and then they pass the ball in a confident motion, garnering basket after basket after basket. The dance, the arc, the *swoosh*.

Northampton would go on to the state tournament.

And the Amherst girls?

The Amherst girls could stay home and they could do whatever there is to do in a town whose official seal is a book and a plow.

* * *

24

Amherst is a college town, home to Amherst College, the University of Massachusetts, and Hampshire College, with the usual self-absorbed loftiness that makes such places as maddening as they are charming and livable. The communities surrounding Amherst range from the hard and nasty inner-city poverty of Holyoke, the empty factories in Chicopee, and the blue-collar solidity of Agawam to the cornfields and strawberry patches in Whately and Hatfield and Hadley and the shoppers' mecca that is Northampton. They tend to look on Amherst with eye-rolling puzzlement and occasional contempt as the town that fell to earth.

When the chamber of commerce sponsored a contest for town motto, Coach Moyer submitted several that he still thinks should have won—"A Volvo in every garage," "Where adolescence lasts forever," and his personal favorite, "Amherst: Where sexuality is an option and reality is an alternative." Townspeople often refer to Amherst, fondly, as "Never-never land." The chamber of commerce ended up choosing as its motto "There's no place like downtown Amherst." Downtown consists mostly of pizza joints, Chinese restaurants, ice-cream parlors, bookstores, and not much else. It has the world's slowest deli. The businesses that don't begin with the word *Pioneer* often end with the word *Valley*. It's hard to find a needle and thread, but if you wish, you can go to the Global Trader and purchase for four dollars a dish towel with a rain-forest theme.

Amherst is an achingly democratic sort of place in which tryouts for Little League, with their inevitable rejections, have caused people to suggest that more teams should be created so that no one is left out. There are always some parents who sit on the bleachers reading their well-thumbed copies of William James's *Essays in Pragmatism* or rereading Trollope, who look up just in time to greet their child's good catch or hard drive to the center with an airy cry of "Deft!" rather than "Way to go!"

Coach Moyer finds it ironic that the same people who disparage athletic competition, sometimes wrinkling their noses as if the very word had an off odor, were sufficiently driven to get 800s on their Graduate Record Exams. They use words like *deobscurantize* when they mean *make clear*, and at parent-teacher meetings for kindergarten-age children they ask if their youngster will be taught not just how to spell, but also the history of spelling.

"In Amherst," says Coach Moyer, "people are so sophisticated that when one first grader said to the other, 'Guess what, I found a condom on the patio,' her friend wanted to know, 'What's a patio?'"

Coach Moyer has proposed some politically correct trash talk just for those who seek to avoid the rough language of the fray:

"I'm going to meet you outside the game and refuse to mediate."

"You ignore your inner child."

"And so's your co-parent."

Every year in August the Rotary Club hosts a Teddy Bear Rally on the town common: 190 booths featuring bears as well as bear furniture, bear clothes, bear books, and other bear sundries.

The church Moyer's wife attends uses an "inclusive language" hymnal, invented in Amherst, which replaces patriarchal references to *Our Father* with the word *creator* and which tones down imagery with a male bias, employing small subtle shifts, such as "Onward, Christian Stalwarts."

It's the last place in America where you can find people who still think *politically correct* is a compliment. The program notes for the high school spring musical, *Kiss Me, Kate,* pointed out politely that *The Taming of the Shrew,* on which it is based, was "well, Shakespearean in its attitude toward the sexes."

Political action is approved, even among the very young.

A few years ago a second-grade class at Fort River School mounted a successful campaign to get the state's Turnpike Authority to abolish the symbol that had lined the road that goes from Stockbridge to Boston since its opening in 1957, a pilgrim's hat with an arrow shot through it. These days it's just a plain old pilgrim's hat. Jen Pariseau has a theory about how Amherst got to be so PC: "It all goes back to this guy Jeffrey Amherst."

The man from whom the town took its name in 1759 was commander in chief and field marshal of the English armies.

"Some people say he was a womanizer and a drunk. The one thing we know for sure is that he tried to wipe out the Indians by giving them blankets infected with smallpox. Ever since, we've been trying to make up for him."

In the sixties Amherst College managed to lose all its Jeffrey Amherst dinner plates, with their frieze showing the white military officer from England in an eternal rout of the Indians. But it has yet to lose its fight song, a somewhat airbrushed version of the life of Lord Jeff, "a soldier of the king." After touchdowns at football games and at the parties afterward you can hear it being sung, in a low register filled with, often, inebriated conviction, a tribute to an old order in which boys were boys, men were men, and girls didn't go to Amherst College. Women entered Amherst College for the first time as transfer students in 1975 and as freshmen in 1976, a fact that used to merit a sentence in the catalogue but is no longer considered newsworthy.

Oh, Lord Jeffrey Amherst was the man who gave his name
　　　To our college on the hill;
And the story of his loyalty and bravery and fame
　　　Abides here among us still—
Abides here among us still.

You may talk about your Johnnies and your Elis and the rest,
 For they are names that time can never dim,
But give us our only Jeffrey, he's the noblest and the best,
 To the end we will stand fast for him.

The town is, for the most part, smoke free, nuclear free, and eager to free Tibet. Ponchos with those little projectiles of fleece have never gone out of style. Birkenstocks (called Birkies), clogs, capes, Doc Marten's, woven tops, and tie-dyed anything are all still the rage. With the exception of Cambridge, Massachusetts, Amherst is probably the only place in the United States where men can wear berets and not get beaten up. The common nickname for the area is the Happy Valley. In good weather, freeze-dried hippies, men and women in their forties and fifties, clinging to their long hair and their beards the way World War II marines used to cling to crew cuts, line the sidewalks with their wares: multicolored candles shaped like pyramids, tin earrings, colorful beads, incense.

The biggest product is invisible. Not widgets or beams or fenders, it is process itself: The two most common jobs are teacher and therapist. People worry constantly about "sending the wrong message," and many conversations are launched with elaborate, back-bending polite disclaimers: "Not that I'm saying you don't have a right to your opinion, but . . ."

The college kids stroll down the main drag, South Pleasant Street, with an air of entitlement: souls afloat in the ocean of knowledge. Some professors call them "time vampires," and as proof they offer anecdotes that, even if they aren't true, have the truth of folklore: "So this student came to my office and asked if he could enroll in two classes that met at the same time on Monday, Wednesday, and Friday from nine to ten, and when I said, 'Sure, if you could be in two places at once,' the kid smiled and said, 'Great.' "

The therapist's version of the same phenomenon has the patient being told that her hour is up, only to respond: "Oh, I can stay. I don't have to be anywhere until eleven-thirty."

Dogs are often named after writers or abstract ideals: Dickens, Chaucer, Harmony. An oboe player who graduated from Hampshire College had a dog named Doggerel. Dogs in Amherst have their own drinking fountain on the town common, a granite basin attached to a fountain for humans, installed by the Women's Christian Temperance Union to encourage people to drink water rather than liquor.

Children have the usual names, but also names like Trillium, Zephyr, Sage, Morningstar, Jett, Orpheus, Willow.

Amherst has the international distinction of being the only town in the world that makes an organized effort to save spotted salamanders. On Henry Street special tunnels, similar to airport runway drains and about six inches in diameter, guarantee a safe escort for these homely creatures who consist mostly of wide mouths and slithering torsos. On one spring night a year, when the atmospheric conditions are just right, a light rain combined with a temperature well above freezing, they leave the hillsides and migrate to the lowest vernal pool they can find to claim a mate. When the rain stops, they go back uphill to a life of abstinence and, of course, all those young 'uns. There's a new band in town called Salamander Crossing; heavy metal it's not.

Two miles from the center of town is Bread & Circus, the self-proclaimed world's largest health food store. Old-fashioned molasses and sun-dried cranberries coexist happily: Fannie Farmer meets the New Age. Food-dazed shoppers proceed down the aisles in a trance, beguiled by blue cheese aged in a cave in Iowa or the *Cabrales* from Spain wrapped in sycamore leaves, by turkeys raised in a free-roaming, hormone-free environment and twenty-two different kinds of granola. One time a child wearing a Burger King crown was accosted by a customer: "Poor thing, she has meat on her breath." The store, nicknamed Bread & Checkbook, has the air of a sacred temple, and even the most harried cashiers have a smiley, pristine look. Like the rest of the Amherst area, with its widespread faith in the efficacy of language, Bread & Circus is filled with signs hailing the "organic special of the week" as well as what's wheat-free and salt-free and fat-free, but not, of course, truly free.

Notices flutter from telephone poles and crowd bulletin boards, announcing Scottish country dance groups and lessons in Zen Shiatsu massage, support groups such as "Writes of Passage" (specializing in techniques that "gather and deepen the relationship to the inner child"), the need for a host family to take in a Bosnian Teen Refugee, or counseling by therapists with names like "Singingtree." In one of those cross-references so common in a small town, Singingtree is the mother of one of the Hurricanes. Her real name is Sally Hardman Shore. Her daughter is the Emily whose nickname is Gumby, and she calls herself Singingtree on those occasions when she is conducting a "vision quest."

Bumper stickers abound. They can be categorized with the same checklist used by birders.

Common; large number seen every year:
QUESTION AUTHORITY
I BELIEVE *HER*
LIVE SIMPLY SO THAT OTHERS MAY SIMPLY LIVE
NUCLEAR ARMS ARE NOT FOR HUGGING

Uncommon; occurs in limited numbers and is not certain to be
   seen:
IT'S A CHILD, NOT A CHOICE
MY KID CAN BEAT UP YOUR HONOR STUDENT

*Rare; as many as four reports per year, but sometimes not
    reported for several consecutive years:*
DON'T BLAME ME: I VOTED FOR BUSH

Accidental; extremely rare, occurrence unpredictable:
THEY CAN TAKE MY GUN AWAY WHEN THEY PRY MY DEAD
    COLD FINGERS OFF OF IT
GOAT ROPERS NEED LOVE TOO

Banners often stretch across South Pleasant Street at the
town common, including the vintage SPAY OR NEUTER YOUR PET,
PREVENT ABANDONMENT AND SUFFERING and ABORTION: KEEP IT
LEGAL, SAFE AND FUNDED.

Some classic headlines from the *Amherst Bulletin*:

WELL-DRESSED MAN ROBS AMHERST BANK
DOES AMHERST HAVE TOO MANY COMMITTEES?
FED BY SOME, FEARED BY OTHERS, A THOUSAND FERAL CATS
    ROAM AMHERST

In almost any other community the photo caption "Hidden
Harvest" would indicate marijuana or some other contraband;
in Amherst it means potatoes.

The police report in the *Bulletin* documents domestic violence and creepy phone calls and break-ins. Someone called in
once about a cow on the loose on Northeast Street; another call
reported a raccoon "behaving strangely in the median strip." It
turned out to be dead. On Friday and Saturday nights license
plates are stolen on a lark with some frequency. Fights are reported, usually just as the bars are beginning to close, outside
and inside Antonio's Pizza or the Pub or Delaney's or Twisters
Tavern. Drunken college kids are often discovered passed out in
someone's yard. Once on a summer night a lovelorn young man

was found banging his head against a tree. The paper reported, "Fortunately there was no damage to the perpetrator or to the tree." Sometimes there are brawls late at night with two hundred kids watching and cheering; in one case, the two kids in the fight not only slugged each other but also bit each other's nose and chest. Illegal bars, in private apartments and spilling out into yards and sidewalks and even roads, often blossom with seeming spontaneity in the good weather, catering to a clientele that reaches into the thousands. One such gathering, called the Hobart Hoedown because it was held on Hobart Lane, was videotaped by the police and then shown, with favorable results, at a town meeting in which the agenda included a request for more officers.

Debate is constant. The concerns can be global and unanswerable: "Whither activism in El Salvador?" or local and also unanswerable: "Which has better Chinese food, Panda East or Am Chi?" On almost any weekday when the colleges are in session, one can choose among lectures with titles like "Studies of the Distortion of the Director Field in Nematic Solutions of a Rodlike Polymer" or "Optimality and Grounded Phonology: Vowel Harmony in Yoruba Dialects" or "Developmental Changes in Inter-Limb Coordination: Transition to Hands-to-Knee Crawling." Even topics whose frank popularity cannot be ignored get to have Latin in their titles: "Saint Elvis: Graceland as *Locus Sanctus*."

Recently, a tongue-in-cheek application to live in Amherst circulated throughout the town; you could check off, for example, your favorite beverage (ginseng rush, jug wine, goat's milk) and recreation (pouring sand into loggers' fuel tanks, strapping yourself to deer, meditating).

Other questions:

- Is it OK to wear Birkenstocks without socks?
  ( ) True ( ) False

- When you watch people eating meat, can you hear the screams of the source animal echoing in your head?

- Do you tie your ponytail with leather thongs, rubber bands, recycled twine, or twine made from celery fibers grown in your own garden?

- How many letters have you written to the editor in the past month? ( ) 2–9 ( ) 10–19 ( ) 20–39 ( ) 40–59 ( ) >60

- Your current house is lit with:
  ( ) Oil lamps ( ) Candles ( ) Fireflies

Despite the external exuberance created by the students, there's a wariness toward outsiders; as Frost observed, "Good fences make good neighbors." It takes a long time to feel accepted. The third wife of a professor in the English department at Amherst College, who used to be a singer in Los Angeles, says, "After eight years, the town starts to grow on you."

Most residents tend to keep to themselves. In the winter, people really do become hermits. No one comes to your door with false offers of friendship. In fact no one comes to your door, except, oddly enough—given that such intrusions are a form of pollution—environmental activists wanting money and an audience. The spiels are always so earnest; typically, the young person at your door might urge the boycott of whale watches because the noise from the boats disturbs the animals in their natural habitat, concluding with a rousing cheer of "Win one for the Flipper!"

The seasons in New England give a focus to time the way a tent with bright stripes focuses a garden party.

Spring that year after the loss to Hamp was no real comfort, a traitorous time with its trick of warm days followed by record-making blizzards, the end of winter in name only. The wind was like glass—sharp, transparent, deadly.

Then April, brown and quiet.

The snow melted, and pussy willows grew in the woods.

If you were desperate for an outing, you could have donned your raincoat and grabbed your flashlight and helped out at the annual salamander crossing.

In May, Hawthorne's vegetable stand up on East Pleasant reopened, as did the farmers' market on the common, with their sparse and hopeful midspring offerings of houseplants and seedlings and early greens.

A sign sprung up outside one house:

PERENNIALS

HERBS

EVERLASTING

The smell of manure in the fields was overruled by the lilacs, and scraggly yellow blossoms appeared on twiggy bushes.

By the third weekend in May the hibernation of the previous winter seemed to have been a hallucination.

The annual police auction was held, supervised by Captain Charlie Scherpa, looking sharp with his blue uniform, gray hair, and large imperious nose as he directed the bids. The goods sold at this annual event are precisely the crop of detritus one would expect in a college town: a cassette holder and tapes, work gloves, a pair of Tecnico women's hiking boots, a diamondlike stud earring, Cross pen and case, 4 CDs, Notre Dame sweatshirt, Seiko men's watch, men's wedding band, lawn ornament, black backpack, beanbag chair, Technics turntable, baseball hat, K-2 skis, and bikes—lots of bikes, men's and women's, by Univega, Columbia, Huffy, Peugeot, Schwinn, Ross, Raleigh, Shelby, Vista, Sears, and Fuji, in varying states of repair and disrepair, in purple and red and blue and brown and green and black and yellow and orange and chrome. One time, back when he was eight, a towhead named Thor Wilcox stood by shyly, and Captain Scherpa made sure he was the only person allowed to make a bid on a decent bike, which he ended up getting for two dollars. Implicit in the tableau of this auction is a genuine longing for a different, older, vanished America—marred, ever so faintly, by a trace of self-consciousness and self-congratulation, a sense of having out-Rockwelled Rockwell.

That same May weekend, the town fair arrived, and the children truly thawed out from the winter, experiencing a footloose freedom they hadn't enjoyed since Halloween. The fair is a rinky-dink event beloved by the citizens because its very tackiness throws into relief Amherst's superior grace, with rides whose menace is all in the name: the Scrambler and the Satellite and Wipe-Out. As always, Thursday was daredevil night, Friday afternoon was for little kids, and Friday evening was shaving-cream night, a junior high ritual that persists even though none of the merchants in town have sold any shaving cream to under-age kids for several weeks. The purpose is to cover one's victims with the sticky lather.

A middle-aged woman with long candidly gray straight hair and glasses, someone who would never honk in traffic or neglect to recycle her cans and bottles, whose single excess is to belong to more than one book group, sighed and asked another, "Do you remember the time the bride came to the fair?"

It must have been a half-dozen years ago that a bride and groom wandered away from their wedding at the Lord Jeff Hotel across the street and bought tickets for the Ferris wheel. The fairgoers, including even the most impatient little children, had stepped back and let them go to the head of the line. In the distance you could hear the commotion from the Senior Splash, all those squeals of the high school girls, in bathing suits sometimes covered by T-shirts, as people paid to immerse them in water,

35

and you could smell the flour sizzling in oil from the fried-dough booth run by the Mormons in their only public fund-raiser all year. The couple in their finery had mounted the air in set increments as the other riders were ushered off so that the bride and groom were at last alone, those nameless two, and the operator, with his tattoo and his pot belly and his scowl, hardly the type to encourage whimsy, cranked up the machine and allowed them to go round and round and round, while on the ground a crowd of admirers stood, clapping each time the cart reached the top and then plunged downward.

The Jones Library posted a sign inviting the public to join in on a walk—a "light-hearted springtime excursion"—to Emily Dickinson's grave, held every year on the Saturday nearest the fifteenth of May, the day on which the poet died in 1886. Everyone is encouraged to bring a flower to place on her grave and a Dickinson poem to read.

In late May all the graduations took place, a gushing wave of parties and anguished good-byes. As always, the town girded for the students' departure, sad and glad to see them leave, showing the odd mix of ingratiation and contempt found in most tourist economies.

It is the worst time of year for the police: midnight crowds throng the center of town, each collective entity so massive that human gridlock occurs. One year, newspapers as far away as Boston were filled with dire stories about traffic on Route 9 and the impossibility of finding lodgings all the way from Greenfield, near the Vermont border, to Hartford, across the state line in Connecticut.

In May 1992 there weren't any demonstrations, but often there are. The police face the pressure of providing special escorts for celebrity speakers and celebrity parents. Captain Scherpa has provided security for Geraldine Ferraro and Johnny Carson. One time he guarded Hubert Humphrey at breakfast, who asked the officer to join him. He's done a couple of favors for Coretta King, and he is a favorite of the Dalai Lama, who appreciates the Karmic rightness of the officer's last name: In Tibet the same name, spelled *Sherpa*, denotes a skilled mountain climber: "He thinks I'm some kind of monk." The offspring of Winnie Mandela, Princess Grace, Bob Dylan, Linda Ellerbee, Dwight D. Eisenhower, and Richard Nixon have been enrolled at the various colleges at various times. Just when the townspeople finally acknowledged that they had been won over by the students, charmed if not by their music then by their vitality, they disappeared, leaving in their wake a strange emptiness.

It was as if they'd never really existed, and Amherst was left to itself.

By Memorial Day Amherst could be mistaken for almost any small town, almost anywhere. A parade was held in which Scouts and Legionnaires marched from the center of town to Memorial Pool at the high school and assembled on the now-green grass for a ceremony with all the classic ingredients of patriotic music, windy speeches, and a gunfire salute. For years the spectacle has been enhanced by a teacher from Wildwood Elementary School, slim and brown-haired, dressed in red, white, and blue with a flag pin on her blazer, who escorts her first-grade class on a day when school is not even in session so that they can lend their thin, childish presence to the tribute to the war dead.

As usual, the Friday evening following Memorial Day saw the spring dinner at the South Congregational Church on the South Amherst Common. For more than half a century the menu has not varied: steamed asparagus grown locally in Hadley (considered by gourmands the best in the world), chicken salad, pickles, rolls, chips, and shortcake with berries. In June, the same newspapers that couldn't get enough of hypothermia the previous winter now couldn't get enough of rhubarb. Using sympathy-ploy headlines, calling it "The Cinderella of the Garden," papers urged their readers to delight in this potassium-rich fibrous stalk, to cook it with sugar and ginger and dried figs and apricots and to turn it into soup and chutney and tarts. At the solstice, the evenings lasted until almost nine at night. The children gathered at Mill River or Kiwanis Park or Ziomek Field. The yelps of the college students as they departed from town with their diplomas were replaced by the sounds of summer in a small town: mowers going, hammers pounding, bikes zooming, balls against bats, whoops, cheers, and boos—and, of course, this being Amherst, occasional outbursts of "Deft!"

Teenagers headed to Silver Bridge up in Leverett and leapt off into the deep part, challenging themselves to miss the hard flat wet rocks that could kill them, or they went to Puffer's Pond, where the shadowed surface could hide a swimmer beneath its depths and had a menace easy to ignore amid the squeals of small children and the towels spread out like faded postage stamps in one of Lucia's albums. Sometimes up in North Amherst on a certain country road the most unearthly sound could be heard emanating from an otherwise-plain house: the mournful sighs, the rousing fillips, and the heavy-lidded schmoozing of Archie Schepp, jazz man, practicing the sax.

It was a slow season for growing that summer, but even in a year with perfect conditions the local corn is never ready on the Fourth, although everyone is sure it used to be. Many days were damp and sullen, and as a result the corn was especially late and the tomatoes came in tough and tasteless. In summer 1992 in the Pioneer Valley, the hours moved forward at a measured sluggish pace. Time was fat like a cow basking in the sun.

2

Late Night
When the Phone Rang

Jen and Jamila, who had already been selected as co-captains of the Hurricanes for the upcoming season, passed through the months of June and July and August in an uneasy truce, mostly apart from each other except for an Amateur Athletic Union event in Clovis, New Mexico. Although they felt emotionally distant from each other, they were cordial, and their team did well. During the final three years that Jen and Jamila were members of the Central Mass Cougars, an all-star team composed of high school players, the team finished fourth, second, and again second in the nation.

They returned home from AAU that year excited, filled with harrowing stories about how they had survived tornadoes and lightning and hail. The most overtly negative moment in the ten days did not involve the two friends, but rather Jamila's father, who, in search of a margarita to celebrate the team's triumph, went to a place called Kelley's; the guy collecting the cover charge, consulting with a partner, told the tall black novelist (a former Rhodes scholar who had played basketball while at Oxford, the winner of two PEN/Faulkner awards and a MacArthur fellowship) that he would not be served unless he removed his hat with the X in front.

Kelley's suddenly had a dress code.

In an article he later wrote about the incident in *McCall's* magazine, John Wideman said he'd thought of teasing them out of their stand with a show of humor: " 'Hey, Spike Lee. That hat you gave me on the set of the Malcolm movie in Cairo ain't legal in Clovis.' " He thought of giving them a quick history lesson: "You probably don't know much about Malcolm. The incredible metamorphoses of his thinking, his soul. By the time he was assassinated he wasn't a racist, didn't advocate violence. He was trying to make sense of America's history, free himself, free us from the crippling legacy of race hatred and oppression."

The writer was pulled back from a confrontation by the image of the girls' faces: "Girls of all colors, sizes, shapes, gritty kids bonding through hard clean competition." He passed on Kelley's.

When Jamila, the youngest of three children, was born in Denver in 1975, the doctors did not think she would live. Judy Wideman's pregnancy was compromised by a condition called placenta previa, which had necessitated a premature birth for Jamila by cesarean section, later described as a "long and bloody" ordeal by Jamila's father in *Brothers and Keepers* (a nonfiction meditation about his brother who is serving a life sentence for a murder committed during an armed robbery).

Her father wrote about how Jamila had been kept alive in the preemie ward, a room "full of tiny, naked, wrinkled infants, each enclosed in a glass cage. Festooned with tubes and needles, they looked less like babies than some ancient, shrunken little men and women, prisoners gathered for some bizarre reason to die together under the sizzling lights."

[Jamila's] arms and legs were thinner than my thinnest finger. . . . Each time she received an injection or had her veins probed for an I.V., Jamila would holler as if she'd received the final insult, as if after all the willpower she'd expended enduring the pain and discomfort of birth, no one had anything better to do than jab her one more time. What made her cries even harder to bear was their tininess. In my mind her cries rocked the foundations of the universe. . . . In fact, the high-pitched squeaks were barely audible a few feet from her glass cage. You could see them better than hear them because the effort of producing each cry wracked her body.

Eventually she would grow into a slender five feet, six inches and 130 pounds. She had distinctive curly eyelashes, framing eyes that appeared to look inward and outward with the same clear vision. On the court, the bones on her narrow sculpted face functioned like a flag, demanding to be heeded. Her father has written that her name means "beautiful" in Arabic: "Not so much outer good looks as inner peace, harmony. At least that's what I've been told. Neither Judy nor I knew the significance of the name when we chose it. We just liked the sound. It turns out to fit perfectly."

Jamila's father got a job teaching in the master of fine arts program at U Mass in 1986; he joined other black intellectuals and writers and musicians at the university, including Julius Lester, James Baldwin, and Max Roach.

Jamila became mysterious and legendary almost upon her arrival in Amherst, instantly known in the town's basketball circles as the only girl on the fifth- and sixth-grade traveling team. Diane Stanton has a son the same age as Jamila: Chris, who would go on to become the captain of the boys' team during their senior year. Diane remembers asking Jamila's oldest brother how she got to be so good.

"When she was little," he told her, "we let her play with us whenever she wanted, but we didn't give her any breaks."

Jamila tells people she started playing basketball the minute she was born. When she was a toddler, she watched the game being played incessantly. She finally felt like a real player when she was six or seven: "The first time I made an overhead shot as opposed to shoveling it under."

When she tried out for the varsity team in the seventh grade, there was no question about her making it.

"Jamila wasn't trying out. I was," says Coach Moyer. "Judy wanted to make sure her daughter was being coached by someone she approved of."

Two high school seniors on the team took Coach Moyer aside after seeing Jamila in action.

"You're going to keep her, right?"

"Who?" he asked.

"The little one. She's unbelievable. We want her on our team."

Tennis almost won Jamila over. During her one season as a varsity tennis player, she was Western Massachusetts champion.

In a 1993 cover story entitled "Queen of the Court" in *Hampshire Life*, a magazine pull-out section of the local *Daily Hampshire Gazette*, her former tennis coach Geoff McDonald (now the women's coach at Duke University) said, "She was one of the best athletes I've ever seen: she got stuff so fast it was frightening. She had the ability to come out of concentration, perfectly mimic what I showed her, and get right back into concentrating." Even in her friendships with the other Hurricanes, when she was out of town for an extended time and seemed to forget about them, her teammates sensed it had less to do with forgetting about them than with her unique ability to "be in the now, to live in the moment."

In the eleventh grade, she was the javelin champ in her league and also the Western Mass one-hundred-yard-dash champ.

42

If Jamila ended up taking on her father's game, she did so with her mother's wiry build and some measure of her intensity.

Jamila hoped to study law and African-American studies in college. Her mother was in her second year at Western New England Law School, and they joked about starting a firm called Wideman and Wideman. As a child of mixed races, Jamila was often asked by interviewers whether she identified more with being white or with being black. She answered that she identified most with being herself. Still, her bedroom featured pictures of Winnie Mandela, Jesse Jackson, and the children of Soweto. After the riot in Los Angeles, she wrote several poems, including this excerpt from "Black":

I walk the tightrope between the fires
Does anyone know where I fall through?
Their forked daggers of rage reflect my eye
Their physical destruction passes me by
Why does the fire call me?

Jamila's mother, with her long dark hair and glasses, a video camera hoisted on her small shoulders, was a fixture at all the games. She underwrote the purchase of new uniforms until the school and team's fund-raising efforts could afford to reimburse her; these were uniforms, chosen by Jen and Jamila, from a collegiate catalog. They liked the Stanford style, with its long wide legs, in large sizes. "Mr. Moyer," Jamila wrote in a note, "As Jen and I (Jamila) paused to observe a catalog we were struck by the beauty and elegance and class of the Stanford uniform example. Except those wretched socks. The rest we will take." "Yes," said Jen, "we want loose and big. Nothing tight. We want to be able to exhale. Inhale, too."

It was Judy Wideman who almost always prepared the pregame carbo-loading feast for the Hurricanes. After experimenting with several recipes, she settled on chicken sautéed in oil with garlic and lemon juice, served on pasta. John Wideman sometimes gave the play-by-play for the local cable network, and he always tried to work the many demands on his schedule as a lecturer and reader around his daughter's season. At the games his voice, with its distinctive blend of the street and the academy, could often be heard booming above all the others: "Go to the hole! D! Don't forget D! Oh, oh. Here comes the Brute," referring to Lauren Demski. It seemed to please him that in the sporting circles in which his daughter excelled, his work as a writer and the precise meaning of his awards were not always understood; he was once referred to as "Jamila's dad, winner of the prestigious Ken Faulkner award."

Jamila had a reputation for being treated protectively by her parents, and there was a myth that Jamila's parents did not allow her to ride in cars driven by people under twenty-five years old. At home she ate healthy food; at school she sometimes indulged her hankering for candy, and when during her junior year she made her thousandth point, she was honored by her friends with a thousand M&M's. Her favorite meal was breakfast; when she and her friends went out in a group, she tried to orchestrate their selections so the morning meal would be Chinese style—a pancake, a waffle, a piece of French toast for everyone, plus eggs and regular toast and juice.

One of Jamila's signature expressions was "Knock on wood." She carried a purple nylon fanny pack to all her games stuffed with mementos and amulets. She had a medallion that displayed a map of Africa in the colors of the ANC flag (black, green, and gold) and a miniature African mask, both from her mother. She had a blank book autographed by Nelson Mandela and Winnie Mandela and Desmond Tutu, given to her father on the day Mandela was released. She had Kenny Anderson's autograph; he was, like her, a left-handed point guard—he had played for Georgia Tech before joining the Nets. She had a necklace from one of her brothers—a peach pit carved so that it looked like two monkeys, a mother and a baby. She had an old silver spoon (she doesn't remember who gave it to her or why), as well as some lucky dice, a picture of Michael Jordan, and a page of quotes from him, including the one that most perfectly describes what it is to be a gifted individual on a team. "Basically, Jordan says the formula of success is learning how to balance being selfish in order to reach a certain level with being part of a team."

All of her teammates described Jamila as someone who leads by example. She often preferred to express herself outside language, in her actions as the Hurricanes' point guard. Her uncanny ability to know the narrative of a play, the plots and subplots, well before almost everyone else on the floor did, had attracted the attention of the local press when she was still in junior high.

Coach Moyer has a habit of referring to his strongest players as "leaders," but outsiders often called Jamila the "star" of the team, unaware that something about that word *star* made everyone on the Hurricanes, including Jamila, flinch. It was ignorant, or, as the teenagers like to say, clueless, annoying in the same way as people who persist in pronouncing the silent *h* in *Amherst*. For the same reason, periodic efforts to attach nicknames to her, by those who did not know better, never really took. Jamila was Jamila. It was that pure.

Jen Pariseau was known locally as the best thing that ever happened to Pelham, which to most people was nothing but a twinge of highway on Route 9; the sign that says ENTERING PELHAM is followed up so quickly by the one that says ENTERING BELCHERTOWN that Pelham appears to be not so much a real place as geographic sleight of hand. Now you see it, now you don't.

Compared to Amherst, Pelham has an outlaw quality

45

upheld by its history as the place where Daniel Shays led the local farmers in a tax rebellion in 1787. Angry because so many farmers were being turned into debtors, Shays and his men, called a regiment or a mob depending on whose point of view you support, marched all the way from Pelham to Springfield, closing down a session of the state's supreme court authorizing even more foreclosures. A riotous night followed, in placid South Hadley of all places, site of Mount Holyoke (the oldest women's college in the nation, with its famed tradition of "gracious dining" at least once a month and pianos and chandeliers in the dorms)—a riotous night that may have involved garroting and definitely involved rum.

There's a small general store near Jen's house where you can get soda and wine and doughnuts. "If you look hard, you can find something without dust on it. There are a couple of bait shops, a turkey farm, and lots of rocks with big dents supposedly caused by dinosaurs."

Pelham is so hilly that Jen was one of the few Hurricanes not to have some kind of hoop in her yard, no matter how rusty or weather-beaten.

"Why bother? The ball would just roll downhill to Amherst."

To an outsider, Amherst and its neighbors in the Pioneer Valley of the Holyoke mountain range look like just one place, a series of small towns and cities united in geographical fate. The locals know better, know how all the little towns and small cities in the Pioneer Valley vary depending on accidents of politics and geology, luck and the lack of it, depending on who got the rich farmland and who got the river, who got the university or the prison or the mental hospital or the state school for the retarded, but most especially, on who got drowned. The drowning happened in the thirties when the citizens of Boston, worried about their water supply, decided to ensure copious quantities by creating the Quabbin Reservoir. Four towns were given no-tice of their eventual demise: Greenwich, Dana, Enfield, and Prescott. Houses were razed, town halls torn down, cemeteries dismantled, stone by stone. In the year preceding the flooding, humans were forbidden to live in the valley, and the land was cleared of trees and bushes and any remnants of construction. Even so, the rumor persists that if you stare long and hard enough at the waters of the Quabbin, you will see schools and steeples and sidewalks. On December 31, 1939, the final town would be covered by water from the Swift River, a roar of liq-uid. The town of Pelham was spared, barely. Boston would not drown it, but instead used the state's powers of eminent domain to seize more than five thousand acres to provide the reservoir with a scenic border. As rugged and lovely as the Quabbin Res-ervoir is, the price was high, and for over half a century one of the deepest bonds in Western Massachusetts has been the re-sentment aimed at the eastern part of the state, perceived as high-handed and bullying.

"Those people in the East, they're different" is the usual tight-lipped code for the ongoing anger at the amputation of Pel-ham and the annihilation of four fine towns. But once you ac-knowledge a shared distrust for the eastern part of the state, the towns divide into self-standing units, filled with their own nu-ances and traditions.

The people who live in Pelham take a certain cantankerous pride in being next to, but nothing like, Amherst, and when they offer the name of their hometown, there is always a silent beat before they intone that name, bell-like yet faintly belligerent: "I'm from . . . Pelham." During her frequent visits to Pelham, Jamila found the people there to be more outgoing, looser than those in Amherst. As she once told her parents, "Everyone in Pelham is funny."

Jen had been raised by her father since she was two and her

brother, Chris, was four. Her father was a former basketball player himself—for the nuns back at Holy Family of New Bedford. He is tall, with curly hair that reinforces the good cheer of a round face quick to smile. The hats he habitually wears hide a hairline that his loyal friend Coach Moyer says is "fading as fast as his jump shot." Only if you really press Bob Pariseau will he admit, in an accent faintly flavored with the broad A's of his southeastern Massachusetts upbringing, that his team was called the Blue Waves, a name that owed its inspiration to the nearby ocean. He's more eager to tell you about his team going all the way to the finals in 1967, only to lose in Boston Garden. Every now and then Jen wore his letter jacket. Once someone asked Jen if the jacket belonged to her boyfriend: "It would be pretty illegal if it did."

Occasionally she tells people ahead of time that he has a stutter: "It goes away, for some strange reason, when he's really angry or upset about something. That's one way you can tell," she says, letting her eyes bug out menacingly in imitation of the anger. The loyalty runs deep. When, during the recruiting process for college, a representative of one of the Ivies wouldn't let her father finish his sentences, Jen decided to turn the school down then and there.

Sometimes Jen teases her father, tells him there should be a statute of limitations on embarrassing childhood stories, especially the one about the day—after driving an hour that morning to drop both children at day care before getting to his work and an hour again in the evening to get everyone back home—he'd walked into the house, overwhelmed by the demands of dinner and laundry and a diaper to change.

"Jenny," he'd said. She'd looked up, with her small freckled face and dark cap of hair. "I can't deal with these anymore. Use the toilet . . ."

From then on there were no more diapers. Years later as a

student at the Pelham School, when asked to fill out a report about what others did for you, she didn't bother to hand one in.

"But, Jenny," her teacher had protested, "what's up? You always hand in your schoolwork."

"It's just that I do everything myself."

"She was," says her father, "always very independent."

As a teenager she was tall (five feet, nine inches), taut, and tightly built. She joked about being flat-chested, and when during a sports physical a nurse-practitioner asked if her family had a history of breast cancer, she said, "Ma'am, we don't have a history of breasts."

Across the road from Jen's house is a trail leading to a waterfall where Jen liked to sit and think what she called "fruity thoughts." Every now and then when exploring these woods one encounters a column of bricks sticking up out of the ground unconnected to anything else. The strange druidic sight of what Jen called "random chimneys" is deeply New England; they are relics of houses in the woods lost, usually, to fire. Sometimes Jen stopped off at the Pelham graveyard, a gold mine of lore for scholars of moldering stones, engraved with jingles like

Death is a debt to Nature due
Which I have paid and so must you.

The burial ground in Pelham has in it a soldier from the Revolutionary War, and it offers proof that even in death we are not all equal. Only men were allowed to be pictured in their carved likenesses with buttons, the more the better. Buttons meant wealth. During that summer before her senior year, Jen often found time to slip off and run on trails of her own making. With her trademark running style she would frequently travel down these private paths of her own invention, speeding along in a kind of glide, never faltering over the easy traps of rocks or roots.

This was where she felt peace come dropping slow. "In the woods," as she always says, "everyone's a poet."

She started playing tennis at the age of three with a whiffle ball and a racquet. When she was six or seven, she played T-ball. She loved Little League, where at first the boys on the opposing teams would poke each other in the ribs at the sight of a girl on the mound: "Ha, ha. We're not going to let that girl strike us out." Soon these comments changed to "Oh, no, we gotta go against Jenny! Again!" By the time she was in the sixth grade she knew she wanted to be an athlete, but her budding career met with a rebuff that she still can't bring herself to fully forgive. An ace shortshop and the only girl on a Little League team called the Red Sox, she was passed over when it came time to name the all-star team. "I'd been playing for three years. I was a pitcher, a first baseman, and a shortstop. But when it came time to pick the all-star team, I didn't make it. I was told it was because I couldn't bunt. It left a bitter taste about being excluded." She lamented the coverage of female athletes in sports magazines and papers: First, there was so little; second, what there was tended to include adjectives like *lithe* and *winsome* and *gorgeous*, which she thought should be outlawed in favor of more pertinent descriptions.

"You know. Words like *strong*."

She hated the way female athletes were presented in magazine photos too. "Whenever possible," she said, using one of her many funny accents, this time to imitate a publishing honcho giving mock directives, "they should be pictured wearing next to nothing. The poses should stress anatomy rather than skill, and ideally female athletes should be given a ton of attention only during negative times, especially when they are victims. Common examples? Like they're stabbed by a fan or something bad happens with their boyfriend."

* * *

Jen and Jamila both remembered what it was like at the beginning of basketball, when Coach Moyer had trouble convincing players and their families of the seriousness of the commitment to the girls' basketball team. In junior high they'd played varsity games when the gym would be empty of spectators except for maybe their parents and a few lost souls who had missed the late bus. Coach Moyer was always getting upset at girls who cut practice to go to their boyfriends' games. A few years ago, during play-offs, a captain had left to go on a school-sponsored cultural exchange for three weeks in the former Soviet Union (with Moyer's reluctant permission). Since then his standards had changed, and so had girls' basketball. As far as he's concerned, the current policy could not be clearer: You want cultural exchange? You can have it with Hamp.

Even during their junior year when the stands had started to fill out in the scruffy but hopeful fashion of a tree in spring, the announcers still had trouble with both their names: "And here we have, representing the Lady Hurricanes, number eleven, Jamilia Whitman, and number twenty-two, Jen Parisio."

It was during junior year that Jen had grappled with the sensation that her friendship with Jamila was slipping away. It was hard not to feel the blade of resentment when Jamila's picture showed up in the *Gazette,* surrounded by a tumble of paper. SCHOOLS ARE LINING UP FOR WIDEMAN, said the headline, and the caption under her photo read, "The recruiting mail addressed to Jamila Wideman pours in at the rate of about a dozen pieces a day." Jamila had more than 150 recruitment letters from colleges. The *Blue Star Index,* a ratings guide of athletes, said she was the nation's second best guard. She was a *Parade* magazine first team all-American, a *USA Today* first team all-American, a Converse, Nike, and Kodak all-American.

The two girls were used to each other's company. On occasion, Jamila had joined the Pariseaus on Cape Cod during their two weeks there every summer. Jen's father, who supervises the reservoirs and water supply for the town of Amherst, has a habit on these vacations of pointing out even the most unpromising puddle and gushing about "primordial swamps."

The Widemans had taken Jen on several family trips to Maine and to Pittsburgh, John Wideman's hometown and the setting of his semiautobiographical *Homewood Trilogy*, a scruffy, steep-hilled, no-nonsense, hard-labor kind of town filled with the memory of smoke and sweat. Jen remembered sitting on the porch of Jamila's grandmother's house with her extended family and watching people in the neighborhood do a double take at the sight of her small grinning white face: "You could almost hear them say, 'What's wrong with this picture?'" There the two girls sometimes slipped away to one of the local hoops where, pretending to be novices, they would ask, innocently, if they could join a group of guys in a game.

Once they'd gone to a fancy literary gathering in Florida where Jamila's father was a featured speaker, along with Tracy Kidder and Jane Smiley. Jen and Jamila never recovered from the hostesses who prattled about the gold-plated plumbing on their yachts. John Wideman was introduced as having just returned "from meeting Nelson Mandela with Reggie Jackson in South Africa." To smooth over the gaffe (all Jacksons are the same), he added his own humor.

"Are you sure you don't mean Michael?" Jamila's father had said with a grin, knowing of course it had been Jesse.

Now, it felt to Jen as if just getting to see her old friend was difficult. It was like being one of the masses at the deli at Stop & Shop: Take a number, stand in line.

Two skinny dark-haired girls, all bones and ponytails, they were easily twinned. In Amherst the names of JennyandJamila were often spoken of in just one word. There was euphony in the sound, it had lilt, it sang, but in some ways it obscured the differences in their styles both on and off the court. Jamila was the "gown" kid, the one whose father was the force at the university, who led a life international in its scope. On court she was the breadwinner who always drove the basket home.

Jen was the "town" kid. Sitting outdoors at the tables in front of Bonducci's coffee shop next to Hastings, drinking the ritual juice or water favored by the Hurricanes, she would keep one eye out for the town trucks to see if she knew any of the drivers through her father and his work. Often she would fling her arm up and give a big wave and a smile, gestures always returned in kind. With her teammates she had unerring radar for the kid who needed a successful bucket, for the kid who needed a shoulder to cry on.

Jen dreaded the fall, and the return to school and to everyone else's excited forecasts about this year's Hurricanes:

Hey, maybe this could be the big year, at last.

People had been predicting that for the past couple of years.

The bountiful blue balmy days at the end of summer in New England are tender because they are so short-lived, and she was feeling that tenderness within herself as if it had physical reality, a sore that would not heal. What if she felt as bad this year as she had the last? She was, with luck, coming up soon on her thousand-point milestone. She recalled with sickening ease the wave of emptiness she'd felt where there should have been joy on the day Jamila had reached her thousandth point. Instead of being excited that her friend was so good, Jen had castigated herself for not being good enough. Would Jamila feel the same mix of would-be goodwill and actual discomfort that Jen had experienced?

Sometimes at the end of a long day, she would stretch out on the water bed in her room. Jen prided herself on her efficiency; she had an engineer's creativity when it came to objects and space. Once, on a long trip with her teammate Emily "Jones-bones" Jones and Emily's mother, Bernadette, when everyone was sure there was way too much stuff, she'd figured out which book bags could be foot rests, which sleeping bags could be unfurled as seat cushions and which could be used as blankets.

As for the most efficient way to store her own huge assortment of T-shirts, this was her trick:

"You could stack them in big piles in drawers that are never big enough, or you could lay them flat on the floor, fold them lengthwise into thirds, then take the remaining panel and fold that into thirds, then roll the fabric into cylinders with the logo showing, saving space and eventually time, because it's now so much easier to find what you're looking for, such as the one Lucia designed for us that says, WE'RE BUSTING OURS . . . SO WE CAN KICK YOURS, or how about this one: REAL MEN MARRY ATHLETES."

She recently saw one that she would like to add to her wardrobe: FEMINISM IS THE CRAZY NOTION THAT WOMEN ARE PEOPLE.

On the wall she had a picture of a basketball hoop drawn by Lucia with a poem written by another Hurricane, Rita Powell. Above her head was her aforementioned "strong women" wall, including pictures of Texas governor Ann Richards, writers Toni Morrison and Maya Angelou, actress Candice Bergen, and singer Bonnie Raitt. She also had copies of the Nike inspirational ads: JUST DO IT!

And from Jamila's father, who had interviewed Michael Jordan for a cover story in Esquire ("Is He Our New DiMaggio?"), she had the autograph of the former Bulls' starring guard. She knew the first lines of Jamila's father's article by heart: "When it's played the way it's spozed to be played, basketball happens in the air, the pure air."

By her bedside she kept a clothbound book—given to her by her teammate Rita—in which she wrote her favorite quotes, a customized *Bartlett's*.

MARILYN MONROE: "If I'm going to be alone, I'd rather be by myself."

COLETTE: "You will do foolish things, but do them with enthusiasm."

LILY TOMLIN: "Just remember. We're all in this alone."

ZORA NEALE HURSTON: "The Dream is the Truth."

Jen was a girl who had Definite Opinions, such as that spandex is a sin against society, and so are hair spray, cats, and the Beatles. Teva sandals are ostentatious, when plain old thongs are just as good. The person who invented mesh was a genius. Jen liked to manufacture her own aphorisms, and one time she gave Rita a list of eight of "life's little instructions according to Jen." The final bit of advice was set apart from the others in large aching capital letters:

1. Don't sweat the small stuff.
2. Everything is small stuff.
3. Fix what's broken.
4. Don't put on deodorant when you need to take a shower.
5. A day without laughter is a day wasted.
6. Always check the toilet before you sit down to make sure no one left the plunger in it.
7. No amount of pain is insignificant except a pain in the ass.
8. NEVER GIVE ALL OF YOURSELF TO ANYONE.

Most adolescents tend to one or the other of two emotional styles, surly insurrection or, as in the case of Jen, brooding self-definition. On a birthday card to Rita she offered "Jen's Philosophy 101":

The first time a bird flies into a window, he didn't see it.
The second time, he didn't know it was there.
Third time, then Jen walks away, because that bird is an
    idiot.

Jen liked to make people laugh. She had set pieces about
commercials that got on her nerves, like the one with the Ener-
gizer rabbit. She told dumb jokes about how diarrhea runs in the
genes, and then she would say, "That's my opinion, and everyone is entitled to my opinion." She would tell her friends:
"These are just some of the things I think about while the
teacher's talking."

Lying on her back on her bed, with her row of stuffed
Gummi Bears staring outward on the shelf above, she would
drift into that space where you're not really awake but you're
not really asleep either.

She was helping out a lot at Coach Moyer's summer camps.
Under town supervision, these sessions in which young children
were treated like future Hurricanes were a popular activity in
Amherst. Although there had been all-boy camps and coed
camps, this was the first summer a girls-only session had been
offered.

Many of Ron Moyer's current and past players were hired
to work at the camps, but Jen stood out as the most hospitable
to the very young kids, treating them as equals, or as equal as it
is possible for someone half her size to actually be.

She applauded their moves on the court, she let them shoot
with her, she laughed at their riddles as if they were funny and as
if she'd never heard them before.

During such moments the feelings of alienation from the
previous season would vanish. For three hours in the morning
five days a week, the ball in her hand would assume a familiar
reassuring heft, and out of her hands it would move with a fluid-

ity missing from that final game with Hamp. Sometimes at the end of a session the little kids would ask if she would consider dropping by their birthday party as a special guest, and at first she thought it was strange, but then it started to occur to her that the difference between a role model and an idol was that a role model was someone you could touch. Sometimes they asked if they could write papers about her for school. "Please be my pen pal," asked one little girl. "You don't even have to write back."

"What kind of pen pal is that? Of course I'll write back to you!"

She would tease the small girls and ask *them* if she could write papers about them, and she called them goddesses. She had a theory that every female could be a goddess of something, whether lowly or exalted. If you were little and never sure of what to say, you could be the goddess of giggling. If you wore braces, you could be the goddess of shackled teeth. If you were smart and nice and wore size-fourteen shoes, like Jonesbones, then you qualified for a triple crown as the goddess of advanced calculus and of kindness and of really big feet. Jen's own ability to put up a three with enough air to graze the gym rafters or touch the sky had earned her the nickname of "Cloudy." She would like to be known as the goddess of the three-point shot, the home run of basketball.

A scent of celebrity now followed Jen, that unseen but palpable buzz whenever she popped into town to pick up the paper at Hastings or indulge in a piece of pizza. She was always running into some little kid whose eyes lit up at the sight of her. She and Jamila had volunteered as peer counselors at Wildwood Elementary School; children who lived up to their behavior-management contracts (basically innocent documents in which fidgety children made a pledge to fidget less) were rewarded with the chance to play pickup ball with the co-captains. Even if Jen couldn't place the child or summon the right name instantly, she had a politician's instinct for working a crowd. To the little boys she would say, "How's it going, big guy?"; to the girls, "You go, girl." And if they found themselves speechless in the presence of such a glittering personage, Jen would say, "Come on, you can talk to me. What's the matter? Do you have constipation of articulation?"

And so it was that after a typically busy summer day, at around midnight, Jen's seventeen-year-old self tired from coaching, lifting, running, and reflecting, the phone rang.

"Hi."

Jen recognized Jamila's voice right away. Still, it was a surprise. She knew Jamila was in Maine, and Jamila had that way of living in the present: When she was out of town, you knew better than to count on a phone call or a letter. That quality, of being there for the moment and squeezing the life out of it, could sometimes be a trial during a friendship but was probably one of her biggest assets on the floor. When Jamila was there, she was *there*.

"I'm up here in Maine, and I've been thinking a lot about you. We have to talk."

The pause that followed was almost imperceptible, but in its infinitesimal nature hung the balance of a friendship.

Jen glanced at the receiver, and then twisted her head backward to see the eyes of all those strong women bearing down upon her.

When she found her voice, it was clear and strong: "You're right. We do."

"I wish you were up here too."

Jen listened, coiled as a telephone cord.

"I'm here with a couple of friends, and my mom wouldn't let me bring more than two people."

Jen knew the absence of an invitation had to do with more than mere maternal edict, even if Jamila's mom was known for a certain control over her daughter's schedule and whereabouts.

Jamila went on, "I want things to be better between us next year. . . ."

The inner terrain of teenage girls tends to change every thirty seconds or so, but on this occasion Jen became Totally Serious, and she stayed that way a long time.

When Jen got serious, her entire face, her whole body, every fiber and sinew, showed it. As Jamila continued, in her pleasant even voice with its deeply American, almost geographically generic, pilotlike use of dropped endings and expressions like *y'all*, Jen got very still, except for the eyes, as lively as two small gray animals.

When teenagers communicate on the phone, it's not always the content of the conversation but the fact of its having occurred that carries the deepest meaning. They are at an age and in an economic bracket where a long-distance call still carries cachet.

Two hours later, a feeling of relief combined with the heavy weight of fatigue, that cumbersome sagging force, was the only reason they both hung up.

3

Onions and Metal Nets

The gods of hoop had been kind to Coach Moyer.

In a small town it's always a thrill to have athletes of the quality of a Jamila Wideman or a Jen Pariseau but to have both of them on one team was a kind of miracle, like some new and rare hybrid discovered by the research scientists at the university creating a two-headed stalk of corn. Their presence on the Hurricanes, their continuous struggle to maintain excellence and to diminish the lash of rivalry that rises up naturally between two talented people, had a curious and ameliorating effect on the rest of the girls in town who aspired to play high school hoop.

That summer, they all made an individual decision to improve, to excel, to push themselves to the limit, and beyond.

Their crusade had, in many ways, a cheerful component. The image used by one local townsperson was of the dog alert at the end of *101 Dalmatians*, but instead of warning one another of danger, they were alerting one another to opportunity:

"Just do it!" they seemed to croon and bark to one another and to the Holyoke mountain range that embraces Amherst at its south border and the Pelham hills to the east.

If you did not live in Amherst and you were just passing

through, the sight of the individual girls would be simple and unmemorable, a girl with a ponytail running, a girl with a ponytail lifting weights, a girl with a ponytail running up and down the steps at the U Mass stadium. But if you knew them, knew these girls, knew their parents and their brothers and their sisters, knew about their secret goal, it became a kind of subtext in the town, a way of reading reality that might be lost on those not yet literate in the alphabet of a certain kind of young, female, athletic ambition.

The girls who were working so hard were not necessarily going to be the starters; some, like Rita Powell, would be grateful to return to the junior varsity.

Rita had a plan.

As one of the younger girls on the junior varsity, a sort of diva in waiting, she had listened carefully to Coach's final talk in March 1992, taking his words as a kind of spiritual injunction:

Dedicate some time . . . get yourself ready . . . challenges next year.

Like Lucia and the other young players—Jan Klenowski and Carrie Tharp and Jessi Denis—she had studied the older girls on the Hurricanes as if they were a painting or some kind of fascinating rock formation. Also a freshman, she wished that she, like Lucia, had been moved up for the postseason from junior varsity to varsity. Of course she was not the equal of Jen and Jamila ("No way!"). Her goal for the coming 1992–93 season was to be moved up to varsity in the postseason. She was appalled by that final game with Hamp; it made her shudder to recall the image of Jamila racing back and forth on the court, coast to coast, a human boomerang, going it all alone, looking, in Rita's eyes, "insane." Jamila had given up on her team ever coming to life, and so she had tried to do it all herself. Rita wanted powerfully to avenge that memory, to expunge it forever. And Jen was just as significant a figure as Jamila. Why, in her own journals,

Rita had called the dark-haired senior with the light eyes beneath the thick bushy brows the "most dynamic person I have ever met." Rita listened to Jen carefully and often recorded her remarks. To Jen they may have been mere asides; to Rita they shimmered with intimacy: "Jen is such a giving person. 'If I can make five people smile every day, I'm happy. That's what floats my boat,' she told me. Another time she said, 'My problems aren't me. I don't let them define me.' "

An only child, Rita lived with her mother and father and several cats in a cozy house in which she had a choice of two rooms to call her own. One was spacious but dark. The other was minuscule, with not even enough floor space left over after the bed and bureau and a couple of bookshelves were in position for a friend to camp out in a sleeping bag. But it had two windows, facing south and west, so that the room often filled up with the sun or the moon. The window to the south looked out on a large field. She chose the room with the light.

Rita Powell was not a wealthy person, but she has been known all her life for her intensity. "Even when she was a baby, when she wanted something, nothing got in her way. The first time she learned to use a cup, it was *cupcupcup* all day long," said her mother, Anne Teschner.

And this summer she wanted nothing so much as to spend a week at a basketball camp in the eastern part of the state run by a former center for the Boston Celtics that she'd heard about from Jan Klenowski, a point guard on the junior varsity. She wrote away for a brochure and memorized it, not just the words, but also the glossy picture, a shot of the floor of the gym, showing just the feet and the hands of someone dribbling a ball on the shiny hardwood. There were four sets of Puma-clad feet (plus legs) in all, black ones and white ones, and the soft focus made it hard to know for certain whether they belonged to males or females. "Play ball," it said, ". . . with Dave

Cowens and friends at the 20th Annual Dave Cowens Basketball School." The camp commenced on a Sunday at 1 P.M. and ended the following Saturday with a tournament. Most days followed the same schedule:

7:15 A.M. wake-up
8:00 A.M. breakfast
9:00 A.M. roll call
9:05 A.M. lecture/demonstration
9:35 A.M. calisthenics/stretching
9:50 A.M. practice/drill stations/3 on 3
10:45 A.M. games/free throws
12:00 noon lunch
1:15 P.M. roll call
1:20 P.M. lecture/demonstration
2:00 P.M. calisthenics/stretching
2:15 P.M. practice/drill stations/3 on 3
3:00 P.M. games/free throws
4:20 P.M. swimming/free time
5:00 P.M. dinner
6:20 P.M. calisthenics/stretching
6:30–8:30 P.M. practice/drill stations/3 on 3
8:30 P.M. canteen opens, movies/free time
9:45 P.M. canteen closes
10:00 P.M. settle down and relax

The only impediment to Rita's plan was the price: three hundred and ninety-five dollars for a resident camper.

So, right after the loss to Hamp, she set about earning money. From eight until eleven in the morning every Sunday, she could be seen outside Saint Brigid's Catholic Church with its formal Italianate exterior (named for the saint who'd founded Ireland's first nunnery), selling the *Springfield Union*, the *Boston*

Globe, and the *New York Times*. She arrived as bundled up as her wares. "I wore, oh my God, *many* clothes. Two pairs of long johns." Early spring can be just as cold as winter, with the added bonus that the air is often filled with the fine dust that comes from previously frozen mud. Her fingers fumbled over the freezing metal coins. "Oh my God."

Rita Powell owned the innate good cheer that seems to attach to people who can sing. She had a habit of doodling the air with random bits of music that ranged from children's songs on an old Sara Pirtle tape to the kinds of complicated music she sings in chorale, including the crazy mélange of pitches and rhythms, the calculated discordance and odd rests of Peter Schickele's *After Spring Sunset*. But her baby-sitting job for three little boys five and under who fought all the time managed to dent those high spirits. "They annoyed me, they jumped on me, they would never do anything constructive like go for a walk." They agreed about nothing except that girls are yucky, an opinion they proffered to Rita with irritating frequency. "Oh my God, the way they fought!"

Rita worked for her uncle who made Birch Hill Country Foods barbecue sauce. She cut up onions, mounds and mounds of them: "Oh my God, *many* onions."

Rita was a thrifty sort. She disapproved of how juniors and seniors always spend a fortune renting limousines to go to the prom; when she accepted an invitation to a dance, she did not buy a new dress but instead found a reasonably priced vintage dress that had a strapless peach-colored bodice connected to a drapey black floor-length skirt.

Slowly the money began to accumulate—twenty dollars on Sunday mornings, five dollars an hour with the kids, fifty for a couple of days of onions.

When she finally got to Dave Cowen's camp, she loved it. Her goal at the camp was to be "just like Jen Pariseau, totally outgoing" and to meet everybody there by the end of the week, which she managed to do. Because she was so busy, she could not find a spare moment to write in the journals she normally kept so faithfully, those dozen or so paper- and clothbound books, with covers that catch her fancy. These are her earthly treasures, and she keeps them in plain view on her bookcase, with full faith that neither of her parents would ever read them. "That would be too violating," she says, using a favorite word of the Hurricanes that has random (another favorite word) applications, referring to anything from true violations to mere annoyances, like unmatched socks or the wrong flavor cereal. Rita has a tradition of writing the same faintly formal words on the second to the last page of each volume: "As is my custom, I leave this last page blank that my writing may never cease . . ."

In these books she confided about her boyfriends, and her teammates, and her parents—especially if they'd had a fight or they wouldn't let her do something—and her deepest ambitions, such as how she hopes to be either the "first female president" or a "weird reclusive herbalist." She did manage to dash off one note to her parents:

Hey Guys!
How you doin'? I'm having a ball! The basketball is excellent! My team—Stanford—is three and one. I'm averaging eight points a game. I am playing low post which is fun! I am also meeting nine million people so I am *always* busy! One of my best friends here is Megan Cowens—she's really funny. Last night, this other girl—Tasha—taught all of us to sing *Lean on Me* in harmony sort of. There's this kid named Ben who says "In like Flynn" like you, Mom. There's Monika who'll be an eighth grader and who's already six feet tall (she's on my team). There's Kristi who wears a bun on top of

her head while she plays and talks with me in a made up language. Well, anyhow, if I kept talking about everyone I met I'd be here forever. I got your letter delivered to my room, and I got a letter from Megan Carpenter. Well, guys, I have to shower so I'll catch you later. Bye.

Love,

Rita.

Lucia Maraniss also had a plan.

All her life Lucia had loved to draw. She possessed a dissecting eye, often studying what it is precisely that makes up an appearance. Coach Moyer, for instance, had spindly legs and thick graying brown hair that flopped over his head in a youthful fringe. She noticed people's gestures and their tics. Whenever Coach Moyer told a joke, you had to laugh, because there would be a pause when his face flooded with expectation. The bluish gray eyes joined yours; time stopped while he awaited a response. He always looked neat to her, almost as if he were hanging from a coat hanger. It had something to do with the boxy elongated head on top of a torso with a similar configuration. The sense he gave of being wide as well as tall had nothing to do with excess girth; it came from the shoulders and from the lips, which stretched across the bottom of his face in a narrow band, giving him easy access to expressions of distractedness, deep thought, or disapproval. One time, Patri Abad, a girl who used to be on the team but had moved away (dear Patri, kind, talented, beautiful Patri stuck now in Chicago rather than here in Amherst where she belonged) had called him Rectangle Man, but not, of course, to his face.

To his face he was Coach, Coach Moyer, and the Big Guy.

One day Lucia took her art utensils and some paper and

some tiny scraps of wallpaper and decided to create what was not so much a letter as a work of art to send to her friend Patri in Chicago. She planned to take the paper and cut it into stamp-sized squares to create a border around the rectangle of words.

Lucia adored Patri's family. She had an older brother, Tony, and two younger brothers, Jose and Reggie. Patri's mother, Ilene, was Puerto Rican, her father was Cuban, and her stepfather (with whom her mother had had Reggie) was black. Lucia's mother, Gigi Kaeser, who worked as a preschool teacher and a photographer, was considering asking them to be part of a project that she planned to entitle "(✓) Other: Portraits of Multiracial Families."

The team needed Patri. It was that simple. Everyone wanted her back in town. She was the one teammate everyone agreed about: She was funny, she was energetic, she defused tensions simply by existing. No matter what she did or said, she made you laugh. In town at the Pub for a meal, she would amuse her dining companions by taking a tomato slice and turning it into a smiley face. Once on a car trip with her teammates Patri had tried to warn the car alongside them that the cap was off their gas tank. She kept twisting her hand back and forth. With everyone laughing, Jen had finally begged her to stop: "The guy thinks you're telling him to feel up his wife." So she stopped, and then she and Kathleen Poe, the driver, engaged in another highway trick. Kathleen laid her head down on the driver's side, pretending to be asleep, while Patri steered.

Patri was light, Patri was harmony, Patri was a riot, Patri was a necessary component to the success of the upcoming season.

Lucia wrote:

Patri,
    You should always remember to follow your dreams. Do you remember when we were playing

basketball outside at Amherst College, and you told me what you wanted to do in the future? You should definitely open up a five-story nightclub place with different music on every floor, after you become a biologist. Then after that maybe you'll have a few kids. But after that, you should look me up (I'm going to be a college professor in England) and we'll take a trip together or something.

Patri, I will always remember you as one of the wisest, most caring and compassionate people I've ever met. I'm going to miss you very, very, very, very, very, very, very, very, very, very, very, very, very, very, very much . . .

♥ always from your buddy: Lucia.

Kim Warner also had a secret strategy.

"Mom, can I borrow the car?"

"Where are you going?"

"Out."

"Just out?"

"Sort of."

"Ballpark figure when you'll get back?"

"Not late."

"Be careful. I know, everyone says this is Amherst, nothing bad ever happens here, but remember what happened at the mall."

Sue Warner also worked two nights a week at a department store at the Hadley Mall. It was there in December 1989, in an act of violence that did much to erode the sense of security, even complacency, in the community, that the body of a young woman who had been shopping for the holidays was discovered in her car, stabbed repeatedly, a day after her sorority sisters at the university had reported her missing. For months afterward, female employees of the store where Sue Warner worked would not venture into the parking lot at night except in a group.

"Mom, don't worry, I'll be careful."

Kim took the keys to the 1986 Dodge Lancer, and sliding into the driver's seat, she thought about the upcoming season.

Kim was going to be a senior in the fall. Most seniors hope that this will be the year, at last, to be a starter, but Kim had no such fantasies.

Her goal was simply to be part of a steady rotation off the bench, to be someone her teammates could count on when they needed fresh oxygen the most. Sometimes even that ambition, as modest as it might seem to some, struck her as impossible. All summer she could not shake the feelings of disappointment that had dogged her after that last game of the 1992 season.

The memory was alive and writhing, a fish that she wished she could just throw back in the river.

She had arrived home that night after the final game, said good night to her mother, and waited for the profound quiet of sleep to seep through the house; then, gliding silently out of bed and down the hall, she went into the bathroom, and with a light touch of her hand she whispered the light on.

She forced herself to gaze in the mirror.

Once again she'd let the team down.

With only thirty seconds to go against Hamp, Coach had given her the signal to join the action.

"Whatever you do, Kim, don't get called for a foul."

She had been nursing an ankle injury, and he didn't want her to get hurt again.

She'd walked out onto the floor, with the big C for Cathedral painted in the middle, and within seconds she was elbowed by the Blue Devils' Lauren Demski (called "Truck" and "the Brute" and "Space Eater" by the Hurricanes, because of her fearsome style). She fell on the floor, and while she was lying there outstretched and helpless, a crab on its back, the ref called a foul. On Kim.

Later, in the locker room, Kim lied.

"God, Kim, were you hurt?" asked one teammate. "Are you okay?" another inquired.

"I'm fine," she told them, "nothing happened." And on the bus ride back to Amherst she'd been grateful to the darkness for camouflaging the discoloration all over the inside of her chin.

But examined in the bright light of her own bathroom, which her mother had decorated with tulip wallpaper and lace curtains, the bruise was more than "nothing": It was huge and blue and swollen, a relief map of every time she failed to deliver on the court, every time she froze in the paint and missed a shot and disappointed Jen and Jamila and especially Kathleen Poe, the Hurricane she had known the longest, a senior who hoped to be a forward starter. The students in Amherst's public schools get out early on Wednesdays, and during grade school they'd spent every Wednesday afternoon together. She knew all kinds of stray information about Kathleen's past, including that she used to be a pickle fanatic, able to eat an entire jar in one sitting.

Coach Moyer had given me a million chances to prove I want to be a part of the team. All he asked was that I not foul. When we were down by twenty he urged us: "Let's get this within twelve points, not for the fans, but for you guys."

Kim had looked at herself in the mirror. Her face had character and dignity, with a balanced purity to the features, but was it a face that could mean business?

She'd tightened her lips. All along her style had been to avoid contact, to put up jump shots instead of driving. But now she vowed:

I'm not going to be a passive player forever.

Then late that night she'd thrust the chin upward, as much of a salute as if she'd raised both fists:

NO MORE!

Five feet, ten inches tall with broad shoulders and plenty of upper-arm strength, she looked like a natural.

The youngest child in a family of four, she was brought up by her mother, Sue Warner. As far back as Kim could remember, her mother had worked two jobs. Her full-time job was as a secretary in personnel at the university. Because of budget cuts authorized by the state legislature in Boston, Kim's mother, like everyone else, had not received a raise in four years. Morale was low, and the feelings of disgruntlement had had a trickle-down effect on the entire Amherst community. In the eighties, real estate and faith in the future had been the drugs of choice in Amherst. It was a time of view, view, view—dream houses sprouting up all over town, with their cedar exteriors and Jenn-Aire stoves and Corian counters. But as the university goes, so goes Amherst; now the university was in a cut-your-losses mentality, and so was the whole town. Parts of the campus were in a state of shocking disrepair: leaking ceilings, walls with holes, exposed sockets, and that most potent sign of institutional depression, broken clocks. One faculty member dubbed it the "University of Dead Lightbulbs," adding that this was not a reference to the students. Lacking the money for niceties, one department served graduating students and their parents an official precommencement breakfast consisting of Dunkin' Donuts on paper plates with a Christmas theme. Once in a while, at least at the beginning of all the belt-tightening, veteran staffers put on brave faces and drew a comparison between the school and the land, praising the pruning, talking about how it is possible to overplant and how an interval of fallowness often precedes the richest crops.

The children in Kim's family are all exactly two years apart. The oldest two are married, and the Hurricanes often speculated, since Kim had the most serious ongoing relationship with a boy, that she might be the first Hurricane to get married. She was certainly the most domestically inclined. She was the one Coach Moyer would ask to sew patches onto the uniforms, and she brought the best homemade chocolate chip and sugar cookies to practices. She expected to go to one of the state colleges, though not to U Mass, which she thought was too big. After she graduated, she wanted to work with children, to be "someone special" for them, the same way Ms. Bouley at Crocker Farm Elementary School had been there for her when Kim was in kindergarten and she would get to leave her regular class for special time in Ms. Bouley's Resource Room. It wasn't because Kim was hyper or disruptive; in fact her problem was the opposite. She was too quiet, steeped in a profound silence, at least in public. Ms. Bouley has always saved a small school photo showing Kim in a jumper with a Winnie the Pooh theme, which Kim gave to her as a gift; in Ms. Bouley's experience as a teacher, students were glad to give you a photo if you asked, but only a few offered, and those she always saved. Kim had been told that when she was ready to student-teach, she had a classroom waiting.

Kim had taken her first baby-sitting jobs in the fifth grade. When she was fifteen she went to town hall and got a permit to work at Cushman's General Store in North Amherst for twenty hours a week.

Kim's father had left the family when she was nine, and she did not see him from fourth through eighth grade.

"One night he happened to be back in Amherst, and he called. I was the one who answered the phone, and I dropped it. My mom picked it up, and he must have asked if he could visit because she said, 'I don't know. Let me ask them.' "

Kim remembered saying she wanted to see him. But when he arrived, her oldest sister had felt differently.

73

"Sherri's room was in the basement. She wouldn't come up. My dad thought Pam was Sherri, and he thought I was Pam. It was a tough situation. My own dad didn't even know me. Then, he sat us down and talked to us. I sat on the couch between my brother and my mother, and my brother had his arm around me, and I had my head on my mom's shoulder. He tried to explain."

Kim had grown up in South Amherst in a small well-cared-for starter house that ended up a finish house as well, in a neighborhood with streets whose names embody a tweedy longing for what appears to be a British-flavored town-and-country ideal: Squire Lane, Atwater Circle, Brookside Court, Greenwich and Longmeadow and Farmington. When she was little, the neighborhood was all families, but lately people had moved away, and some of the houses were being rented to students. Sometimes she wished her mother, whose hobbies were crafts and changing the wallpaper and the window treatments in their small house, would move to a nice safe compact condo.

Kim always appreciated how hard her mother worked, and over the years she and the other children in the family had planned surprises for her. They'd schemed to give her a VCR, a microwave, a brass headboard for her bed, and a piece of jewelry known as a mother's ring, a gold band set with the birthstones of all four children. One time they'd really surprised her with four new tires.

Kim pulled out of the driveway of their ranch house and headed up Route 116 to Crocker Farm, where she had been an elementary school student along with numerous other Hurricanes, including Kathleen Poe, Emily Shore, and Rita Powell.

Wearing a T-shirt, shorts, and her game sneakers, she pulled into the dark parking lot and backed the car up so that the headlights would throw the greatest light possible on the hoops she had used as a child.

She got out of the car and gave the empty courts and fields a sweeping look. Good: She was alone.

She walked onto the court and dribbled in a fashion that might seem aimless to an outsider; but in fact she was glancing at parts of the pavement, imagining:

This is where Jen will throw me the ball, here is where Jamila will pull up and dish it off, here is where Kathleen might miss a shot, and this is where I have to be for the rebound.

She moved carefully, methodically, trying not to stress either of her ankles. Surgery was inevitable, but she wanted to make it through the 1992–93 season first. She inched her way closer to the basket:

Eight feet is too far away; shoot from eight and Coach will put me back on the bench just like he did in that last game against Hamp. Six feet. That's better. Right side off the backboard, through the chain-metal net. Left side, rattle it through. Over and over, spin right, dribble, jump. Drop step, pivot, shoot.

Applauded only by the mosquitoes and the crickets, she would take the ball and pound it on the asphalt and set up and shoot. Despite the noise from the bugs and the drone of traffic on Route 116, she heard nothing except the thud of the ball and the pulsing inside her chest, the steady beat of pride and exhaustion, the old brag of the athlete's heart.

For Kathleen Poe, it was torture waiting for the season to officially start. Sometimes to blunt the anxiety, she went running.

Nothing suited her more than to slip on her running shoes and set forth from her mother's ranch house with the big picture window in the living room and to run from South Amherst up to U Mass, to the football stadium where she did stairs and sprints in a routine she had cooked up on her own. Endorphin home brew, someone had called it.

Senior year would be fun, but it would also be emotional; everything was the Last Time for this, Last Time for that. She spent a lot of time thinking about where she would apply to college. Duke, probably; her parents had both gone there, but in recent years no one from Amherst had gotten in. Haverford and Williams sounded small and inviting. She would apply to Dartmouth as a reach, Bucknell as her safety school.

She had lived in only two places besides Amherst: Ithaca, where she'd been born while her father was a graduate student in social science, and Canterbury, England, where the family had spent a sabbatical semester when she was eight.

"Culturally, England wasn't so different from here except that at school the children wore uniforms, and boys and girls always lined up separately. In gym I remember how my classmates were impressed by my flexibility and how they could not believe I wanted to climb the rope. The only thing I hated were the butcher shops. They were so violating. It's not like here where everything is in packages and covered with cellophane."

When she'd made the connection between the hunks of flesh hanging from the ceiling and the polite chop on her plate dressed with parsley in a piece of fluted paper, she decided that she could not abide the thought of eating meat ever again.

Her father often teased her about the decision. "You're the only vegetarian I know who doesn't eat vegetables."

It grated on her that his attitude would not change when, as a professor at Hampshire College, he taught a course called Attitude Change.

This was one subject guaranteed to bring out the fight in her. "Dad, that's an old joke. Besides, the only two vegetables you cook I don't like: tomatoes and avocados."

"Now, Kathleen."

"At least I don't sneak those candy bars."

"Not anymore," he'd say, patting his belly. "I'm watching it."

Kathleen had progressed through school with nothing but accolades. Her report cards over and over reflected a child who'd been a pleasure to teach. She was "enthusiastic," "helpful," "consistently cheerful," "positive," "cooperative," "industrious," an "avid reader," an "absolute delight," and "a joy!"

Shortly after the family's return from England, her parents had separated; her father then sent a note to the school that read:

"Please allow my daughter Kathleen to take bus 2 to Hampshire College on Wednesdays and alternate Fridays as she is living with me on the Hampshire campus part-time."

The Hampshire College campus in the southernmost part of town is instantly recognizable as different, partly because of the proud nakedness of the buildings where few walls are covered with the traditional ivy. The first class had been admitted in 1970. The "mods," or apartments where the students live, are named Enfield, Greenwich, Prescott, and Dana after the lost towns of the Quabbin. The students refer to the school as Camp Hamp, and it prides itself on being a place where "it's okay to go outside the lines." No one gets upset if classes begin a few minutes late and then extend beyond the allotted time; students design their own curriculum, and classes are just another resource, like the library or the public lectures in the valley. There are no grades, just evaluations at the end of a course. Hampshire has no football team; the popular sports are kayaking and the martial arts. Until recently you could have pets in your room, and there were dogs, cats, bugs, and snakes. In recent years a major social event has been a Halloween dance where everyone goes in drag called the Drag Ball. Its most prominent graduates are in film and include people like Ken Burns, the creator of the PBS series on the Civil War. The only time bells are rung on campus is in honor of the one sacred moment at Hampshire, when a student completes the major project required for graduation. In the eighties a student did his on Frisbees, calling them "Flying Disc Entertainment." When Kathleen and her brother had visited the campus as kids, their favorite mischief was to sneak up the ramp to where the bell is housed and ring it just for fun.

"It was like really cool to do."

At U Mass she would enter the arena and look up at the stands, those stacks of seats against the sky. The emptiness was exhilarating; without the music and the fans and the thud of bodies, it was as if it all belonged to her.

First she would run up and down a bunch of stairs one step at a time, and even as she pursued her training for the upcoming season, her thoughts were as always drawn back in time to the ooze of that memory:

Humiliated, again. Nobody knew what was inside of us, and we had just lost our second-to-last chance to prove ourselves. Like Coach said at halftime: "The only people who believe that we can win this game are in this locker room right now."

Then she'd skip a step, taking two at a time, bounding upward:

To leave the floor with regrets is disheartening. To leave the floor with regrets and no more opportunities to do better is absolutely unbearable. This indignant feeling of lost time rose in my throat as I looked at Brenda, who had no more chances to show her stuff, to prove those obnoxious fans wrong.

Finally triples, huge lumbering movements, awkward greedy lunges just like the giant steps doled out in the children's game of Mother, May I?:

I was left wanting to throw myself in front of the doors, to refuse to let the crowd leave. I just wanted to make them go inside and sit down for ten more minutes; the game was lost, but I wanted some pride back. *No, really, we can play the game. Boy, can we play it. Let us put our skills where our mouths are. We're ready for the test. We WANT the test. But the test comes once a year and only for a few years. And we just blew it, again.*

Sometimes Kathleen would feel so pumped from the stairs, she would decide to forgo the sprints and challenge herself even more, with a long swing up North Pleasant all the way to Cushman Village, a wink of a place with a railroad crossing and the small general store where Kim used to work (that had the best homemade shepherd's pies back when it was in business), across the railroad tracks on Pine Street, and then down Henry Street over the place in the road where those world-renowned tunnels escort the salamanders for their wild night of lizard love.

Kathleen traveled over hills, past farms, past fields. When she finally raised her eyes she was amazed at the way the miles added up.

Her placid expression fled, replaced by a toothy grin suffused with triumph.

Her body felt hard and lean; her mind was filled finally with but one thought: Oh my goodness, look how far I got.

Rita with her onions, Lucia with her letter to Patri, Kim at night in the parking lot of her old school, Kathleen up and down those steps: *cupcupcup* all summer long.

4

Feel the Fire

Fall arrived in Amherst in early September, when the air took on a discernible chill. Labor Day is generally regarded as the beginning of the new year because the passage of time is dictated by the colleges, and that's when approximately thirty thousand students showed up at the University of Massachusetts, Amherst College, and Hampshire College, as well as several thousand more at the all-women's colleges of Mount Holyoke in South Hadley and Smith in Northampton. Like the surrounding towns, each school is idiosyncratic, catering to a different clientele. At Amherst College, small, private, pricey, and supremely self-confident, the joke is that when the professor walks in and says, "Good morning," the students answer, "Prove it." At Mount Holyoke, considered more sheltered and conservative, when the professor says, "Good morning," the students take it down. At Smith, considered somehow more tony, the presumed response is social: "Good morning to you, and perhaps you'd like a croissant and some cappuccino." At experimental Hampshire, founded in 1970, there is no response because no one bothers to show up for class. And at the University of Massachusetts, huge, unpampered, urban, with its highrise dorms and the world's tallest red-brick library, the students want to know, "Will that be on the final?"

The students returned as always to farm stands weighed down, at long last, with a plethora of corn and ripe tomatoes. Up on Flat Hills Road, a farmer set out extra cukes and corn and squash on a wobbly table with a hand-lettered sign: FREE. The roadside stands operated on their usual honor system, with a price list protected from the wind by a tin can containing the day's receipts.

At least one moving van got stuck in an underpass because a youthful driver assumed that the words "low clearance" didn't apply to him. The kids took over the aisles at the Stop & Shop, depleting the shelves of expensive single-serving novelty ice cream and of chips and of ramen noodles, and bellowed out, in voices as strident as the loudspeaker, "Where's the friggin' Cheez-Its?"

"You might expect, the first weekend after they get back, to find the town hopping, but it doesn't really get bad until the third weekend," said Captain Charlie Scherpa of the police department. "The first two weekends after they come back, they still think they're going to be on the dean's list."

Year-round residents—accustomed in the summer to a green and dreamy interlude, sunsets all to themselves, quiet unclogged roads, and nearly empty restaurants—railed about the inconveniences caused by the fall onslaught of students.

"Guess what I just saw. The three most disconcerting words in the English language."

"What's that?"

"A sign in front of the bank, WELCOME BACK STUDENTS."

"Yo, Kristin. Can we talk?"

On a sunny fall day tinged with a hint of hay and embers, Coach Moyer was standing in the crowded corridor at Amherst Regional High School, a building of such deep institutional blandness that some might wonder if perhaps it had wandered from the U Mass campus to its current site off Triangle Street.

In the corridors boys in backwards baseball caps and girls with mini–jewelry stores in their earlobes swirled about in that crippling confusion that somehow, a minute later, ended up miraculously with everyone in the right class. A tall girl with the tiniest scar near her right eye returned his greeting.

"Sure, Coach. When?"

"Anytime. Just drop by. Now?"

"Sure."

"How was your summer?"

"It was okay." No basketball camp for Kristin, no Cape Cod, no Maine, no Clovis, New Mexico. What can you say about a summer at McDonald's but "okay"?

Kristin Marvin hated her job at McDonald's, but it meant money, money meant gasoline, gasoline meant freedom.

She had a long résumé when it came to classic teenage jobs. She'd worked in town in Amherst at the CVS, where "most of the customers, at least the young ones, come in to buy two things: condoms and something to make it look as if they don't want just condoms." She had also been a market researcher at the mall: "You know, those annoying people with clipboards who ask all those questions." At McDonald's she had the ex-alted title of crew trainer, and she worked every possible shift, from early morning to late night. She did birthday parties ("the pits"), she did drive-through, she was a cashier and a clean-up person. She scrubbed the sundae machine, she mopped, she swept, she wiped down tables, and she restocked from the base-ment, all the while, and this was the ignominious part, wearing "ugly gray polyester bell-bottom pants too short for my legs, a fifty-fifty T-shirt, no jewelry or anything like that, and a wretched tall hat with a flat brim."

Coach Moyer always called her his city kid, which she considered "pretty funny if you think about it." Of all the Hurricanes, including Jen in Pelham, she lived the farthest out, in Shutesbury, a town filled with dirt roads, one little school, and no stores, just a bar for hunters and over-the-hill softball players that's called the Shutesbury Athletic Club. Kristin was the only Hurricane with her own car; a vehicle was the birthright of any kid old enough to have a license in Shutesbury, just as in Amherst a Volvo is in effect a voter registration card. Hers was an old brown VW Rabbit that her stepfather had found for her: "He's really good at cars." Yet for some reason her car ate alternators the way some cars drink oil; part of the rite of having Kristin baby-sit was picking her up at the local Mobil or helping her jump-start her car.

Kristin was well suited to the wildness of Shutesbury and lamented its recent discovery by young professionals whom she called "cruppies": "That's short for *crunchy*, as in granola, and *yuppies*, you know, those young families who live in big wood and glass houses. They don't want to live in Amherst and deal with the students. They have culture on the walls, you know, posters from Africa, and they drive Toyota station wagons, and they have one or two children named Zach or Emma, and they are very into the New England thing, blah, blah, blah . . ." Kristin had a way of sometimes abandoning sentences in the middle if for some reason the thought had lost her interest. It wasn't a sign of ditsiness but rather one of impatience.

Kristin's father and her mother were high school sweethearts who early in their marriage had cultivated a mutual devotion to the Montessori system of schooling. They'd split up when she was two, and her father had remarried soon afterward to a woman with a five-year-old daughter. Later they'd had two more children together. During most of Kristin's childhood, David Marvin was a bus or a plane ride away: "I have no memory of living with him."

Kristin's mother, Wheezie (short for Marie Louise), was the daughter of the writer Clay Blair.

Kristin felt she had led a "hippie childhood," an interpretation that was somewhat annoying to her mother: "We were, shall we say, financially disadvantaged for part of the time, and I did take her to a Grateful Dead concert when she was about four and danced with her on my hip, and for about a year I didn't shave my legs, but we weren't hippies."

"Well," said Kristin, "we didn't have a TV until halfway through my childhood when I was eight or nine, and even then it was a little black-and-white, which is pretty unusual for someone of my generation." She remembered a childhood in which she "grew up not knowing what was going to happen next, where we'd be living, who with. I hated not knowing. That's why I like medicine. It's filled with answers." She'd had a reputation as a child for being self-sufficient. She hadn't minded playing alone for hours and daydreaming or reading quietly. For five years after the divorce, she and her mother had lived in Maryland, but they'd moved back to Amherst when her mother got tired of a commute that included thirty-five stoplights.

She stood out from the rest of her teammates as the most experimental and the most independent. She thought it was "sort of funny" when someone joked that in the yearbook under her name, instead of saying "Most likely to succeed," it should say "Most likely to."

Kristin lived with her stepfather and mother, who worked as a computer consultant in the department of engineering at the university, in a low-key, behind-the-scenes job that helped set the stage for the more public activities.

Kristin's stepfather had been previously married to Kristin's stepmother, and the marital realignment resulted in a circumstance in which their daughter from that first union was now Kristin's double stepsister.

The house was in a perpetual state of construction; her stepfather, Dale Houle, earned his living as a contractor, and an unsung occupational hazard of his line of work is that your house gets worked on last. He was fond of saying the problem is always one of time and money: Either you have the time and no money, or you have the money and no time. As a result, the stairs had makeshift treads and no risers, the flooring had yet to be installed in the living room, and the siding was missing from the front of the house, so it was covered with flaps of Tyvek house wrap to protect the plywood from the elements. A wood-burning stove in the dining area was the sole source of heat, and Kristin used to like to curl up with her textbooks next to it to do her homework. She told her friends to come to the side door: "The front door will eventually be usable," but for now there was a mattress propped up against it.

Her friends were often surprised to learn that she kept her room as organized as she did. "It may look cluttered, but everything has its place." Her walls were covered with an assortment of Absolut ads, which she liked because they were so "you know, like, effective." Her shelves contained a Coca-Cola bottle filled with the dried petals from the roses her father had given her on her birthday and a troll doll dressed in a surgeon's outfit. At first she'd wanted to be a lawyer. "Ever since she learned the Constitution in the eighth grade, we were dead," said her mother. But once she'd started getting 98s in biology, she gravitated toward medicine. At fifteen she'd volunteered at a local hospital and had the opportunity to witness an operation: Part of a woman's infected colon had been removed. All those glistening innards! Not only did medicine strike her as fascinating, but its air of certainty was also deeply pleasing. She wanted when she grew up not to marry somebody who was rich but to be "somebody rich." Like Jen (rule eight: NEVER GIVE ALL OF YOURSELF TO ANYONE), she believed you should never count on anybody but yourself.

She had delicate light skin that was quick to flush under the exertion of a fierce game. Sometimes her teammates called her "Bad News" and "Graceless" ("Grace" for short), misinterpreting her tenacity as clumsiness. They also called her "Jolly" and "Jolly Green." Kristin was five feet, ten and a half inches; of all the Hurricanes, only Jonesbones (five-eleven) was taller.

On the court she saw herself as a tiger or a gorilla, all stealth and snarl and strength. She had, when pressured, a style that could be just as fearsome as those Blue Devils, and if someone had called her "Truck" or "Brute," she would have said, "Hey, great."

She knew she would never be as good as the other senior starters, Jen and Jamila and Kathleen Poe, the forward who could barely scrape herself off the floor at Cathedral High School during that last game of the 1992 season.

She would never get their minutes and she would never get their points.

Her job was to make her friends look good.

She didn't have an ego problem; it was fine by her to set the stage for their more glamorous moments.

Her concern was mostly how to be more like Jamila, not so much in her skills as in her spirit. Where do you find it, that peculiar supply of adrenaline and cunning, that makes you keep going, going, going?

Sometimes as she stood in McDonald's during her eighteenth summer, dressed in that painfully ill-fitting uniform with the ludicrous hat, surprised by how eager she was for fall and for basketball and even for Coach Moyer's jokes, she felt like screaming at the French fries as she immersed them in their wire basket in a vat of hot oil, or at the fish fillets as they crisped up, or at those all-beef patties spitting grease on the grill, and most of all at herself: "Feel it! Feel the fire!"

* * *

Coach Moyer folded his arms in front of him. His office, which faced an alley, had one big window and an array of coaching mementos. He had a habit of writing his name in big block letters on objects such as the phone book, a holdover from his childhood when his mother struggled to supply him with one of everything but made it clear that lost or misplaced items would not be replaced. He also had a habit of reflexive generosity on a modest scale, like an ancient maiden aunt dispensing mints or a nickel. You couldn't show up in his guidance office without being shown a press clipping touting the success of a former Amherst athlete or told about a new bumper sticker ("Did you see the one that says COMPOST HAPPENS?")

"How's senior year so far?"

"Great."

"Grades from last semester?"

"They're up there."

"What colleges are you thinking about?"

"I'm applying to the premed program at Holy Cross."

"What are your goals this season?"

"I am really looking forward to playing this year."

"I see you as my starting center." His plan was to start with Kristin, to have her sprint off the line and push the other center off the block. He wanted to keep her in for the first five minutes of every game, let her set the tone, and then when she needed a break, he'd sub with a younger kid like Jonesbones, whom he thought of as Mother Teresa with a hard drive to the basket. "We need your toughness and determination. I'm going to need you at every practice. You know, it's a big commitment. I understand you had a pretty social summer. I hope you're not partying a lot."

"Mr. Moyer, I'm not going to, like, mislead you or anything. When the season's not happening, I'm going to go out with my friends. But during the season, I'm, like, totally psyched. All my social friends understand that basketball comes first. The ones who really like to party drop me off at tryouts in November and they say, 'See you in March.' "

"I'm glad to hear it. Let's make this a great year."

"No problem, Mr. Moyer. I'm not going to neg out on you."

Fall that year did neg out. Many of the leaves were slow to peak, and then, whipped by the wind, they died before their time. The cold settled in mean and early. The Christmas tree farms, with their weathered signs that said BLUE SPRUCE, WHITE SPRUCE, SCOTCH PINE were open for tagging. Provident shoppers chose their trees early to get the ideal fatness and height; otherwise, you had to wait in line in the cold down at Atkins Farm & Fruit Bowl in deep South Amherst or at the Boy Scouts' stand in the center of town.

In October the leaves rusted, they rustled, and they fell. The rusting caused the usual alarm, especially among newcomers to the area who called Bob Pariseau, director of water resources, to complain about the color of the water from the tap. In that strong low voice of his, made oddly stronger and more commanding because of its hesitancy, he patiently explained that the leaves steeped like tea in the reservoir: "There's nothing to worry about. It happens every fall; it won't hurt you. A new filtration system will probably clear up the problem in the future."

On Halloween the children dressed as witches and skeletons, although one boy threw on a sheet and went as the ghost of the Boston Red Sox. Some college students stole pumpkins off the residential porches of stately old houses on Lincoln Avenue only to return them, several days later, carved and leering. Most homeowners thought it was funny, the first time.

The papers published the first of what is always an onslaught of features about seasonal affective disorder (SAD) syndrome, warning about what happens to sunlight-energized people when they are deprived of it: lethargy, depression, even suicide. By the end of the month the trees were bare except for the oaks, the last to turn, still red in a gray and brown world.

"Welcome, hi, come on in." The Big Guy stood outside the door to the guidance office, welcoming the press, looking like a bouncer with a heart of gold.

It was a big day.

Jamila was about to announce that after much consideration, with the University of Connecticut running a close second, she had decided to go to Stanford, where she had been offered a full scholarship. The Stanford Cardinals were the defending Division 1 champions.

Coach Moyer was expansive, proprietary.

The presence of the media transformed the drab anteroom outside his office—where kids often studied, or pretended to, or looked at college catalogues and dreamed of futures with dormitories and no curfews—into a jostling mecca. Standing at least one if not two heads above most of the gathering, Coach Moyer rallied to the cake and carnival. For the press, too, it was a happy moment: High School Athlete Makes Good.

Photographers jockeyed for the perfect angle for their pictures, and the pencil press scribbled Jamila's quotes and their own impressions on narrow pads of paper: *confident, composed, joyful, just like on the court.*

Coach Moyer joked about how the real announcement today was that Jamila had decided to "forgo her first year of college to stay for a record seventh year at Amherst."

Her teammates looked on, applauding their friend, peering at the cameras.

Jen joined the appreciative reaction when Jamila said: "The truth is I couldn't bear the thought of never wearing the Hurricane colors of maroon and white after this year, so the closest match I could find was cardinal and white."

And when Jamila thanked a number of people for their support, especially her "best friend, Jen," the wide grin on Jen's face was a cover for even deeper feelings. From Jen's point of view, the verbal nod, buried in the hot lights and the whir of the cameras, lost to most people amid the outpouring of congratulations, was like one of those random chimneys in the woods. It showed that something sturdy had endured the onslaught. She felt fortified.

Coach Moyer, with his jocular style ("If people from Poland are called Poles, what do you call people from Holland?") and ranging frame, long-legged and short-waisted in the classic manner of male basketball players, had come to Western Massachusetts within weeks of his graduation from Lafayette College in Pennsylvania, moving to the hometown of his bride, Betsy Rodgers, a graduate of Amherst High (class of 1965) and of U Mass. As time went on, he had developed the domesticated swagger of a small-town mayor. Abroad in Amherst, at Rafters (the sports bar near the university) or at dinner in town or at the Hampshire Fitness Club during his off season, he was expected to respond to greetings with the latest local sports information about who was playing, at which school or gym, and when: "Boys. Chicopee Comp. Tuesday night." "Girls. At Feiker at Hamp. Thursday."

His first job in the valley was as a stockboy in 1972 at the old Zayre's, where Stop & Shop is now. After he'd been on the job a couple of weeks and made a little over a hundred dollars, he and his wife got in their VW bug and drove to Philadelphia, where he made good on a debt to his old high school coach.

"Hey, I wasn't expecting to see this again," Harry Silcox had said, touched that the kid remembered.

"It's yours," Moyer had replied, "and you deserve to get it back. Thanks."

Coach Silcox had talked Ron Moyer out of going to Temple, where he had signed a letter of intent. Although Silcox was himself a Temple grad, and it would have been a plum to send a kid along to his school, Silcox thought it was too close to home, too close to the possibility of peer trouble, and through a series of magic phone calls, he'd been able to get Moyer accepted at Lafayette on a full scholarship. The only hitch was the one-hundred-dollar damage deposit required of all incoming freshmen; it was that fee that Ron Moyer returned to his old mentor.

The life Ron Moyer had created for himself in the valley could not have been much more different from the one he'd left behind. The broad outlines of the story he shared readily: youngest of four children, single mom, saved by a coach. It could be inferred that his mother had been an unusually strong person and that perhaps his delight in coaching the girls at Amherst was connected to the wish to make them strong in her mode.

But whenever he was caught in one of those contemplative moods that sprang up like the first cold clamp of frost, he readily acknowledged a more complicated, less sanguine version of the past. His mother had been dealt a bad hand. She was, in the fifties, that most dicey of beings, a woman alone without any reasonable means of support, well before the days of peppy phrases like "single mom" and "alternative parenting styles" to describe circumstances that are anything but peppy or stylish.

* * *

What strength she had came from wielding her weakness like a weapon.

He could easily summon the house where he'd grown up, and he recalled the strange dispossessed feeling of living in a building in which every room, even the garage, was rented out. He could see Edna (when had he stopped referring to her as "Mother"?)—large, looming, with that lost look in her eyes, counting the rent. This was her only income, and since she never reported it, she was always certain the government was about to arrest her at any minute. Some of the tenants were short-timers, but others stayed on for years, like poor Mrs. Helen McClosky, an alcoholic who appeared to have no family and whom he called "Aunt Helen." Ron had been given a space in the basement, roped off by a curtain, next to the furnace, as his room.

He had been a save-the-marriage baby who did save it until he was about three, when his father left, in the company of another woman, for Florida, sunshine, and golf, bequeathing Edna the baby, a ten-year-old daughter, and two teenaged sons—and the row house, about which Ron Moyer always had one question: "Who owns the middle wall?"

Edna had nursed the fantasy that her husband would return. She'd never taken the names Mr. and Mrs. James R. Moyer off the mailbox. She called all the boys Jim, not just the oldest son, whose name really *was* Jim. Bill was Jim-Bill; Ron, Jim-Ron. When he got to be a teenager he sometimes called her "Jim-Mom," and he introduced his sister as Jim-Marion. Edna did not seem to mind. He was known as the humorist in the family. It had started inadvertently when he was seven; he and his mother were taking the train to the welfare department, and he saw a sign advertising suburban lots for sale. "Lots of what?" he had asked because he really didn't get it, but after that his wit was never questioned.

His mother had lived her life in fear that one day a big car or truck was going to come and possess the house.

You couldn't blame her for not knowing how to manage. Her own mother had died when she was in the eighth grade, and she'd been forced to leave school in the ninth to take care of her father, who committed suicide when she was fifteen. She married when she was eighteen. James Moyer Sr. came from a big family—eleven siblings, mostly no-counts, gamblers, two-bit crooks, even prostitutes. Ron's brother Bill remembered once going to one of those sideshows held beneath the old Steele Pier at Atlantic City and paying money to see the Frozen Lady, a skinny dark-haired woman with blue lips wearing just a bikini beneath a slab of ice, only to be overtaken by a sudden jolt of recognition. Cousin June!

Edna had two passions: the gravelly voice of Arthur Godfrey on the radio and bingo, which she played at least once a week. She died at the age of seventy-five after suffering a heart attack in the middle of a phone call about bingo. On the way to her death there had been many illnesses, some real, some imagined, all disabling. She was hospitalized for catatonia and other psychological disorders. One time she became distraught because she was sure that the blood in her body was circulating in the wrong direction.

There had been one magazine in the house, *Reader's Digest*. As a boy, Coach Moyer took the It Pays to Enrich Your Word Power section seriously and increased his by reading it, sprinkling his current conversations with oddly erudite words, like *erudite*. There had been a couple of show books by Ellery Queen and also a set of encyclopedias.

His mother wore too much makeup; she did everything in excess. Her iced tea contained more sugar than liquid. Like many people for whom time proceeds forward without many other high points, the holidays swelled up with meaning. All year long whenever she'd had any discretionary income, she invested in cans of pumpkin for the making of her famous pumpkin pie. "I am famous," she would tell people in her one moment of unimpeded imperiousness, "for my pumpkin pie." There'd been a cupboard in the kitchen that she would quietly stock all year long with supplies intended only for Thanksgiving and Christmas, days at last worth marking and heralding and celebrating.

There were few visitors to the house, mostly bill collectors and Jehovah's Witnesses who sat in the living room for hours reading passages from the Bible and the *Watchtower* pamphlets. It was a two-way street: She was as grateful for their company as they were for an audience. "Now let's go over some of the Scriptures that prove Judgment Day is upon us," the sincere visitor would say, and Edna, perched on a chair in her parlor, would lean over eagerly and say, "But first may I sweeten your tea?"

There'd been only one rule in his house when he was growing up: You can do whatever you want as long as the police don't bring you home. When the children were grown and on their own, she explained, "I just always assumed that eventually you would get tired and have to come home." When he was in high school there was a place where you could bowl all night for five dollars. He was always surprised when he asked his pals to join him, and they'd say they had to ask their parents. "What's the matter? Are they against bowling?"

James Moyer had been sporadic at best about sending the required twelve dollars a week for the support of his youngest son. Ron Moyer remembered the hand-wringing scenes, the waiting for the checks, and the silence that had surrounded the mailing of the letters she sometimes sent, to no avail, to the Metro Justice Building in Dade County, Florida, asking that someone locate her husband, who she knew for a fact was living somewhere in Miami in a trailer.

When he was twelve or so, his mother launched a couple of minor business ventures. Her first effort consisted of crocheting bonnets for toilet paper. Her customers had their choice of yarn: They picked the main color, and then a contrasting one for the plastic flower on the brim. When they went out Edna had him trail her with a wagon containing samples in the hope of attracting a clientele. Eventually, as he always put it, Edna had diversified, making similar covers for liquor bottles out of shocking pink yarn in the shape of poodles, which she modeled on Mrs. McClosky's empties. "I guess you could say Aunt Helen was a silent partner."

The most notorious expression had been "The car will get you there." She herself did not drive, and since she always seemed to get wherever she wished, she was right. The car, which she had no control over, did get her there. But at what price?

He owed a lot to his brother Bill, sixteen years his senior. His brother was the first person in his family to finish college. Bill had taken him to the dentist for the first time when he was twelve. He had thirteen cavities, and three teeth were pulled, two without Novocain because that cost a dollar extra. It was Bill who'd said that as wrong as his father was to leave, it never would have been right between him and Edna.

Bill had played basketball with him all the time. For years Ron Moyer labored under the somewhat parochial impression that if you could beat Bill Moyer in basketball, you could beat anyone.

The playground ball served him well when he was in high school and came under the tutelage of Coach Silcox, who let him know he was a good kid, a hard worker: "You move slow, you can't jump, but at least you listen."

Silcox, a first-team college all-American, had been coached by Harry Litwak, an Austrian-born Hall of Famer who'd coached at Temple University from 1952 to 1973. He had 373 wins, 193 losses, thirteen postseason tournaments, and six

NCAA play-offs, with only one losing season. Harry Litwak was famous for doing "more with less," for taking teams of little or no promise and helping them find within themselves their hidden superiority. It was one of the profound satisfactions of Ron Moyer's life, right up there with his marriage and the births of his children, that he had such an august athletic ancestry: "The kids on the Hurricanes might not recognize it, but they've been exposed to good genes, coaching-wise."

While in college, from 7 to 9 A.M. Monday through Saturday, he had a job in the kitchen washing dishes, earning seventy-five dollars every other week, all of which he set aside for his mother. He would wait for her to call or write, the usual communications with their heavy mix of hypochondria and emergencies and threats: "You'll miss me when I'm dead." All his earnings went for her support except the ten-dollar per diem given to members of the basketball team during away games. Instead of going out to dinner with the team, he would eat the leftover box lunches that the other kids had passed on and use the per diem money to cover his own incidental expenses. Although Lafayette had returned the damage deposit, minus twenty dollars levied on everyone in his class for some kind of vandalism during the Lafayette-Lehigh weekend his freshman year, his mother had cashed the check.

Ron Moyer had met his wife at a summer camp in the Poconos where they both had jobs as counselors. Like him, she was an athlete, and he always described her as someone who'd played three sports in high school back when only three sports were offered to girls: basketball, volleyball, and softball.

Eventually he'd gotten his master's in counseling. "When I took Abnormal Psych in college, I thought, this could have been our family history."

He was hired first by the public high school in Hadley and later by Amherst as a social studies teacher, guidance counselor, and coach.

If his life had one organizing principle, it was basketball. He still sometimes snuck a look at a couple of scrapbooks he'd kept during his three years as a starter for Lafayette's Coach Hal Wissel. The pages bulged with varsity schedules and team photos that would be ageless except for the Beatle hairdos and long sideburns. Yellowing news clips from papers like the *Express* in Easton, Pennsylvania, were preserved with the most relevant passages underlined in blue ink with a ruler: "Moyer, who had a deadly short range push shot, missed only one of his nine floor shots as he contributed 17 points and 10 rebounds." On December 6, 1969, he'd gotten to play at Madison Square Garden against Seton Hall; he also saved an old program from that historic event, a slick brochure filled with ads for steak restaurants and several varieties of Scotch and various whiskies as well as a photo of folksinger Judy Collins whose "melodic tones graced The Felt Forum during her recent appearance." Through it all, the location that felt best to him, most like some kind of ideal home, was the gym. With its high ceilings and stale air, it was familiar, friendly, a flannel-shirt of a place. In college he'd distinguished himself on the court: He was the leader in rebounding for his team three years in a row, and on December 12, 1970 he amassed thirty-three rebounds against Gettysburg, a single game high and a record that still stands today, a tag line he loved to attach to himself, the same way ancient Greeks and Romans always liked to say what town they were from: Hector of Troy, Moyer of thirty-three rebounds. In his office at the high school, in addition to the sign that said THE ONLY DIFFERENCE BETWEEN THIS PLACE AND THE *TITANIC* IS THEY HAD A BAND, he kept a small red media guide with tiny print attesting to his collegiate exploits. Even more than the row house in Philly where he'd lived through adolescence and the house on the hill in Pelham where he resided as an adult, the gym was the place he was calling from, his true hometown, his deep-down address.

5

TEAM,
Underlined and Capitalized

The first organizational meeting for the 1992–93 season was held in mid-November.

Already a dramatic, precipitous pulling-in had taken place all over the valley. Furnaces were checked, windows caulked, chimneys examined for creosote, mittens matched. Wood was stacked, outside, under a tarp as a guard against rain and snow. The Saturday morning farmers' market on the common closed down on the second Saturday of the month. The roadside stands had all disappeared except Hawthorne's on South Pleasant, with its hand-lettered note next to the scale: IN GOD WE TRUST. ALL OTHERS PAY CASH. Hawthorne's planned to hold out until Thanksgiving. "We used to stay open and sell a few Christmas trees," said the man who operates the stand, a laconic Yankee type of indeterminate years always dressed in his green gabardine work clothes, himself a seasonal landmark. "But there's no point competing with the Scouts."

With the arrival of the cold, eating habits changed. You indulged in your neighbor's gift of homemade raspberry jam with its unmistakable taste of thrift and sunshine. Root vegetables, pulpy and medicinal, were welcomed at the table—sweet potatoes and celeriac and parsnips and turnips.

Coming in from outside, stamping their feet, blowing hot

air on cold hands, a group of coltish girls (getting these kids in shape, thought Coach Moyer, will have more to do with harnessing their spirit than breaking it) gathered in room 4 at Amherst Regional High School, a large nondescript classroom facing out on the front parking lot and the scene, whenever possible, of the Hurricane team meetings. Coach Moyer believes in tradition and consistency, even down to where the group goes for the ritual pregame pep talk.

The word was already out. Coach Moyer planned to run a tight ship this year. Dire visions of "suicides," also known as "gassers" and "back-and-downs," sprang up in the heads of the Hurricane hopefuls. These were sprints, sometimes meted out as punishment, during which a player had to run up and down every line on the court, bending and touching them at the ends.

A hierarchy was already in effect. The girls who were certain to make the team—Jen and Jamila and Kristin and Kathleen—were seated up front, talking and giggling, doing their imitations of the killer Buffalo Bill in *Silence of the Lambs* summoning his dog, "Precious . . . Precious." They were filled with the ease of the truly confident.

Those who were younger or less sure of their athletic abilities cowered in the outskirts, crouched beneath windowsills or hidden in the back row, heads down, pretending to memorize the "Amherst Girls Hoops Candidate Application, 1992–93 season." Coach Moyer scanned the group to see if there were any surprises. In a town like Amherst you always hope for the ringer, a great athlete who moved here unexpectedly over the summer because one of her parents had an unforeseen opportunity to become chancellor or provost or president of something. But what he saw was a mostly familiar array of eager faces, among whom were a fair share of what he categorized as "quiet kids, no dad in the picture." Over the years he had often been called on to assume a parent role.

"Kids have a built-in need to be parented. They take it

wherever they can get it, and I accept that role. I tell them that if they have a problem, come to the Big Guy. I'll try to help." Applicants to the 1992–93 Hurricanes were asked to give their height and weight and age, to circle the position they hoped to attain (point guard, shooting guard, center, rebounding forward, scoring forward), to list their best hoop skills and the skills that needed working on most, to "please discuss any after school commitments other than Hoop," and to "list all day/night/weekends not available for practices or scrimmages" including any "travel/vacation/holiday plans." They also had to give their course schedule, the names of their teachers, and their estimated grade for the first quarter.

"Be generous with yourselves," said the coach, in one of his usual gambits. "Nobody else will."

A sports participation fee of sixty dollars was required of every student who played a varsity or junior varsity sport.

"Some of you may be thinking: 'That's a lot of money. I don't know if I can afford to try out.' When I was a kid, it would have been a lot of money to me too."

He said this every year. It was hard to know if they really believed him; even his own kids used to react skeptically to his stories of bringing bundles of old papers to the junkyard, making certain he'd dampened the middle so they would weigh more. Or trailing his mother and her wagon filled with its crocheted hope for betterment. It had been a goal, with his own kids, to make sure they didn't have to scrape the way he had been forced to do. He didn't want them to worry about everything from orange juice to tuition. But his antenna for a certain kind of poverty was still sharp, and he could see from their downcast glances that a couple of kids were already worried about the money.

"You don't have to pay the fee to try out. And if you make the team, we do have a waiver procedure. No one will lose a place on the team because of financial hardship.

"I just want to thank all of you for coming today. Some of you are probably wondering what I'm looking for in a member of the Hurricanes. Well, to put it simply, I'm looking for good people with good credentials. From what you told me about yourselves on those forms I had you fill out a couple of weeks ago, some of you are athletes without a portfolio. If you've never played on a team before, if this is the first time you've tried a sport, I've got to be honest with you. That's tough, that's hard. But DYB, and we'll see what happens. Being part of a team is not something your grandparents can buy for you. No one can give this to you as a gift. You have to earn it yourselves.

"My method of coaching is simple. The accent is on team, <u>TEAM</u>, underlined and capitalized. I don't want the kind of people I call team-busters. They make snide comments, they count the syllables in the newspaper to see who's getting more attention than someone else. They're filled with a lot of looks and stares that try to put people down. Attitude is every bit as important as athleticism. During the tryouts, show us your best attitude.

"To win at games I need dependable people. If you can't remember to bring a paper that gets you into tryouts, how can I expect you to remember our plays, which are a lot more complicated than that?

"You have to get your priorities straight in terms of your life. Your first obligation is to your family, and then to your schoolwork, and then to basketball. Now that I've said that, you should recognize that basketball is such a huge commitment that you should try out only if you can meet your obligations to the first two, because my role is to see that you don't cheat the team.

"I have a friend, the coach over in Agawam, Lou Conte, who always tells his players, 'Little eyes are watching you.' I want you to be role models on the court, off the court, and in the locker room.

"This is a winter sport. We play over Christmas vacation and vacation week in February. Don't come up to me and tell me you have to take an emergency trip to Florida. First of all, I'd like to know how you come up with those tickets in the middle of winter.

"Last year we lost far too much time waiting to start practices. Either be serious about being on a winning team or don't come out. There are two kinds of players: Those that are on the bus or not on the bus. The bus rolls at two-thirty every weekday. It's been five years since we've had a winning junior varsity team. It's been six years since we've had a winning junior high team. It's been a lot longer since we've won a Western Massachusetts regional final. This year we're going to change all three of those things."

Later that night, he passed the white trailer across the street from his house, up the steep driveway, glancing to the right beyond the above-ground pool with its winter cover that dominated the front yard to see if the lights were on in the house next door, occupied by his wife's parents. (Whenever people asked him if it was hard to live next door to his mother-in-law, whom he called "Hurricane Marge" because of her tendency to pop in unexpectedly and sweep through the house, he would reply, "Not a bit. Besides, we're getting an invisible electric fence.") He realized how eager he was to get this year's team in place. People often wanted to know if his daughters—Kristin, a freshman at the high school, and Courtney, a senior day student at Deerfield Academy—played basketball. They had both chosen swimming instead, and together they had set seven records in the individual medley, freestyle, and relay events in the town of Amherst.

Coach Moyer sat in the small family room with the comfortable armchair across from the TV set and pored over the forms. Jamila wanted to be point guard; no surprises there. This would be her sixth year in the job; she had started out in this position in the seventh grade at four and a half feet tall and weighing eighty pounds. Whenever people asked him how long he'd been coaching Jamila he would answer, "Oh, about one foot."

She listed "court sense, passing, and the 'J' " as her best court skills. She felt she needed to work on "defense (passing lanes), learning when to take shots, setting a pace appropriate for a game according to our strengths and losses."

In the space provided for "after school commitments other than Hoop" she wrote in the largest letters possible: "NONE."

Jen Pariseau said she wanted to be a shooting guard and a scoring forward and the water girl. She had made that same joke every year since the eighth grade, and she felt compelled to jot it down now, if only for sentiment's sake. She listed as her "travel/vacation/holiday plans" a "trip to Vermont around New Year's." This was partly a nostalgic reference to the shared family vacations of the Pariseaus and the Moyers when the children were younger, before athletic commitments took up most of their free time, and it was also a joke. Jen hated skiing and bore a grudge against one evil slope where, on the last run during spring skiing, she'd broken her leg. Jen, who loved to laugh, never did whenever people pointed out that if she'd broken her leg, of course it was the last run. Coach Moyer read the notation and thought it was a good sign, an acknowledgment of the closeness between the two families.

Courtney Moyer and Jen had been close friends since they were three and part of a play group Betsy Moyer had organized. During grade school they'd walked on a path in the woods back to the Moyers' house every day. They played constantly. One Halloween they dressed up as basketball players. Now that they were older, they liked to tease their parents with tales of their miscreant pastimes: how they'd tied nooses around Kristin Moyer's pound puppy, set traps by digging holes in the yard and filling them with leaves, run rummage sales at which the Pariseaus and the Moyers were forced to buy back their own belongings, made a miniature golf course out of an old croquet set and charged admission.

The two families consulted freely with each other on that peculiar surliness that can infect a child especially during early adolescence. The Moyers went through it when Courtney was in the ninth grade: "I don't know why I acted the way I did. I love my parents. But I wouldn't talk to them. I would say: 'Yes.' 'No.' No emotion. If they asked me if I had a good day at school, I said: 'I guess.' At the age of fifteen Jen was similarly hard on her stepmother, but Betsy Moyer, in her usual direct and enthusiastic manner, told Tracy Osbahr, "If she won't talk to you, that's good. It means she accepts you."

Jen's acceptance of her stepmother eventually took on many forms, including the birthday and Mother's Day cards whose purchase and inscription she would labor over. "TRACY," said one, in huge letters in honor of her fortieth birthday, "I am using big writing because I heard that when you're forty your sight goes." Inside Jen offered to buy her a beige band for her watch; she had the money but she just needed Tracy to take her shopping. An older Jen thanked Tracy for helping her pick out a dress ("I couldn't have done it myself") and for teaching her the difference between "there, their and they're." It was her stepmother who had carefully stored Jen's school papers over the years, including the xeroxed literary magazine published at Pelham Elementary. Jen and her brother, Chris, often spent weekends with their mother in nearby Belchertown, but in recent times, with the heavy commitment to sports, Jen most often saw her mother, Terry Coty, in the bleachers, where she was an increasingly faithful presence.

Over the years, Jen had come to refer to Betsy Moyer as her third mother. With her soothing voice, double pierced ears, and short sandy brown hair in an easy but stylish cut, Betsy Moyer remained in her forties a strong athlete. She liked step classes, downhill skiing, and especially tennis. Her signature shot was so powerful that even Jen had to hustle to return it.

The Moyers and Jen's father and stepmother socialized often, sharing prime season's seats next to each other at the U Mass men's basketball games.

Coach Moyer could see that it had been hard for Jen to sit by and witness Jamila's growing prominence, partly because she was so close to being just as good. She was right to be miffed at him; he had been all over her, as he put it, like white on rice all last season. And he would be this year too if need be. With Jen, this season, it would be a matter of getting her to believe in herself all the time, every minute, especially on the floor. She couldn't tune in and tune out. It had to be constant.

Kristin Marvin, no longer wearing a McDonald's uniform and on time despite the mood swings of that brown VW Rabbit, wrote that she was trying out for center, and she gave as her best skills rebounding, defense, and heart. He liked that. It wasn't a brag; it was the truth. He was glad to have Kristin on board. You worried with Kristin that she might roar off into the sunset on a Harley Davidson, but if she didn't, what an ally.

Kathleen Poe, her legs feeling stronger and harder than they ever had from all that running in the summer, all that stepping at the stadium, wrote that she wanted to work on dribbling and shooting while pressured. She gave as her height five feet, ten inches followed by a written sigh, "Well . . . ALMOST."

As the number three player, Kathleen Poe was the depth the team needed, that extra layer of offense that could make the Hurricanes impenetrable at the top. She had the makings of a great natural athlete. She was tall and strong and a glorious runner.

She had a straight back, and she possessed what used to be called a wonderful carriage. Thanks in part to a beauty mark on her right cheek, she radiated elegance, although she of course complained ("I have no nose, no nose!"). She embodied that old lost virtue of instinctive graciousness, the type of kid who at someone's beach house will help put away the groceries while everyone else is changing into a suit and racing to the beach, and she'll also, as a vegetarian, bring her own can of tofu hot dogs. Her calm, neat appearance inspired her teammate Kim Warner to observe that on the court, when everyone else had degenerated into "a mass of damp hair and a human sweat ball," Kathleen somehow managed to appear less disarranged.

As Coach Moyer told an aging gym rat that fall, "I have the two best guards in the state and probably the nation, but it will all depend on the girls up front. There's an old saying: 'Guards win games, but forwards win championships.' "

There was no way around it: Kathleen was the key. The problem with Kathleen was that her reflexes on the basketball court were exactly the same as in her personal life. She was *too* nice. She had a tendency to stop dead whenever an opponent fell down, to offer her hand and apologize even if she had nothing to do with the tumble.

As a former boys' coach, Ron Moyer knew what he would have done if Kathleen had been a guy: He would have yelled and screamed and strutted and carried on, and it probably would have worked. But with Kathleen, as with most of the girls he had coached, that kind of fireworks usually didn't work. You had to be gentle, constructive. The more he coached, the more he believed boys could benefit just as much from a positive approach. He'd once read about a study where some players were shown videos of foul shots that they'd made and others were shown videos of foul shots that they'd missed. Across the board, male and female, the players bombarded with the positive model improved their percentages, which did not surprise him: "Whenever you fill your mind with a lot of don'ts, the don'ts dominate your thinking. You're programming yourself to do it wrong."

This season marked Ron Moyer's ninth year of coaching the Lady Hurricanes. At Hopkins Academy, the public school in Hadley, he'd coached the boys from 1971 to 1977, and in 1975 they'd won a league title. He had also coached coed youth soccer for eight years, and Lassie League softball for four. His camps on summer mornings, run through Leisure Services in the town of Amherst, were often the first introduction to organized sports for the children in Amherst. He kept a Rolodex in his head of former players who'd gone on to join college teams: Rhonda Jackson at Virginia Commonwealth, Jody Fink at Harvard, Melissa Osborn at Williams, Heather Richards at Columbia, Tom Witkos at U Mass. Whenever he learned that one of them, like Rhonda Jackson (who had inspired Jen and Jamila when they were little), had been made captain, it suddenly all seemed worth it—all those bus rides, all that time spent waiting for the last kid to be picked up, the frowns and the smiles feigned by way of displeasure or encouragement, the repetitious lectures, the laborious drills.

In October, as a way of psyching himself for the season, he and coaching friend Mike Thomas had attended a seminar in which he got to hear Al McGuire, the former coach of the Marquette University basketball team back when it had won the 1977 national championship.

Coach Moyer loved his comments.

- Don't ever have any vendettas in basketball, just love affairs.
- Don't lie to your kids. Lies can break up a battalion.
- Every season has at least seven or eight crises. Sprained ankles, games canceled due to the weather, infuriated parents,

kids who fade away in the middle of the season. A certain amount is normal, but when you get fifteen or twenty, it grinds you down to just surviving. Anticipate the crises and work with them, but don't let them throw you off course.

- If you want to win, get your players to love the game. Coach your personality.
- No coach wins a game by what he or she knows; you win by what your players have learned.
- A coach who starts out listening to the fans ends up sitting next to them.

Coach Moyer glanced at the rest of the forms. Under skills that needed work: "outside shots," "low post moves," "comprehension of plays," "confidence." There was one good laugh. Someone had written, under best hoop skills:

"Lucky shots."

6

You Can
All Clap Now

It rained on Thanksgiving. The Amherst high school football team played its second annual holiday match against Minnechaug in a sparsely attended away game. The day after Thanksgiving, notorious as the most popular shopping day in most of America, was, as always, according to Captain Scherpa, the quietest day of the year in Amherst.

"It's dead, and we love it."

Kim Warner, frustrated that it was too cold and too wet to play hoop outside at Crocker Farm, spent much of the weekend at her job at A. J. Hastings Newsdealer in the center of town, the closest equivalent in Amherst to a common meeting place. The venerable old store sells Amherst College T-shirts, tobacco and ink, newspapers and periodicals and stationery. Stodgy and cluttered, with its original wood floors in the back, it was here that townspeople came to rely on Kim as a sort of personal radio, asking her about the upcoming season and inquiring if everyone's ankles and knees and elbows were doing all right.

In a place filled with transients, Kim represented a certain continuity to the Hurricanes, a bridge that extended from the old-time settlers and farming community to the interloping newcomers. Her mother had graduated from Amherst Regional

High School in 1968, and her mother's parents still lived in the house over by the high school where her mother had grown up. Her father's folks lived in Pelham.

"So," her customers would ask, "when are tryouts?"

"This Monday. They are always on the Monday after Thanksgiving break."

"That's soon."

"Not soon enough. I can't wait."

Kim had one of those wide yet timid smiles that invite consoling remarks.

"Oh, you don't have to worry. You're a senior. Of course you'll make it."

Kim always tried to respond with a look of confidence. In the ninth and tenth grades she'd been moved up in the postseason, and in her junior year she was on varsity. But she took nothing for granted. She forced herself to react positively to her customers.

Of course! Smile. That's right! Smile. No problem! Smile.

"The first rule of tryouts is don't hurt the Big Guy."

About sixty girls stood side by side.

"Okay, please organize yourself into some layup lines, and let's see what you can do."

The girls divided into small groups, and stationing themselves at the six baskets throughout the gym, they pounded the ball against the floor.

"That's right," shouted the coach. "Dribble in. Don't travel. If you travel, you'll lose the ball to Agawam." Whenever he spun a scenario of doom, it was always against the Brownies of Agawam or the Blue Devils of Northampton, the Hurricanes' chief competitors. He never said Chicopee Comp or West Side, schools with weaker teams.

"Don't be afraid to mess up. Basketball is a game of mistakes. Assume you're going to make some mistakes, and don't start kicking yourself until about the fifth one. My rule is that the only mistake that's going to get you off the floor is not hustling."

Jen and Jamila passed the ball back and forth to each other with great verve; they even fooled around with some fancy behind-the-back stuff. Kathleen looked as if she didn't know how *not* to make a basket, and Kristin chugged away, strapping and steady.

Coach Moyer had his eye on Gumby, a junior, as his fifth starter.

Her playing style most reminded him of his own in his heyday: the way she stuck to it, posted herself beneath the basket, prevented buckets for the other guy, and fed her teammates plenty of opportunities to look good.

She wasn't as quick as some of the kids, but she had soul and she had staying power.

With her dark ponytail and face filled with circles, beginning with the huge round dark eyes, Gumby made layup after layup. What shyness she felt about being linked to the seniors (Kathleen had been her idol ever since she could remember) vanished on the floor.

Gumby was born strong.

She had been the biggest baby in the nursery: nine pounds, nine and one-fourth ounces. She was able to whale a whiffle ball out of the yard by the age of two. She'd always loved games—card games, board games, athletic pursuits. At six, she'd joined her first soccer team.

Her father, Stan, a professor of chemistry at Springfield College, recalled "how Emmie used to laugh on every exhale. She eagerly played offense and defense, but her favorite position was what she called 'the goldie.'"

Now when she gave people directions to her house, she told them to go down Southeast, turn onto Mechanic, and then proceed to Chapel Road: "The house is this disgusting blue-green, I think my mother got the paint free or something, and surprise! There's a basketball hoop."

All summer she had worked out, first at Hampshire Fitness Club, a sunlit haven in puritanical Amherst famous for its hot tub, where in the winter pasty patrons steep in the steam and cheerfully offer their solutions to the world's most pressing problems. Gumby's bailiwick was the weight room, where she trained every other day. She would often leave the club and wander over to one of several of Amherst's weather-ravaged outdoor basketball courts, insinuating herself into a game with a group of guys whose initial reluctance would change to grudging admiration, especially after she drained a shot in their faces.

Gumby and Jonesbones, the other Emily, both wanted to be sports doctors or orthopedic surgeons. Sometimes they spoke with glee about how much fun it would be to crunch up someone's knees or decrunch them, as the case may be.

"But, you have to," one always reminded the other, "give up, like, your twenties."

"As long as I'm not the kind of doctor that sticks needles into little kids," Gumby always said with great emphasis. She'd had enough of that kind when she was eleven and had to be hospitalized for two months in Boston. She remembered the great feeling of finally being allowed to go home. "I'll never forget. I came home on December eighth. Or maybe it was the seventh. It was the same day some big military thing happened."

Gumby's parents were loyal fixtures in the stands, and although they had been divorced for several years, they often sat side by side. They were interesting opposites. He was dark and a scientist, keen on quantifiable inquiry, and she was light and one of those New Age therapists. Sally Shore was "Singingtree," whose flyers fluttered from the bulletin boards in town: "Have you ever experienced a time during which you felt an inner harmony and a luminous awareness of being precisely where you needed to be in your life in order to more fully live from your essence? . . . If so, you have felt the melody and beauty of your song. My work honors the deep reservoirs of transformational energy that exist within each of us."

Seeing their daughter play with such strength stirred up memories of other, more vulnerable times.

She'd gotten sick as a child, something to do with excess acid, a condition called reflux esophagitis. Her father explained, "It seems to happen more with people like Emmie who have type O blood."

She'd taken medication, slept with her head on an incline, and mostly soldiered on. Starting in the fourth grade, she played on a coed basketball team at her school under the supervision of Coach Noel Kurtz.

In the beginning of sixth grade there'd been a sudden weakness, some vomiting, a lethargy that wouldn't go away. Ten separate visits to the doctor all yielded the same false surmise: "It must be a particularly virulent strain of the flu." What made her so mad was that she'd intended to be captain of her elementary school basketball team that year.

She had been vomiting so much that one day Stan Shore took an exact measure of both her liquid intake and what she'd spit up; the two were the same. No nourishment was getting through.

They sought the help of a specialist in Boston.

During the two-hour drive, she'd grown more and more pale and kept nodding off.

Her mother would lean over and tug at her arm:

"Wake up, Emily, wake up. Oh, look, over there, isn't that the place we stopped and had lunch the time. . . . Emily, please, honey, open your eyes."

The child had arrived at Mass General, dozing in her seat, with a barely discernible pulse.

The intake staff reacted by grabbing a gurney, barking orders, rushing the slumped form of the child to the intensive care unit. Eventually she'd been diagnosed as having a serious ulcer. The acid in her body was eating out her duodenum.

Medication was dripped onto the ulcer through tubes for ten weeks, but it refused to heal. The parents had tag-teamed each other up and down the Mass Pike for twenty-four-hour shifts at her side. Someone (Stan Shore was vague about who it had been), had taken over his labs at the school, and a neighbor they knew from the South Congregational Church took care of Emily's younger brother every day after school.

Nothing was healing. Surgery was the only option. There was a children's surgeon at Mass General named Hardie Hendron who was so good and so steady and so single-minded that his nickname was Hardly Human. Emily was scheduled to go to him.

A day or two before that appointment they'd given her a day out. Her father had lifted her into his car. She didn't have much strength. The large eyes of the father and the daughter and the darkness of their hair resembled each other in a way that was amiable, almost comic. Together, they'd driven around, including a stop at Fenway, where he bought her a shirt, a Red Sox shirt, the best, a replica of the actual shirt the team wears when it plays. It was a man's size small, and of course it was too big for her. He just wanted to do something. They'd driven into a parking lot, where he wanted to make a turn, but then he saw a cop and he didn't want to make a mistake in front of a cop, so he said, "Is it okay to make a right turn?" The cop had looked at

Stan Shore, at his pale, ailing daughter, and said softly, "You can do whatever you want."

The doctors told them the surgery would last three or four hours. " 'You never know beforehand exactly what you're going to find. You make judgments at the scene.'

"She was in surgery for, I don't know, it must have been seven or eight hours. When they finally brought her into the recovery room, she had a big tube in her mouth, and she was very drugged up and in pain, but the recovery progressed quickly. She could have played the role of an invalid and gone on being delicate. That's a very powerful role. But, no, she wanted to come home as soon as she could. All fall, even when she was the most sick, all she could talk about was basketball, basketball, basketball, and how sad she was to miss the opening of the season because this year, as a sixth grader, she wanted to be captain of the team. Well, it was too late to be captain, but her coach let her back on the team in January."

January 6, to be exact, she'd started playing again.

"Something was driving me. I've always loved sports. Mr. Kurtz encouraged everyone to play, girls especially."

Unlike others in his family, Stan Shore did not think of himself as religious in a formal sense. He did not believe in a personal human-type God. But he did have spiritual thoughts and he did believe in small miracles.

The memory of his daughter's illness would fade away, but never completely. If she were hurt or not feeling well, the terror resurfaced.

The majority of the Hurricanes were from families in which the original parents had divorced, or some other major stress meant they'd never be called "the Waltons," the team's nickname for Emily ("Jonesbones") Jones's family.

As the head pediatrician for the local health maintenance organization, Emlen Jones enjoyed a limited local fame similar to Coach Moyer's, but instead of knowing all the scores and all the upcoming games, he knew about your child's immunizations and scoliosis and ear infections. Because of his height and heft, it was widely assumed that Emily's prowess on the court had come from him in a direct genetic transmission. While he was not bad at volleyball, the legacy that created in Emily a formidable stamina as well as a daunting under-the-basket presence actually came from her mother, Bernadette. Of all the mothers of the Hurricanes, she was the only one who had played basketball in high school and in college with any degree of seriousness.

Coach Moyer paced the gym, clipboard in hand. He had his starters, Jen and Jamila and Kathleen and Kristin and Gumby. He had his height in Jonesbones. He had dependability and desire in Kim Warner.

At the end of the second day of tryouts each girl was called up and given her own conference with Coach Moyer and with the others, such as Trish Lea, coach of the junior varsity, who helped make the selection. One by one the players approached the grown-ups, who appeared diminutive as they sat huddled over their ever-present clipboards in chairs at a table in the middle of the large gym. It was easy this year. Most of the kids cut themselves, and the few who didn't were shifted over to managers.

Lucia approached the table with wide eyes.

Coach Moyer thought that Lucia looked as if the summer had been good to her. She'd gotten bigger, stronger-looking. Something was driving that kid.

He had good news for her.

"Sophie King."

A blond girl walked up to the table and after a brief huddle broke into a big smile. Sophie was another quiet kid willing to work hard. Her parents had met in the Peace Corps in Tibet, and they had a FREE TIBET sticker on their car now. For a while they had tried farming out in Hardwick, but they gave that up to move to "town" partly for the schools and the after-school activities. Her mother was an acupuncturist and her father sold lumber. The family maintained its activist streak. Sophia had spent the summer in Worcester working for Habitat for Humanity. It was, if memory served Coach Moyer right, Jen who had been responsible for getting Sophie to try out for the Hurricanes back when she was in the ninth grade and Jen was in the tenth. Instead of saying hello in the hallways at school, Jen would ask, "You trying out?" Sophie had been eager for a new activity. She had just given up the ballet she'd studied since the age of five, first as physical therapy and then for fun and finally, during the best times, as art.

Her family had attended a concert at a church in Boston's Back Bay when she was four and a half. Growing tired of the music, Sophie and the other children ran outside to play on the sidewalk. But because she had grown up on a remote farm at the end of a dead-end street, she had no sense of city traffic. The driver of the truck that crushed her leg was not to blame for failing to see her. Gangrene had almost claimed the limb; she'd undergone so many skin grafts that the injured leg from the knee down remained marbled and misshapen and discolored, paler than the rest. She said that people who noticed it for the first time had one of two reactions: "Did something bite you?" or "Gross. What's wrong with your leg?" She'd decided to give up ballet at the end of eighth grade when her teacher told her there was no point in continuing: Sophie was too tall, and her head was too big.

Then Jen had given her an approving slap on the back: "Forget ballet. You're a Hurricane."

Jade Sharpe was picked for her promise.

Her portfolio was slim. She had never touched a basketball until, as a lark, she'd decided to try out for the seventh-grade team. Despite the absence of early training, Jade had great style on the court; the other Hurricanes called her "Octopus arms." She had great style off the court as well. She often wore her hair in extensions; with it swept off her face, the emphasis was on her large wide-set eyes. She was famous on team bus rides for her imitations of, among others, Aretha Franklin.

She was also local. Her parents were from the city of Springfield, but they settled out in the country after her father had gotten his degree at U Mass. Her mother, Cheryl, worked as a nurse, and Avery Sharpe was a jazz musician mentored when he was young by no less an eminence than Archie Schepp.

Jade was the oldest in a family with two boys and two girls. For a while the family had lived in one of those nearly all-white towns that border Amherst, but when it became clear that Jade would be only the second black child in a school system with 527 children, the Sharpes moved to the Amherst district. Still, it wasn't as if the minority population of Amherst was so large that it was easy to get lost. Jade hoped to go to college in a city like Atlanta, where it would be a relief not to know every black person walking down the street by name.

Her family had settled in a house surrounded by trees.

"When you live in the woods," her mother always said, "you can stop buying toys. The children can use a stick for a flagpole to wave a banner, a bow and arrow, a staff for walking."

The Amherst area was, she said, "not a fairy tale, but at least there aren't as many kids lost by the wayside here as in other places."

Jade was the only Hurricane who'd attended the Common School in Amherst, a private progressive elementary school filled with gentle rituals: a Halloween parade in which the costumes were awarded a prize that was not licorice or fireballs but instead an adjective (a child dressed as milkmaid, for instance, once received "most lacteal"); a May Day celebration to which grandparents were invited, with everyone making baskets full of origami flowers; and Friday Sing, in which someone had once led the entire school in a song he'd written, with the refrain "There's nothing wrong with right field."

Jan Klenowski, a frail but fierce tenth-grade guard, would be on the varsity, but to get more game experience, she would play JV during the first part of the season. She had missed most of her ninth-grade season because of a broken collarbone suffered during a game.

Coach Moyer added up the names on the roster: Jen, Jamila, Kristin, Kathleen, Gumby, Kim, Jonesbones, Lucia, Sophie, Jade, Jan.

There was one more opening.

Patri Abad wanted that space.

Patri was back in town.

Patri had managed to leave out in the open Lucia Maraniss's letter with its ornate decorations and sentiments, the avowals of admiration and that spray of *verys*.

Patri's mother later told people that her daughter would sometimes walk outside the family's apartment, combining piety with desperation, reciting the Rosary to the Holy Mother, but that was not how it went according to Patri.

"I'm not a nun. My mother likes to exaggerate."

Neither Patri nor her mother argued about the moment when, caught in thick urban traffic, Patri had seen a bumper sticker that she pointed out with a great gesticulating commotion. "See, Mommy, read what it says. GOD ALLOWS U-TURNS."

Whether it was Lucia's fourteenth *very*, or divine intercession from the Virgin, or a miracle bumper sticker, Patri's mother had relented. The family moved back during the summer before Patri's senior year.

From Coach Moyer's point of view, Patri had missed a crucial year in her development as a basketball player. But she was eager, and the other kids adored her. It was optimistic of her to even try out.

"Hey, does anyone know my definition of an optimist?" asked Coach Moyer. "That's a guy who rides to his appointment for a vasectomy on a bike."

When the shakedown was complete, like the Macs at Atkins Orchards blowing off a tree in a storm, eleven girls stood together: the 1992–93 Hurricanes, minus one.

As for the twelfth and final member of the team, Coach Moyer made a special announcement.

"Okay," he said, a big grin creasing his face. "You can all clap. Patri made it."

The whoops that followed were pure and uninhibited, and yet a mere hint of the kind of adrenaline that would kick in during the good times in the upcoming season.

"Tryouts are over. We start regular practices tomorrow."

School ended at two-fifteen, and Coach Moyer expected his players to be on the floor right away, stretching, shooting, loosening up.

At two-thirty he blew the whistle.

Then he went through his short announcements, filling the kids in on league developments, standings, changes in the schedule, little bits of news that they might need. The purpose of this was to get them focused. He scheduled a minimum of four practices a week. A two-hour practice on Sunday was left optional.

"Hey, what's wrong with you guys, just standing around acting calmatose?" *Calmatose* was one of Coach Moyer's special made-up words; it meant calm to the point of coma.

"Let's do some stretching exercises before we get stretch marks. What's the matter, Patri? You don't think I'm funny?" Coach Moyer was in typical form.

"I'll never forget last year, down in Agawam, one of their fans turns to my wife, Betsy, and says, 'Your husband's a horse's ass.' So she defended me by replying, 'Whose isn't?' "

"Mr. Moyer, I'm only laughing because if I don't, you'll kick me off the team," said Jen.

"Did you hear about my great-grandmother, she had Lou Gehrig's disease and Alzheimer's? Yeah, she knows she hit a hundred home runs but can't remember when."

Jen motioned to her teammate as if she were a conductor trying to get an orchestra to sing louder. "Everyone, quick, act like you get it. If you don't, he'll make us run suicides."

"Okay, enough fun and games. I know you think I'm dain-bramaged. Did I ever teach you guys about the principle of verticality?"

"That means you're supposed to stick your arms in the other guy's face, right?" said Jen.

"Your humor's beginning to grow on me."

"Yeah. Like warts."

"Time to practice our layups. This isn't humanities camp. This isn't a typical Amherst gathering where everyone forms a committee and stands in a circle and discusses their feelings. This is basketball! We get in lines for basketball. Use the backboard for an easy two. Lunge for the ball. If you're out of breath, that's cool. Just never buy a VCR from someone who's out of breath. There are two things in this world that don't last long. Dogs that chase cars and tournament teams that don't make foul shots."

Then he would announce either "Three lines!" (which would be met with groans) or "Dribble series" (a selection of drills that were much more popular).

The famed dribble series was invented by UCLA Coach John Wooden to increase his players' ball-handling skills. They would play dribble tag or make obstacle courses or dribble while lying down on the floor.

This series often ended with what Jen and Jamila called the "catch of the day," in which one or both guards would come up with some outlandish dribble-pass-catch combination (dribble left-handed, bounce the ball off the head of your partner, who had to catch the ball behind her back . . .).

That was easy compared to the "Three lines!" call.

Designed to teach quickness and balance, these exercises required the Hurricanes to run weaves from basket to basket. Then Coach Moyer had them go zigzagging up the court, using defensive slides. They would practice shuffle steps and foot fires, a special torture in which the player goes into a crouch, one hand down, one up. On the whistle they began jabbing their feet against the floor. The tap, tap, tap sounded like drumsticks on the skin of a snare drum. Then the coach would point—forward, backwards, sideways—and the team would move instantly in shuffle steps, then resume their foot fires.

He also had a series of drills in the half-court, designed to improve man-to-man defense. (He offered to change the term to *person-to-person*, but the girls preferred not to.)

The defensive player would have to play with her hands behind her back. The goal was to force the ball handler to change direction three times, simply by positioning her body, and more important, her feet. There were other one-on-one drills. Over the years, Coach Moyer had discovered that the traditional defensive style, semicrouch, left hand low to prevent the right-handed dribble, right hand high to prevent the shot, wasn't totally right for girls. So he taught them to move their left leg forward (in effect, preventing the dribble with their thigh) and to keep their left hand raised; that way they would automatically have a hand up in the face of their rivals. Most prefer a set shot to a jump shot.

All of Coach Moyer's drills—and as opposed to other coaches, he liked to limit drills—were designed to aid the "transition offense" that he was installing this season, in large part in response to what he'd seen that losing night during the previous March at Cathedral. In his endless ruminations over the summer about what had gone wrong against Hamp, it came down to this: the complete absence of a transition offense that attacked the basket before the defense had a chance to get set. It wouldn't matter how big the other guys were if Jen and Jamila could lay in the ball before the six-one, six-two centers even had a chance to get back. Hamp had beaten Amherst because they had taken one of their players, Johanna Clark, and told her to dog Jamila everywhere. He remembered how Jamila had appeared out of control ("Insane" was Rita's term), everywhere and nowhere at the same time. She had simply been trying to get the offense established with a player in her face.

A transition offense is rare for any high school basketball team, boys' or girls'.

Most coaches like to have their players come down the court into established positions, read the defense, and then go to a series of rigidly set plays to defeat the defense. A transition offense requires great athleticism; its weapons are speed and skill. For the Hurricanes, it meant that as soon as a ball was rebounded or inbounded, each player ran an assigned lane on the court, leaving the middle open to Jamila. She would attack the front rim of the basket. On her right, Kathleen would run wide, then either set a pick against a low post screen for Jen, running the baseline, or an elbow pick, at the foul line, for Jamila to use. If she was open, Jamila would simply dish her ball.

The effect of a transition offense is simple: When run properly, it seems as if the team is *always* running for a fast break. It seems as if someone is *always* open for the easy deuce or the uncontested three-pointer.

During the 1992–93 season, Coach Moyer timed his players. After a basket scored against Amherst, he discovered, his team would score a reply in nine seconds or less (so much for the thirty-second clock). If there wasn't an easy score, he trained Kristin Marvin to come way out to the sideline, take a pass from Jamila, and then return it to her, and they would run a set play. But this was a rarity.

There was one other major drill: Take it to the basket. The Hurricanes had to toughen their game, get into a little more foul trouble, play closer to the paint. As he put it, he had picked over the loss against Northampton "like the bones of a Thanksgiving turkey, and although I saw the negatives that the kids couldn't forget—the way they threw crazy passes to each other as if no one wanted to even touch the ball and how they'd pick and fade three feet away from the basket—I also saw the beginnings of almost everything that could make this season different."

He designed this drill mostly to help Kathleen and Gumby and Jonesbones. It was one on one, with a little jab step, face up and drive, or a crossover step and drive.

He had Jen and Jamila and Kathleen bring the ball up full-court against six or seven defenders.

He also employed what he called his "challenge games." He would say, for example, "Three minutes to go . . ." Then he would put the varsity on the floor against the JV. He would ask the JVs how many points they needed to win, and that would be the handicap the varsity faced.

The losing team in the drills faced the ultimate disgrace. Some coaches might have the losers run wind sprints. The Hurricanes met with a far worse punishment. The losers had to sing to the winners a song of the winners' choosing. Sometimes they named a tune and sometimes just picked themes: a Christmas song, a song with the word *blue* in it, something from *Sesame*

Street. Unless the singing was done by Lucia or Rita or Jade, the quality was so wretched, the winners found themselves begging the losers to stop.

One day during what appeared to be a routine practice, Coach Moyer decided to offer his solution to what he called "the Kathleen problem." Here she was, a starter, and the only thing she was fierce about was being gentle.

If he could only get Kathleen to feel the same intensity about basketball that she did about not eating meat. He had to get her to be fierce about being fierce.

There was not a drop of meanness in Kathleen; she was so sweet, so demure. Basketball has been called a game of subtle felonies, something Kathleen didn't understand.

"Kathleen," Coach Moyer would say, "you gotta cheat a little to win, step on someone's toe, maybe laugh in someone's face."

She would respond with a bland blank look. What was he going to do with her? She constantly backed away from her opponents, she ran around screens; she played in an unconfident way.

He folded his arms and bided his time.

She bumped into someone, and catching herself, she looked up. "Coach, I just said, 'I'm sorry.' I'm sorry."

"Kathleen, what are the two words you never want to hear on a basketball court?"

"*I'm sorry?*"

"What are the two best words to hear on a basketball court?"

"*I'm open?*"

"Kathleen, if this keeps up, I don't know what I'm going to do with you. Sometimes I think what you need is an evil twin."

"I'm sorry."

"Kathleen! This is it. From now on, Kathleen stays home."

Her eyes popped.

"Hey, Mr. Moyer, just kidding, right?" said Kristin. "Just kidding" was another of those trademark expressions of the Hurricanes.

"No, not just kidding. I mean it. I'm getting another player."

The other Hurricanes stopped mid-dribble to eavesdrop.

Coach Moyer did not back off.

"The person I want here instead is . . ."

The horror on her teammates' faces was unmistakable. What was he trying to do? Give it up in the preseason? Everyone knew Kathleen was golden, she was great. Coach Moyer was the one who always called her *key*. No Kathleen?

". . . is . . . the new Hurricane is . . . is named Skippy." Actually, this was a genteel theft. He got the idea from *Doonesbury*, the comic strip, in which George Bush had been pictured as possessing an evil twin by that name. He gave Kathleen an even look. "Okay, Skippy, put on your game face."

She looked startled at first.

"Let's see Skippy take the ball to the basket."

She moved toward the hoop tentatively. Was Coach for real? Then she smiled, ever so crookedly. Something about the strategy, the theater in it, the relief of pretending to be someone else, slowly sank in. It felt right, it felt okay. After that, the hesitancy that had so often hobbled Kathleen even during practice disappeared.

She grabbed the ball.

She stormed forward, her face a seamless mask of concentration.

She bashed the ball in.

"Skippy, I like that mean look. If there's a pick there, knock it over. Let's stay in that frame of mind. Hold that."

This is great, he thought: *I can yell at Skippy.*

But the question was still there. This was, after all, just a dress rehearsal. What would Kathleen be like when faced with the real thing?

For now, he was beguiled by his own ingenuity.

"Roses are red," he said, "violets are blue. I'm schizophrenic, and so am I. Don't forget, Kathleen. In this gym, you're Skippy."

"I won't forget, Coach Moyer."

"Actually, forgetting isn't always so bad. There are advantages to Alzheimer's. You make new friends every day. People let you hide your own Easter eggs . . ."

Practices ended at 5 P.M.

November turned into December; bulky sweaters and raw chapped hands gave way to gloves and parkas. As the Hurricanes hurried to the idling cars driven by parents who often coordinated pickup with the end of their work day, the darkness was thick, almost molecular. The air possessed a bitter dampness. There had already been discrete particles of snow and even light dustings. In Amherst the first real storm holds a special terror for college administrators. For years they have tried to break a dangerous tradition in which kids from U Mass leave their campus, with its disjointed urban mishmash, and march across into town, past the common and Hastings where Hurricane Kim Warner worked and Bonducci's coffee shop where Hurricane Kathleen Poe's father, Don, could often be seen sipping coffee in the front booth (Bob Pariseau, Jen's dad, believed he lived there) toward the Amherst college campus, with its tasteful preppy bricks, accumulating wads of snow as they go so that, in an attack that has been billed as class warfare, students from both places pelt one another with snowballs, a few of which are sometimes filled with rocks. This year the campuses were spared.

The first Friday of Advent was marked by the Lighting of

the Merry Maple on the town common, the last gasp of community-wide warmth and cheer before the ritualistic hibernation, the mass retreat into caves and holes. The same papers that rediscovered seasonal affective disorder each year with such fanfare trotted out the boilerplate about hypothermia and what to do when your toes experience tingling, then pain, then numbness.

Coach Moyer embraced the cold.

Summer was finally over.

7

Smiles on the Floor

For high school students on a team, even on one as determined as the Hurricanes appeared to be, there was still a whole lot of life, and drama, being conducted off the court as well. Adolescence is a time when what to do with your life and a newly discovered blemish can both bear down with seemingly equal pressure, when pimple = apocalypse. Basketball was important, but so were fights with one's parents, fights between one's parents, driver's permits, driver's licenses, boys who asked you out, boys who didn't, money and the lack of it, decisions about sex, drugs, and alcohol.

Who would get the awards at graduation? Jen thought she had a good shot at winning the tool chest awarded to Mr. or Ms. Consumer Auto for excellent work in a course with that title.

Was it true that Julius Lester had been chosen as this year's graduation speaker? Amherst Regional High School always aimed high in that department; Jamila's father had given the speech in the past, and the wish list compiled by the seniors always showed a sense of sophistication and connection. Somebody's grandfather had been Elie Wiesel's personal physician; a student who used to be best friends with Bill Cosby's daughter back when they lived in the area thought she might be able to get him or his wife.

The party after commencement was also discussed at length.

How many friends from outside the school could you take to the all-night graduation party at the football field at Amherst College, where you had to bring your bedrolls and your back-packs ahead of time so that "security" (meaning Coach Moyer and Coach Thomas and other parents and teachers who volunteered) could frisk them for contraband? Was the party as fun as everyone said?

Would the prom be held at some place swank or at a place with only one floor and a drab name like the Quality Inn? Everyone prayed it wouldn't be on a boat in Boston; last year's seniors had chosen that option, and the night turned out to be both wet and freezing. If the Hurricanes attended the prom, should they buy a dress or have one made by seamstress Sara Weeks, who could intuit from looking at a girl whether she should go with green satin or black crêpe, whether the skirt should be puffed or slinky, if the hem should be long or short, or somehow both.

Would they wear heels as a concession to fashion?

And if they did, would they be able to walk?

"The whole college thing" weighed on all of the seniors except Jamila (because of her early decision to go to Stanford).

In most towns the size of Amherst, high school is the pulse, the glue, the last fine time. But in a college town, higher education provides the ultimate romance, the smithy where noble ideas are forged. In this context, high school is in danger of being a footnote within a footnote. Unless the high school elbows its way into public consciousness, it is easy to dismiss, not unlike the tiny print known as agate used by newspapers for the scores of faraway games.

Amherst Regional High School occupies a spacious grassy

setting within walking distance of the center of town—twenty-one acres of wetlands, parking lots, and a flat one-story brick edifice.

There are thirty-two foreign languages spoken in the homes of the students, with Spanish, Khmer, and Chinese as the leading three.

Twenty percent of the students are on free or reduced-fee lunches.

Classes are offered in the usual subjects, but there is also a Child Study program, Auto Shop, Drafting, Advance-Placement Calculus, Physics, Survival Living (the final is a three-day solo in the wilderness), Bible as Literature, Women and Literature, African-American Literature, Latin, Chinese, Classical Greek, German, and Russian, in addition to Spanish and French, The Holocaust, Death and Dying, and The American West. The education that occurs inside the building varies from basic to standard to advanced, although in recent times the system of tracking has been under attack by the NAACP as racist. It was one of the first schools in the country to adopt a policy against sexual harassment, including an antileering clause that prohibited students from staring in an invasive or menacing way. It is not an ordinary high school, if in fact such a place exists.

Soon it was confirmed. The commencement speaker would be Julius Lester.

The school would graduate two hundred and five seniors in its class of 1993. Eighty-nine percent would go on to two- or four-year colleges.

The essay Patri wrote as part of her college application was about her brother Reggie:

As I watch my three-year-old brother grab the spoon out of my mother's hand while she struggles to feed him and say, "I can do it myself, I'm a big boy now," my heart is intoxicated with tremendous pride and delight. He wasn't always the happy, mischievous buck-a-roo he is now. From the day Reggie was born, he was forced to live in the cold, sterile environment of a hospital's intensive care unit. While confined to the limiting barriers of an incubator, he was deprived of the "normal" form of loving which a newborn deserves. . . .

Reggie was born three and a half months premature. During the first few months the only connection between him and our loving touch was a small window on the incubator about four inches in diameter. None of his vital bones or organs were strong enough to be handled frequently. We were in and out of the hospital daily, something with which I was not comfortable. As time passed, I adjusted to the setting. . . .

At first I would compare Reggie to the other children, convincing myself that he was doing better than they were in order to keep my hopes up. There is one particular instance that I wish I could have dealt with differently. I walked into the hospital's playroom where there were many children. A small child about two years old came running towards me and grabbed onto my leg; he was looking for affection from me. When I took a closer look he had a tube coming out of a hole made in his neck and when he breathed he made a loud wheezing noise. Due to my unawareness at the time, he really scared me. I tried to hide my fear from him, but it was too late because he had already noticed my immediate response. Children are good perceivers of emotion. He had a look of rejection on his face as he walked away.

One of the biggest problems in curing a patient seems to me when they lose hope, but it's difficult for a child to keep up hope when parents stop visiting and nurses stop treating them as humans, seeing them as just another patient. To me Reggie was not just another patient, nor another number on some doctor's chart, and every child out there is someone's son or someone's daughter. Seeing all this firsthand has made me realize how important it is that each and every one be treated that way and has increased my desire to become a pediatrician. Today Reggie is as healthy as any other three year old, thanks to the care he received during his first few months. I know I'll see a little bit of him in every child I care for and I know I'll do whatever I can for each one, never giving up and never losing hope.

Jen, with her grade point average of 3.733, was the only other Hurricane besides Jamila being recruited by Division 1 schools. Her advisor at the high school, Carlene Ricelli, wrote a recommendation calling her "an ambassador of goodwill. She will make a difference on your campus. . . . Beneath Jen's easygoing and amicable exterior is an intense drive. As her dad once told me, 'Jen has managed to do everything but sing.' That undoubtedly will be next." Her terrible voice, eager but tuneless, was a team joke.

She had been recruited by a host of good schools, including Princeton and Holy Cross and Rutgers. West Point really wanted her, and although she turned the school down, it was not without some misgivings on the part of the people who knew Jen and her leadership style. One time, a former marine who had served in Vietnam, observing how she got her teammates to hop to and restore to cleanliness a house they'd been enjoying, volunteered that she would make an ace leader of a platoon. People kept fantasizing wholescale upheaval in the military-industrial complex if Jen got anywhere within, as Coach Moyer put it, "shooting range, so to speak."

In the end Dartmouth won out, partly due to the strength of the women's basketball team but also the heightened New Englandness of its campus only two hours away. It also had a strong engineering department, although she sometimes considered majoring in the humanities. She loved to read, especially works that, as her stepmother put it, appealed to her "ethical style," books by women and minorities taught by her favorite teachers at the high school, Ms. Booth and Ms. Saulsberry. Jen kept this secret ambition to herself because she did not want to disappoint her father, who believed that a degree in engineering would guarantee her reasonable employment all her life. Dartmouth required a peer evaluation as part of the application process, and Jen asked Jamila if she would be willing to write one.

Jamila had no problem finding words to describe her friend. She wrote to Dartmouth about the time they had all been in Florida for her father's speech and how afterward Jen had gone up to a table where Tracy Kidder was signing copies of *Among Schoolchildren*, a portrait of a fifth-grade classroom in Holyoke in which deprivation was the norm. What had always struck Jamila about the way Jen approached Tracy Kidder was how she didn't ask him for his autograph. Instead, skinny and thirteen, she'd said, "Tell me what happened to Clarence," referring to a child in the book who was in the greatest danger.

Jamila wrote that she admired her values, her way of sifting through to the important stuff.

When Jamila thought of Jen, she realized that, more than anyone else she'd met, they would be friends forever.

The phone call during the summer had worked the change they both longed for.

For Jamila, "There was a clear understanding that from that point on we were working together. I didn't need her to be me. I needed her to be herself."

* * *

Something was troubling Rita.

Jen could see that she was distracted, less likely to smile or to break into one of her funny songs. They were almost three years apart in age and that can be, for teenagers, a gap of geological magnitude, a rift in the landscape of time akin to a canyon. Rita was still slightly embarrassed about the time when she had turned fourteen and her mother had totally violated the big kid/little kid hierarchy and invited Jen and Jamila to her birthday party as a surprise. Jen remembered Rita as "totally stressed. Totally mortified. She knew us as basketball players, not as friends. When you're younger, you always have this fear older kids think you're dorky, so Jamila and I just kept saying 'This is great!' every minute."

Jen had gotten to know Rita better since the summer. Upon Jen's return from Clovis, Rita had given her a copy of a poem she had written. Jen loved to read and reread it.

Some people's feet never leave the ground.
Some of us soar.
Some people's eyes are on the crowd.
Some of us never notice.
Some people's minds are on the competition.
Some of us don't care.
Some people put their body into it.
Some of us put our heart and soul.

Usually Rita was easy to get through to.

All you had to do was joke about how she might not be the first female president, but she'd surely be the first female president in space.

"Don't worry," Rita would reply. "I'm all over that."

Or, they might recite together word-for-word Judy Tenuta's comedy routine they both loved:

"I was baby-sitting my brother Boscoe and my mom came home from work early and she said, 'Hey, Judy, what was Boscoe's severed arm doing on the table?' Um. Bad paper cut.

"So I was baby-sitting the Clapp twins and I had to put them to bed. For their own good. And they said, 'Oh, no, Judy, don't turn off the lights. There are monsters in the dark.' And I said, Oh, no, those are just your clothes trying to murder you.

"Have you ever been walking down the street and seen someone from your past that you don't want to talk to so you try to rearrange your DNA but they notice you anyway and they say, 'Judy, were you going to walk past me without saying hi?' And I said, Um, no, Mom."

But lately nothing cracked the façade of deep, troubled thought. Finally, one afternoon, in the locker room, Jen asked if they could talk.

"Oh, Jen, it's just that this kid, this boy, well, he keeps bothering me. Really, it's no big deal."

Rita breathed deeply.

"Have you talked to your mother about it?" Jen asked.

Jen liked Rita's mother. Rita had included a quote from her in the blank book she'd given to Jen: "Everyone's pain is real." Anne Teschner told them stories about when she'd played softball in high school. She always shuddered at the memory of her team's uniforms, scanty in the cold weather, scanty whenever you slid into base.

"My mother? I can't talk to her. She's from Worcester." Rita used her mother's pronunciation: "Wuz-tuh," as it is called by natives, truncating the syllables, making the very name of their town a taunt.

"What does that have to do with anything?"

"You have to know Worcester." Rita was thinking about how the city in central Massachusetts is a neighborhoodish place where scores often are settled with quick informality.

"Okay, you can't tell her. Can you tell me? I don't mean to badger you, but it hurts me to see you so hurt."

Rita took a deep breath. "It's probably nothing."

"Can you tell me more about probably nothing?"

"I don't even really know him. See, at first he called me on the phone and he said he liked me, but he wouldn't identify himself. He said if I knew who it was, I wouldn't talk to him, he was such a bad kid. I kept saying, 'Who is this?' and he'd say, 'No one.' And then after a bunch of calls one day, he called again and asked why I wasn't at practice that day. I was in the middle of practicing for cross-country, and there was no way anyone would know if I was in practice or not unless he was watching me. I asked him not to call, but he kept calling and then he started leaving notes, and they really embarrassed me. You know, 'I worship you' notes. So when he called again, I said, 'Look, this is really making me uncomfortable.' And then one day in class this kid walked in and gave me a rose, and it was him. I had never met him. His name didn't mean anything to me. I told him to leave me alone, but then he had one of his friends threaten my boyfriend, and then he paid a friend of mine for information about me. And in the hallway at school, all his friends keep pointing at me, blocking my way. One day I was walking with my boyfriend and we both started laughing at something, I don't know what, and he saw us and he thought we were laughing at him, and he started calling my best friend every night and said, 'She's going to pay for this.' And he said he had a Smith & Wesson and he was going to blow my brains out, and it's pretty known at the high school that he has access to guns. And I don't know what I should do. I mean, is this okay?"

Jen just stared.

"He probably doesn't really mean anything," the younger girl continued.

"I'm probably overreacting . . ."

Jen waited.

All those peer ed classes, that high-minded talk about self-esteem that seemed right now so hopelessly hypothetical.

In class, if someone presented a story like Rita's, your reaction would have a clear crusading purity:

Oh, go kick him in the nuts. Tell him to go screw himself. But when your dear pal is practically in tears talking about how bad she feels and she's trying to convince herself that it's not serious but she's hurt and she's scared and she's worried about the kid who's harassing her because for some weird reason she's concerned about his feelings even though he isn't concerned about hers, it's hard to know what to say, but finally, you say what you think is right.

Rita told Jen the boy's name; she recognized it from similar incidents with other girls.

"This," said Jen, "is not okay. He can't do that. What are you afraid of?"

"I don't like to see someone get in trouble."

"He got himself in trouble. You didn't put him there. Besides, maybe deep down he doesn't like what he's doing either."

"What if his friends bug me in the hallway, call me names, or won't let me get by?"

"Didn't you tell me they're already doing that? I'm sure that if you speak to the dean of students, he'll help. I'm not going to push you because this is your decision, but if you want, I'll tell Mr. Parker you need to talk to him."

Rita's face reflected a mixture of relief and sadness. She looked down at her long fingers.

She nodded. Yes, please tell Mr. Parker about it. Please tell him she needed to talk to him.

Given the pressures of their lives—pressures invisible to outsiders blinded by the peak foliage of youth, the ease, the grace, the beauty of adolescence—some of the Hurricanes found going into the locker room after a day of classes and donning those sneakers the perfect refuge. It was comforting, all those routines and all that drill; even Coach Moyer's trademark patter, which everyone practically knew by heart, had a way of blurring the edges of a bad day.

"Respect your uniforms," he would say, with an air of fresh discovery, as if he'd never said it before. "The only time they hit the floor is when you are in them.

"When I say practice is from ten to twelve, I mean be ready to walk on the floor at ten. Don't waltz in at ten after ten.

"It's a game. I want to see some smiles on the floor. I don't want to see a lot of stick people; when elbows go straight, knees go straight, your weight's all on the back of the heels. Relax and play the game with your legs.

"One of the major elements of this is enthusiasm. Nothing great ever happened without enthusiasm. Basketball is a loose and confident sport. The team that gets loose first usually wins.

"If the other team beats you, go up to them, head up high, and congratulate them.

"If you're one of those really nice people, find a little compartment, take that nice person, that Kathleen, and put it aside for a while. You can take it out when you're baby-sitting or selling Girl Scout cookies.

"Basketball is an opportunity to improve your character, a laboratory for life. You're putting people in an artificial situation and turning them loose.

"Sports is the toy store of life. Run around. Try everything on.

"I want you to love the game. Can't play it so good anymore, but I love it.

"The most important statistic is total points. If you end up with one more point, it's a great game. Jamila, what's the second most important statistic?"

"Shots taken?"

"Just wanted to see if you were listening. After having you hear the same stories and the same jokes for six years, it'll be good when you leave so I can get into the Amherst spirit and recycle."

"You already have the Amherst spirit," said Jen.

"Are you saying I get my jokes from the landfill?"

"No, just dump them."

"Did I ever tell you about that great game my college team played against Moravian?"

Had he ever told them? Breathes there a human being within a hundred-mile radius of Amherst whom he hadn't told? A thousand miles? The world over?

"We went into four overtimes, and I played every minute of all four overtimes, so I was dead. We should have killed them. Finally, our coach calls a time-out, six seconds left, and he tells Mike Miller to shoot and that way we'd win the game. Then he takes me aside and tells me to win it by tapping in the miss. I did. At the buzzer."

Sometimes during practice Coach Moyer said they all had to make ten free throws and after that they could have a drink of water.

"Hey, this is nothing. When I was in college and playing ball for Lafayette, my coach made us make fifty free shots in a row, and he would count the last ten personally. I got so I could do it in . . ."

"Twenty minutes," responded the Hurricanes under their breath. There were certain Coach Moyer stories they had memorized, and this was one.

"Maybe you'll get lucky and you'll beat my record someday. You know what I call luck?"

They all did, and they could all recite it along with him:

"Luck is when preparation meets opportunity."

Then he repeated the saying and added, "Coaches always say things twice. Coaches always say things twice."

"Doh!" said Jen. She was widely acknowledged at Amherst Regional High School as the best imitator of Homer Simpson as he expressed his famous expletive.

Occasionally, one team member would turn to another for coaching, as when Kim said to Jen, "I need help."

"What's the matter, Kim?"

"I'll never get ten free shots."

"Kim, remember that story we all read when we were little kids about the Little Engine That Could?"

"Sure," said Kim, "that and Winnie the Pooh were my two favorites." The ball went in the basket.

"So," said Jen, "how does it go?"

Another basket.

"You know, there's a little train that's trying to get over the mountain to deliver all those toys."

Three and four.

"Right. Remember what the Little Engine kept saying?"

"Sure, I remember."

Five.

"You do? The exact words?"

Six, seven, eight.

"I'm pretty sure I do."

Nine.

"What were they?"

Ten: success, water.

"I think I can. I think I can."

"Okay," bellowed Coach, "everyone can fluid up now. Good work, everybody. Hey, did you hear the one about the two psychologists who met on the street. The first one says, 'You're fine. How am I?'"

*　*　*

Jamila had heard about a team of college women who referred to themselves as "Hoop Phi." Something about the expression, with its two strong syllables, insistent as a drumbeat, insinuated itself into her consciousness, and try as she might to put it aside, it became in her mind the perfect slogan for this year's team, better than the one Coach Moyer was trying to inveigle them into using, something about "a fist and a flag."

He would raise his hand and wave his fingers. "When they're all going in different directions, they're not very powerful, but curl them up into a fist and they're that much more powerful. Only teams that get that close actually win a flag."

Whenever he introduced the phrase, which was fairly often, the girls looked down and around but not at him. Something about it failed to inspire. Jen, for one, couldn't make herself thrill to it, any more than she could to the way Jamila tried to line up everyone behind "Hoop Phi." Jamila would shout "Hoop" hopefully, and Jen would keep on dribbling. But one day at the end of practice a couple of her teammates softly responded. Some say it was Kristin, some say it was Jade, others remember both at once, but the Hurricanes all agree. That first feathered "Phi" was the beginning of something that built and built, becoming, in the end, loud and unmistakable, and soon it became the rallying cry for all of them, including Jen, during the tap drill that ended every practice. The players would line up and tap the ball off the backboard, while in the air alternating cries of "Hoop" and "Phi."

Jen and Jamila were not the first females in Amherst to be known simply by their first names.

That honor goes of course to Emily Dickinson. As the poet

Archibald MacLeish once said, "Most of us are half in love with this dead girl we call by her first name."

All year long, pilgrims came from around the world to visit the poet's home, including on one occasion a Viet vet, who said he wanted to thank "the little gal who helped me get through Nam." Toting guitars and other instruments, they go to her grave to recite her poems and sometimes even sing them, intoning her words, ". . . that thing with feathers" or "Presentiment— is . . . ," often kneeling in the grass as they gaze at the fenced-in stone with this simple legend:

"Called back."

From April to October, twice a week, it is possible to arrange for a tour of the Federal-style Dickinson homestead on Main Street, with the expansive side yard and the trees in front like bars. Children under twelve are admitted free. "They are our *special* visitors," explained one tour guide, who then checked herself as if this might be offensive. "Of course we believe everyone is special."

There's not a child in Amherst who hasn't on the way to Fenton's for sneakers or Bruno's for a sub driven by the place where Dickinson selected her own soul for society, then shut the door of her second-floor bedroom, which looked out on a row of tall soldierly hemlocks.

During her lifetime only seven of her 1,775 poems saw the light of print.

"Publication," she once wrote, "—is the Auction / Of the Mind . . ."

With that attitude, what would she consider basketball was of the body?

Not by nature a team player, she tended in her work to celebrate solitude:

How happy is the little Stone
That rambles in the Road alone

Her notion of sociability was to wave down passing school-children and to lower from her bedroom window a little basket on a string containing gingerbread or raisins. Her custom was to wear nothing but white, a color that in her day was a symbol of renunciation and mourning. The dress that she wore during the last ten years of her life is preserved on a dummy in a glass case in her room. There is occasional talk about a Dickinson scholar, said to be a dignified sort of person, who keeps importuning the trustees of the homestead to let him try on Emily's dress and wear it to a reading, but thus far the diminutive garment, with its narrow shoulders and small patch pocket (where it is surmised she used to tuck incipient poems on precious scraps of paper), has remained on display, safe and prim, headless as a cucumber.

Despite all the pilgrims who come to Amherst, Dickinson is somewhat out of fashion in certain circles, partly because, as a poet, she did not inhabit her body in the way we demand today.

Jen was the most vocal about her trouble understanding Dickinson's elliptical style.

There's a famous photo of the poet, plain-faced and solemn, which has been issued as a postcard. Whenever she saw the card, Jen would announce to anyone within earshot, employing one of the famous accents, lowering her voice, crushing the syllables, using a tone of fake elation: "Doesn't she look like such an exciting woman? I bet that book on the table next to her is entitled: 'If you are confusing enough, people will think you are brilliant.' I know she read it many times."

Coach Moyer himself often wondered, *How can it be poetry when it doesn't even rhyme?* although he wondered less when someone replied that it was for the same reason that a basketball game with low scores can be exciting. It was, he thought, a conundrum at least worth contemplating.

Teachers who faced resistance to the poet sometimes drummed up enthusiasm for the poet's work by pointing out her distaste for normal punctuation, how she preferred dashes to commas and how she was such a rule breaker, she didn't even give her poems titles. There was a U Mass professor who got a big response whenever he shared his discovery that one of her poems may well be about being bitten on the behind by a spider. Dubbed the "outhouse poem," it describes someone

Alone and in a Circumstance
Reluctant to be told
A Spider on my reticence
Assiduously crawled

In his lectures the professor told his students the telltale clue is in the use of the word "assiduously": "A-S-S. Get it?"

One local mother set the poet's most famous work to rap with this intro:

It's no Felony
To worship Emily
Write—Write—Baby.

Followed by:

I'm Nobody! Who are you?
Are you—Nobody—Too?
Then there's pair of us?
Don't tell! they'd advertise—you know!

How dreary—to be—Somebody!
How public—like a Frog—
To tell one's name—the livelong June
To the admiring Bog!

There's no blood in her poetry, no mastectomies, no babies, no beatings, no tongues touching. It would be difficult to imagine her writing about her grandfather, who helped found Amherst College because Harvard was a little too lenient with its boys, or about her father, who was somewhat autocratic and distant, in the haranguing manner of, say, Sylvia Plath, exclaiming, "Daddy, daddy, you bastard."

Yet, if a place belongs as much to the dead as to the living, the influence of Dickinson is profound. She was bound by the limits of her era. She barely left the house, and yet she became in the view of her supporters perhaps the greatest practitioner of a certain kind of metaphysical, nature-based poetry in the world.

"Would Emily Dickinson be a potential Hurricane if she were alive today?" Coach Moyer once asked himself rhetorically. "She certainly has the right first name to be a Hurricane. Physically, she resembles Carrie Tharp—small, dark, frail. She amassed a career total of seventeen hundred poems, even if a lot of them were from close range. She mostly wore white, which indicates she'd probably only be interested in playing the home games. I'd probably play her as a guard, but not a point guard, because she's not a great face-to-face communicator. She had a great fear of being rejected, so she'd probably only shoot threes from long range while wide open. It's a historical fact she went to Mount Holyoke, so the most we could expect of her at the collegiate level is Division Three."

8
Tip-Off

The first game of a season is always a time of testing. You're never certain how good you are until you finally hit the floor against another team. A game in which your team is favored to win is freighted with special intensity.

The pendulum does not swing equally.

Victory is expected.

Loss is a disaster.

"Okay, tonight expect the usual Chuck and Chase from West Side," said Coach Moyer on December 15 as the Hurricanes gathered in room 4 at the high school before heading off to West Springfield for their first game of the season. "Chuck and Chase" was his expression for a team without much in the way of coherent strategy.

"Did any of you happen to see what the *Springfield Union* wrote?" He held a news clip up for all to see. "They picked Northampton to be this season's regional champ."

Coach Moyer could see it was working. He liked to stir them up before a game, let them taste a little indignation. Nothing served the purpose better than a newspaper article that underestimated their abilities.

"You're kidding, right?" said Jen.

"No," he replied. "They wrote, 'Most local experts consider Amherst for a likely third or fourth spot, after Hamp and Agawam and possibly Longmeadow.'"

The Hurricanes were unanimous:

"Well, they're wrong."

The bus ride home was buoyant and loud.

Amherst had won their first game, 59–42, and what was most encouraging was the performance of the forwards, Kathleen and Kristin and Gumby and Jonesbones, their steadfast tilling of the fields so someone else could claim the bloom. The singing was so loud that even Jen's awkward cacophony was easily drowned out.

Jen made a point of asking Rita if she had spoken to Mr. Parker.

Rita said, "Not yet."

Jen told her it was her decision, and she could not make it for her. "I will not walk behind you holding you up. I won't walk in front of you and pull you along. But I'll be right beside you every step of the way."

It was a boost starting out the season with this kind of send-off: Jamila had 17 points, Jen had 11, and so did Emily Shore. Kristin led with 7 rebounds.

As the bus swayed back to Amherst, weightless and merry for the moment, Jen allowed herself the delicious thought:

This was going to be fun.

Again.

Like in the old days.

As the press began to shine its eye on the Hurricanes and their progress, Kim, especially, was thrilled at all the newspaper accounts, even when her name was not mentioned. She would carefully clip each notice, insert it in an envelope, and send it with a short note to her father in Florida.

On December 18 Amherst beat Cathedral, 65–32; on December 21 at Chicopee Comp the Hurricanes won, 60–22. Kim's correspondence headed south at a similar clip.

On December 23 Chicopee High played Amherst at home.

Jen walked on the court during the warm-up in what Kristin always called a "hopped-up" mood. She had the jitters but she was taking the excess drive and turning it into smooth practice shots. Jen always came out for the warm-ups with a slight air of distraction. Her light eyes would sweep the stands, and only when she'd located her father would she—without actually making eye contact—relax.

The first few minutes of the game were devoted to a series of moves that would appear curious to an outsider. Whenever possible, members of the Hurricanes, led by Jamila's example, appeared to be avoiding making baskets of their own in order to give the ball to Jen. Four minutes and fifteen seconds into the game, when the score was 11–5, the action stopped completely and an uproar ensued, underscored by the arrival of someone in a fluffy pink gorilla suit and a bouquet of balloons.

Jen Pariseau, who had entered the season with 944 points, had made her thousandth career point.

She stood in the center of the court. With her wide smile and square shoulders and forthright gait, she shook her head back and forth. She found her father in the stands and gave him a look of rebuke. An ape! How could he? This was so embarrassing! Even her opponents applauded with good cheer as she accepted a plaque honoring her achievement, which Coach Moyer had ordered two months before that night's game. How did he know it would happen that night? "Hey, I'm the coach. I can control when a player gets to leave the bench."

Jen hugged her teammates, especially Jamila, and thought back to a year ago when Jamila had reached this milestone; how she wished she could turn back time and feel the same goodwill toward Jamila that her friend was now showing her. The score that night was 72–45.

Jamila and her parents gave Jen a gold chain with the number twenty-two dangling from it, which soon became her favorite piece of jewelry.

"I hope she doesn't do what my friend did when he got the gold medal," said Coach Moyer. "Took it home and got it bronzed . . ."

Over the Christmas break Kristin decided something was wrong with her game, drastically wrong. The Hurricanes were doing well, but she felt the beginning of the dullness that had sabotaged the team in every other season. A good start followed by a fatal fizzle. As the official supplier of team spirit, if she didn't feel excited, who would?

She needed guidance; of the two captains, Jamila was the one she chose to call. Kristin felt closer to Jamila.

Jen and she often had opposite opinions.

Sometimes when Kristin had a suggestion for a change, Jen would shrug it off. Or, she would give Kristin her worst putdown: "Go sign a petition." To Jen, a petition was a painstakingly democratic, indigenously Amherst way of taking forever. Both Kristin and Jen knew that the problem between them was somehow connected to their mutual stubbornness. Each was always so certain her way was the right way. Yet Kristin suspected that deep down Jen recognized everything she did for the team, not just on court, but off it as well, and she was right. Jen was grateful to Kristin "for grabbing the Hoop Phi puppy and running with it." It was Kristin who organized everyone to wear backwards jeans to school or overalls with baggy shirts or Champion sweatshirts or crazy hats or dress shirts with ties. Before game days it was Kristin who reminded everyone: "Team ritual tomorrow. Wear a dress. Look nice." When a player groaned about how jeans were so much more comfortable, Kristin remained unrelenting. "You too, Jamila."

On the bus rides home following a victory, it was Kristin's voice that often superseded the others:

We're from Amherst,
Couldn't be prouder.
If you can't hear us,
We'll shout a little louder.

It was hard to curb the panic in her voice as she reported to Jamila: "I don't feel it."

"Feel what?"

"You know. The fire."

Kristin knew what it meant to feel hot. Hey, she dove off the low board when she was fifteen months old, the high board when she was two and a half. She could ride a two-wheeler at age three and a half. She dove off a booster seat at a Taco Villa when she was about four or so, thus the little indentation in the flesh near her eye, that speck of imperfection. Kristin dove. Period. But now, with the season under way and even with those Ws (wins), she felt a dilution of the spirit, a flickering of the flame.

"Okay," said Jamila, "let's go to Boyden," referring to the all-purpose gym at U Mass.

"No way. Not there."

"Come on, I go there with my dad all the time."

"I'm not your dad. This is really embarrassing. Someone could see me and wonder, Why is she out here on this floor?"

"The more confidence you have in yourself, the better you're going to play."

"Okay . . ."

And now she turned to her friend Jamila, hoping she could tell her where the adrenaline came from, that special store of energy that kicks your entire being into a kind of animalistic supersensory awareness. How did you do it? How did you find within yourself that kind of passion and cunning?

Employing that survivalist arrogance that accrues to people who pride themselves on knowing all the good backroads, Kristin got in her brown VW and jigjagged over to Jamila's in record time. Together they headed off to the gym at U Mass.

On the way, she realized: *Jamila isn't asking me to be her dad. She's being her dad to me.* Whenever Jamila had a bad game, her father took her to Boyden, where she made two hundred jump shots in a row.

Kristin already felt better as she walked into the cinderblock extravaganza named for Frank Boyden of Deerfield Academy, the subject of a book called *The Headmaster* by John McPhee: "He believed in athletics as, among other things, a way of controlling and blending his boys, and required them to participate throughout the school year. This idea was an educational novelty in 1902."

The two girls stood close to the basket. Jamila kept feeding the ball to Kristin, and Kristin kept making shots, from the right, from the left, in front, looking, not looking, swinging those arms up over and over, yes! *swoosh!* yes! *swoosh!* yes! The hundreds of jump shots she took off stalled feeding passes from Jamila got Kristin back into the rhythm of the game. Hot, sweating, they paused to guzzle some water.

Spotting a couple of guys, they asked if they wanted to join them.

This was the Hurricanes' favorite subterfuge.

The response was the usual twitching and winking symphony of gestures: Eyes were rolled, impatient glances exchanged, and then, reluctantly, they joined in, not so much out of largesse as to show the girls who's who.

And then, the fun began.

On that gray winter afternoon, within the gray confines of Boyden, Jamila was great, and the greatness was contagious. First the two girls squared off against each other, one on one, and then they took on the guys, and then one girl and one guy against another girl and guy. The play was amicable, but furious.

Afterward, all of them were soaked with sweat, floating in the light inner air that follows a rigorous workout.

As Kristin and Jamila prepared to leave, first one of the guys, and then the other, took Kristin aside and asked who Jamila was.

"Just a friend."

"You two home from college on break?"

"Nope. We go to high school in town."

"Come on."

"Really, you can ask anyone. We're seniors."

Jamila just stood to the side, enigmatic as ever. Her teammates agreed that Jamila understood the fine line between being cocky and being sure of yourself, and she danced it with style.

"Come on, who is she?"

"I told you," said Kristin, swinging her hair against her still-damp neck, taking bold strides off the court, tossing the words off behind her back, "she's my friend."

And as the two girls proceeded off the court, the guys stood in the distance still scratching their heads, with dazed expressions, calling out, with a final effort to figure out what had just hit them, in muted pleading voices, an unwitting echo of the reclusive poet in white, "Who are you? Who are you?"

Hamp at home, Hamp at Hamp, always a vintage event, always guaranteed to draw a crowd from both sides of the river.

The first meeting between the Hurricanes and the Blue

Devils took place at home almost halfway through the regular season.

The media gave it top billing.

From the *Daily Hampshire Gazette*, by Jeff Thomas:

The big game of the week will be on television and radio, will be covered by a horde of print reporters, will be played in Amherst and undoubtedly will be a sellout.

UMass men's basketball? Wrong!

Try high school girls basketball. Try Northampton at Amherst Regional, 7:30 tonight. Both 8–0. One the Valley Wheel champion and 20–2 last year, the other the Western Mass. champion and state runner-up.

WHMP-AM will have the game live with George Miller, the voice of the Minutemen. ACTV-10 will be doing the game, to be shown next week on Amherst cable.

Neither coach wants to bill this game as anything other than a regular-season game, but that story won't sell.

"This is the championship of January and the winner gets absolutely nothing," said Hurricane coach Ron Moyer. "Our goal is to be the best team in March."

Last year the Canes were the champions in January and for the rest of the regular season, sweeping the series with the Blue Devils.

But it was Northampton that reigned in March, beating Amherst in the Western Mass. semifinals and going on to beat Agawam in the finals for the Western Mass. crown.

"You want to win every game you play," said Northampton coach Tom Parent. "I only think it's a big game if one of us dominates the other."

One cliché used when these two teams meet is that there are no secrets between them, neither will surprise the other on the court. The coaches know each other, have seen each other's team play and seen films of their opponent. The players know each other and are friendly for the most part.

So it will come down to talent and tactics. Both teams have more talent than some of the other leagues in Western Mass. The distribution of that talent is what will come into play.

The Hurricanes are strong in the back court with everybody's All-American Jamila Wideman and three-point specialist Jenny Pariseau. Their front court isn't as well established, with Kathleen Poe, Emily Shore, and Kristin Marvin starting and Emily Jones the first off the bench.

The Blue Devils are strong all over and deep, a dimension Amherst doesn't have. Beth Kuzmeski, the second best guard in Western Mass., brings the ball up. She's joined by fellow senior Johanna Clark in the back court. Up front the Devils have long-range sniper Liz Moulton and in-the-paint players Kim Frost and Addie Stiles.

There's no good reason why Northampton had become Amherst's bitter rival except, perhaps, force of habit, which in New England can justify decades of silence or animosity between old-timers. As Jen always put it, "Something happens when we play Hamp. Both teams become brutes." Amherst's homecoming float during the preceding fall had featured two Blue Devils in electric chairs.

Hamp is a perfectly reasonable town, filled with stores where you can get Nicole Miller jackets or Cole Haan shoes,

Bauhaus sofas, and real art. The restaurants are plentiful and varied, and between Pearl Street and the Iron Horse, music is too. It is the site of Smith College, which has among its alumnae Sylvia Plath, Gloria Steinem, Julia Child, and Betty Friedan. The images of Barbara Bush, who attended Smith, and Nancy Reagan, who graduated, are shown on the front of a favorite Smith T-shirt; the back says, THERE'S GOT TO BE A BETTER WAY TO GET A SMITHIE TO THE WHITE HOUSE. Another favorite T-shirt, celebrating the school's centennial: ONE HUNDRED YEARS OF WOMEN ON TOP. Another: BEHIND EVERY GREAT WOMAN IS A GREAT WOMEN'S COLLEGE.

Although at least half the students at Smith are on scholarships or work/study, the image of pearls and horses persists, partly because pearls are still popular, and if you wish to bring your horse from home, there are stables available on the campus. On Friday afternoons tea is served in the dorm dining rooms; students have carte blanche to invite faculty to join them for meals, for which no fee is charged. In the old days, each dining room had been equipped with a cubby where a student could store her favorite silver or napkin rings. The quad area, which houses most of the dorms, is the scene of a mock riot for several days every fall. In one of those boisterous yet harmless undergraduate rituals, students march to the president's house on campus demanding Mountain Day *now*. Mountain Day is a traditional interlude at Smith and at Mount Holyoke, announced by the pealing of chapel bells campus-wide. Classes are canceled unexpectedly so students can enjoy the fall foliage, or, just as likely, go shopping in Boston.

Northampton is the longtime residence of Calvin Coolidge and the birthplace of the inventor of the graham cracker; it has that rarest of amenities in modern America, a lively and safe downtown, the jewel of which is a grand old theater with box seats and balconies called the Academy of Music, devoted now to movies.

The town is also known as a friendly location for gay women; in the winter you sometimes see snowmen—snow *people*—with breasts.

"Country-music fans gravitate to the Grand Ole Opry, painters dream of Provence and ski bums settle in Aspen," according to an article in *Newsweek*. "Lesbians have a mecca, too. It's Northampton, Mass, a.k.a. Lesbianville, U.S.A. In a profile of the town last year, the *National Enquirer* claimed that '10,000 cuddling, kissing lesbians call it home sweet home.'"

Sometimes nicknamed "Paradise," Northampton has a history of being an independent, utopian community, home for a time of former slave Sojourner Truth, a feminist and abolitionist who fought to regain her son Peter after he'd been sold: "Oh my god! I know'd I have him again. Why, I felt so tall within—I felt as if the power of a nation was with me."

Amherst had a lot to fear from Hamp this evening.

Northampton's Beth Kuzmeski had been playing against Jamila since junior high, and if anyone could shut her down, Beth could. She'd seen Jamila's behind-the-back move, her dipsy-do on the way to the basket, her pull-up jump shot, and seen them over and over again. In addition, Addie Stiles and Kim Frost of Hamp were top-quality players up front.

At the end of the junior varsity game, the Hurricanes, entering the gym from room 4 rather than the locker room, saw that fans were being turned away. Jen saw some of Beth's family in line, and she asked the ticket takers to give them top priority. They were foes on the floor, but in every other context they admired each other.

Jen could not believe how hot it was inside the gym: "Oh my God," she told her teammates, "it must be about three hundred degrees Fahrenheit." Even when she exaggerated, she did so with such conviction that the hyperbole passed for reality. Weeks later, if you asked any Hurricane, they all swore it had been three hundred in that gym and not one degree less.

The mayor of Northampton and the superintendent of Amherst schools were there, receiving the attention of the local broadcasters, but more significantly so were some of the young girls who were being coached for the first time ever in youth basketball, 140 second through sixth graders on teams with names like Terriers and Wildcats and Cardinals.

The gym possessed that surge of energy, nearly electrical, that occurs in a crowd in which people are scrunched up next to one another, mindless of the hard bleachers, cheering.

"This many people from Amherst, all in one room; they should just lock the door at halftime and hold a meeting on diversity," said one fan.

In the bleachers, this conversation summed up the mood on the Amherst side:

"Mommy, what number is Jamila?"

"Eleven."

"What number is Jenny?"

"Twenty-two."

"What does that add up to?"

"Thirty-three."

"No. Trouble. For Hamp."

But trouble was coming Amherst's way. Not long into the first half, Jamila picked up her third foul.

The reaction from the Northampton side was what you'd expect from fans who drift off to sleep dreaming of the opportunity to demolish those Canes.

The Amherst fans were dispirited.

The last time the two teams had met was at the play-off game at Cathedral in Springfield almost a year ago.

Jamila looked stricken.

This was a rarity for her; in fact the fans often chanted, "Jamila doesn't foul, Jamila doesn't foul."

Anyone who has ever been counted on by members of a

team knows the feeling, knows the emptiness that gnaws at you when you feel as if you have let everybody down.

You feel guilt, you feel anger, you're furious at yourself, the refs, the world in general.

Coach Moyer put her on the bench.

He nodded at Jen, charging her in effect with playing both their positions at once.

Coach Moyer called one of his infrequent time-outs.

It's not unusual to see a player take over a game at the offensive end of the court, to suddenly explode and make every basket, but what Jen did now was to take over both ends of the court.

She stole the ball.

She rebounded missed Northampton shots.

She played an astonishingly fierce defense on the perimeter, and then she went to the point where Northampton double-teamed her, then triple-teamed her, and still she could not be stopped.

She was simply everywhere.

It was really as if for four, five, six interminable minutes she played against Hamp, all five of their players, on her own, with only the most modest assistance from Kristin, Gumby, Kathleen, and Jan Klenowski, subbing for Jamila.

The lead for Amherst was small, a point or two, when Jen entered the floor. When she returned to the bench, drained and exhausted, Amherst had extended its margin by six points.

One fan exclaimed, "This isn't basketball. This is Horatio at the bridge!"

There was an immense cheer when she left the floor.

Realizing that an athletic debt was owed, that her friend Jen had delivered a reprieve and given Jamila another chance to win the game for Amherst, Jamila returned to the floor for the second half. Soon Jamila and Jen and Beth all had four fouls, recalling for some fans the infamous *Mad* magazine satire in which a game ends with the teams walking from one side of the court to the other.

With three minutes and fifty-six seconds left, the score was tied.

A clutch shot by Jonesbones raised Amherst's prospects by two.

With Amherst ahead by two and with the thirty-second-shot clock winding down, Jamila, trailed by Beth Kuzmeski, came off a high screen set by Jen. Liz Moulton, the other Hamp guard, dogged Jamila as well.

Jamila drove to the baseline, attracting a third Blue Devil; she rose up, took about a fourteen-foot jump shot, and drained it for the winning points.

"Beyond big-time," said the same fan who had earlier called Jen "Horatio."

The next day's headlines were sweet as sap: ROUND ONE GOES TO AMHERST, FULL HOUSE SEES CANES TOP HAMP.

On January 20, Amherst beat West Side again, this time 75–44. William Jefferson Clinton was inaugurated as president, and for Jen the best part was Maya Angelou's poem. Kim and her mother bought Jen a copy of *On the Pulse of Morning* with its red cover, gold lettering, and paper of heavy vellum. It took Jen one second to find the page with her favorite line:

> *History, despite its wrenching pain,*
> *Cannot be unlived, but if faced*
> *With courage, need not be lived again.*

Rita took Jen aside in the locker room and told her she had spoken to Mr. Parker and to several Amherst police officers.

None of them thought the situation with the guy harassing her was merely a prankish case of boys will be boys. The next step was whether to pursue this in court, to see if he could be prevented legally from making contact with her on the phone or otherwise.

She tried to tell herself she was absolutely certain he wouldn't bother her again; that is, she was pretty sure, which is to say, maybe it wouldn't happen again if she were lucky.

In the end she decided to go to court.

She kept thinking about the other girls he had bothered in the past, and she worried that in the future he might bother some other girl: *He threatened me, and if I don't do something to stop him, maybe the next person will get more than threatened. If women allow that kind of behavior, it will never stop.*

Sixteen wins into the season, the Hurricanes traveled to Clifford B. Kibbe gymnasium in Agawam to face the Brownies for the first time this season. There was a long history of being intimidated in their gym. Coach Moyer always told his players that you've got to outplay Agawam so convincingly that you take the refs out of it:

"You have to outplay them by twenty to win by one or two. In basketball, as in any sport, there is a home-court advantage: The more the home court is feared, the harder it is for the interlopers. Sometimes the refs participate, wittingly or unwittingly, in the favoritism: You'll be tackled while you're dribbling and called for a walk as the other guy pushes you off the court. It's called home cookin'. You need to have a road warrior syndrome. You have to fight the crowd, the refs. You can't mind the boos. Passive teams get chewed to bits on the road. You can win at home with finesse, but you win on the road with heart."

Coach Moyer and the coach of the Brownies, Lou Conte, were pals on the coach circuit. They had both coached boys' teams and girls' teams, and they agreed on many points. Sometimes before the games in each other's gyms they stood side by side and shared their similar impressions, a sight that puzzled the Hurricanes. If Agawam was the evil empire, how could the coaches be so friendly? Coach Moyer realized that often the Hurricanes failed to understand that the real villains are the ones from within, those tiny voices that cut you down.

"The girls are fun to coach," Coach Conte would say. "Boys are often sometimes there just for the ride. Girls, they tend to appreciate it more."

"They listen," Coach Moyer would reply. "Boys, you have to tear down their ego. With girls, you just have to build up their confidence."

They were in perfect agreement.

"The thing is," Coach Conte would say, "a coach isn't . . ."

". . . just a coach," Coach Moyer would complete the thought.

Coach Conte would grab the rebound.

"A coach is a teacher, a life teacher. You're often the third-most influential person in the child's life. I tell my kids, 'At the end of the day you should thank the good Lord for the things you have, you should have done something good for someone else today, and did you kiss your mother and father before you got into bed tonight?' "

And then the buzzer would sound and the contest begin.

The two teams played within six points of each other the entire game that night.

Agawam was crafty.

The Brownies disdained trying to press or trap Jamila. They double-teamed her. The double-team allowed the biggest of the Brownies, Kim Trudel and Cyndi Stone, to race back and get set up on defense. As soon as the defense was set, Agawam went into a triangle and two. This puts the three big players under the basket in a zone, while the two defenders played Jamila and Jen head to head.

It took Amherst out of the transition and put the game into a slower-paced, slog-it-out affair.

Yet, all in all, with only ten seconds to go and trailing by just two points, Amherst had the ball.

Coach Moyer invoked the old adage: At home play for the tie, on the road go for the win.

Jamila took a long three-pointer.

It rimmed out, agonizingly.

In the end Amherst lost it in the paint. Agawam was a little more rugged, a little more willing to bump and run. Plus they had height, players like Kim Trudel and Cyndi Stone. You can't teach tall.

Once again, thought Coach Moyer as the bus bumped its way back to Amherst, bogged down in Agaswamp. In his parking-lot talk, he accentuated the high points of the game:

"You hung in there. You scrapped for the ball. You didn't give up . . ."

Yet, he worried.

The next day's headline in the *Daily Hampshire Gazette* was as plain and stark as the reality:

AGAWAM HANDS AMHERST FIRST LOSS

Agawam avenged an earlier girls basketball defeat at the hands of Amherst Regional by handing the Hurricanes their first loss of the season, a 52–50 setback last night in Agawam.

Amherst goes to 16–1, tied for first place in the Valley Wheel with Northampton, while Agawam is a game back at 15–2.

The Brownies relied on their strength in the paint,

with twin towers Kim Trudel and Cyndi Stone, to wear down the smaller Hurricanes inside. The 6-foot-2 Stone had 18 points and Trudel notched 16, with every hoop coming from down in close.

"Agawam played a smart physical game. We had trouble keeping them away from the hoop, but that's their game," said Amherst coach Ron Moyer.

Agawam took a 27–23 lead into the lockerroom in a tightly contested first half. The physical nature of the game played right into Agawam's strength, and the Brownies were able to keep the tempo of the game in their favor throughout.

"We tried to bang with them, but in the end they were just a little bit stronger. I thought Kathleen Poe did an especially nice job for us," Moyer said.

Jamila Wideman had another spectacular night for the Hurricanes, with 18 points, 9 rebounds, 6 steals, and 5 assists. Emily Shore and Jen Pariseau each had 9 points.

Coach wondered: *Will this be like last year? Will it be like it's been every year for the past five?*

This season he had assembled one of his best overall teams ever, perhaps the best.

Tonight's defeat was either the beginning of the unraveling, or it was a wake-up call.

From now on, it wasn't just a test of skill. It was a test of who's hungry.

The next day in practice he decided that the loss was probably a blessing. It reminded all the girls of their mortality and took the burden off an undefeated season. He looked at Jen running her hardest in practice, concentrating in a way that appeared deeper than any level he had noticed before. He assumed she was remembering last night's game, thinking about how she'd wanted to take that last shot, could taste it like some kind of ambrosia, but she couldn't free herself.

For everyone, the Agawam game brought back all those bad Hamp loss memories.

But still, as he ran the "take it to the basket" drill, screaming hard at them, he saw there was no backing down. He saw them throwing themselves on the floor for loose balls and slamming into each other in an unladylike fashion. He saw that each of them had made the same decision and that they didn't have to tell anyone what that decision was because they were showing it on the floor.

Teenagers who don't want to discuss something with their parents are like those guard walls in Third World countries topped with shards of glass. When Jen had come home from Agawam, she'd bypassed her father and her stepmother, who were sitting in the addition they had both designed, an airy square room with windows on three sides, decorated in peaceful blues and browns.

Bob Pariseau left the game seriously doubting Amherst would win the league. He and John Wideman had had their usual critique session, and they agreed that it didn't matter how good you were if you choked in the big games. Jen didn't talk about Agawam that night of the Hurricane loss, or the next day, or the next, but one evening after practice when her father picked her up, as they drove up and up Pelham Road past the tall trees into the gloom of the countryside to their house, she burst out: "Daddy, I'm so frustrated."

He remembered what his wife Tracy always said: "When teenagers want to talk, they'll often choose a car at night. It's not face to face, it's a little anonymous, rolling past the countryside. The thing is, when they finally want to open up, you have to be infinitely available. You can't be tired, you can't have a headache, you can't say: 'Not now, it's the end of a day.' It's like having a two-year-old all over again."

"Jen, to win at sports you have to scrap. There are so many instances of Amherst teams who don't have the scrappiness to get the big wins."

He spoke in a torrent, there was no pause to the words now, just a quick tumble of sound.

"I couldn't get my three-point shot off all night."

"What do you expect? You have a reputation as a three-point shooter. They know that. You need to go to the next step. Put the ball on the floor and dribble around them. Then, either shoot or pass off. Basically, you need to create offense. You were playing miss, assist, miss, assist. You have to shoot ten to fifteen shots a game. You're a scoring threat. You can't leave it all up to Jamila."

Jen listened. She was as quiet and still as the ancient pines that lined the road; the words reached as deep as the surrounding darkness.

She nodded; her profile was distinct and jutting even in the shadows.

The defeat in Agawam was, for whatever reason, Jen's last nervous game.

9

Bombs Bursting

Usually by February in western Massachusetts, people are shuttered as effectively as their houses. Skin goes gray; it flakes and itches. Barely muttered salutations, grunts more than words, are exchanged with lidded eyes. Women whose greatest vanity is their pride in the lack of it begin to contemplate cosmetic procedures, incisions and surgeries, tucks and lifts. Men plan escapes, the most benign of which involve golf. Colleagues and neighbors who were friendly in the summer, sharing their hippie bedspreads and their tabouli and their tofu scrambler on the lawn at Porter Phelps Huntington House along the banks of the Connecticut River during the Wednesday evening concerts, now ignore each other as they gingerly navigate streets burdened with snow and ice. The intellectual realization that every day at dawn and at dusk there is almost a minute more of light is of little consolation. The college students have been away for a month, but the peace in that is canceled by the rampant bleakness. Nearly everyone begins to suspect they are suffering from a touch of SAD. Adults converse in tattered scraps of sentences that begin "If it snows one more time," "If the temperature stays below zero one more day," and "If I slip on the ice on this doorstep ever again . . ." The frightening nature of these utterances is not what they convey, but what they don't. The completion is left up to the murderous, the bloody, the despairing imagination of the listener. There is so little to do that Hitchcock Nature Center, which runs a Hug a Bug fair in the clement weather (in which you can touch a hissing cockroach and sing songs like "Kumbaya"), suggests that people go on a walk in the snowy woods and be on the lookout for "dirty patches of snow under trees that appear to be moving—yes, moving!" The locomotion is caused by snow fleas, the only consistently wingless insects on the planet.

But this year was different.

Slowly, throughout the valley, the season was taking many strange and wondrous turns.

With the success of the Hurricanes came an unexpected dividend, a strange gaiety as normally housebound seasonal hermits discovered fraternity in the bleachers. At first as the gym in Amherst began to fill, people appeared awkward, uncertain of which fork to use first, shut-ins on a rare outing. But as the phenomenon of the Hurricanes spread through town, and outside of it, so did the bonhomie and the size of the crowds.

"That was great," the fans would say at the half. "Last time I watched a girls' game was like watching paint dry." Or, "Did you catch Wideman passing the ball to her buddy? That girl's got shake."

A cop was posted at the door of Amherst's gym, unheard of at a girls' game.

"Coach Moyer asked me to come here today and tell you a little bit about what it's like to be on the Hurricanes."

Jen stood in front of about fifty prep leaguers with upturned faces, young girls who wanted to grow up to take her spot on the team. They sat on the floor and looked up.

Jen's talk was a mix of her own words and phrases and some classic comments of Coach Moyer's:

"Hey, I still lose the ball, I still dribble the ball off my feet. I miss six out of ten shots. Being part of a team is not something you're born with, not something someone can give to you, not something you find under your pillow with a note from the tooth fairy.

"You've got to be willing to work for it, willing to produce that heart, that little extra desire. There's no *I* in team. The difference between chump and champ is *U*.

"While everyone else is sleeping late, you're at the gym in the middle of winter when it's fifty degrees indoors and the lights aren't on and you're in your sweats playing, and you have to figure, that's the glory. It's not the headlines, not the fans cheering. It's seeing your breath. Those are the days to live for because those are the days you know you're getting better."

For some observers, the most unusual phenomenon was the sight of the little kids, girls and boys, besieging the Hurricanes after a game, especially Jen and Jamila, and asking them for their autographs. A girl named Mary Kuhn told Jen after the defeat by Agawam, "You'll always be winners in Meg's and I's eyes." Mary and her pal Meg informed Jen and Jamila they wished they'd go to U Mass instead of Stanford and Dartmouth, mispronounced "Dark Myth" by the really little kids.

They'd put out a newspaper called *Hurricane* with this account by Mary and Meg of Jen's thousand-point night (the spelling and the grammar are as presented in the original):

Pariseau has a big smile to any kid who asks for her Augraph she gives a Great big smile. (I should know I ask!) Pariseau only needed 6 more baskets till her career was 1,000. Pariseau only needed six more points to get bouquets of balloons, flower and tons of cheers, just for Jen. But Jen decided to make the crowd sweat a bit. So Jen passes off to Kristin Marvin who shoots for ? points and she makes it. Then Wideman a all-American Basketball player heading for Stanford steal the Ball from Chicopee and passes to Pariseau who instead of shooting she passes to Emily Shore who gets 2 pointers. The crowd was pleased but a bit restless. I've got to concentrate on the game not my goals, I'll get them sooner or later, Pariseau explained. I have the hole night to get 1,000 points! When the clock timer clicks to 13:44 on the gym wall there was a big sign that said Jenny Watch and six, five, four, two. High school students tore off the number of Baskets she had left to get till reaching 1,000. That's when Jen only had 1 more basket until she reached 1,000 in her career. (999 Baskets). Then Wideman does a wonderful steal from Chicopee and she passes of to Jen who scores her final points. And when she reached her points the crowd went CRAZY! My friend (Mary Kuhn) and I saved our voice till that moment.

Older kids wrote long letters filled with preadolescent angst, about life as well as sports. One such letter from a sixth grader at Fort River Elementary School was not much different from dozens and dozens of others to all the Hurricanes from younger kids whose sense of the world, and its possibilities, shifted to a greater sense of optimism in the face of so much success from a group of people who were, if not peers, at least close enough in years to seem approachable. The voice in the letter, the tone and the concerns of the writer, is typical, in some ways, of girls that age, with its combination of gratitude, self-deprecation, eagerness, and altruism. What made it extraordinary to Jen was that in person this girl was "totally shy, and no matter how much I tried to get her to talk she wouldn't, and then she opened up in the letter and it was the first voice of hers I ever heard. It was strange in a very pleasant way, in that she found a medium she could communicate through. It was almost like a diary, and she found the confidence to send it. I was very glad that she did."

January 31, 1993

Dear Jen,

   Thank you so much for coming to our practice. It wasn't really a practice, but I don't know what else to call it. I was surprised you came, because you must have a ton of homework. You are really good at basketball and I don't care what anybody else says, I think you're every bit as good as Jamila.

   I forgot to ask you this at our (sort of) practice, but aren't you scared of going to college? That probably sounds dumb, but I would be scared to death, I mean, leaving all my friends and going somewhere I've never been before.

   I feel like I know you really well, now. I mean, I'm not embarrassed to talk to you anymore. You're kind of like the big sister I've always wanted. I wish we could do something really special together, not like basketball practice, something special. I don't know.

   I'll be at your game next Saturday. We're playing the Panthers, I think. I hope you can ref. See you on Saturday.

Your friend,
Jenny Hurwitz

The postscript that followed was longer than the letter:

P.S. This is going to be long because I just got your letter and I have a lot to say. First of all, thanks for writing. I didn't really expect you to, but I'm glad you did.

Ann and I have had some rough spots, but we've figured out how to avoid them. One thing is not to see so much of each other—last year we were together at *least* six times a week. The other thing is not to get in on anybody else's arguments. We used to do that but it just got us mad.

We've never been mad at each other. We've never been mad at each other for more than an hour I don't think.

I'm so glad you remembered softball camp. I do too and I got so mad at myself for getting sick (that's why I was only there for one day).

I really really want you to meet Ann. She's like you in the way that she has no trouble speaking in public. Sometimes, though, I think she does get a little nervous, and tries to hide it by acting really relaxed and sort of goofy. Actually, I have a lot of friends who really want to meet you. I tell them you're really special and they should go to one of your games.

Ann is really special. In fact, the only thing I can't talk to her about is boys. I don't really know why, I just can't. You're right, I should try to become friends with boys, but they're so hard to talk to. There is one boy who lives across the street from me who I can talk to. His name is Spencer. He doesn't act weird when I talk to him and sometimes I actually feel he tries too hard to get me to notice him. He's pretty popular in school—one girl even said she would pay him twenty dollars to go out with him—so he pretends not to notice me in school when I see him. He's nice out of school though.

Like I said before, you are like the big sister I've always wanted, and I will write or talk to you if I have any questions, problems, or just need to talk. If you ever need to talk you can write or call me. Also, like I said before, I'd love to do something with you if you're ever free. I'm free most of the time on weekends and on Wednesday afternoons. I'm so sorry this is so long, and I really had no intention of writing this much. See you soon.

—Jenny

It was letters like these that lifted Jen, more than anything else, more than the victory over Hamp at home, the rapprochement with Jamila, the mentoring of her younger teammates, and even her father's eager coaching from the sidelines. They were like one of those principles of physics she learned about in Mr. Camp's class; they had a locomotive urgency. They made her boat float.

It was the last home game of the regular season, an otherwise chilly February afternoon when Jamila spoke to the team privately about what the Hurricanes had meant to her. She had written out her comments and she read them with a depth of passion she usually reserved for the action on the floor:

"With all of the media buzzing around in the last few days and Mr. Moyer trying to convince us that it was not distracting I came to realize something. A number of the reporters asked me to explain Hoop Phi. I simply could not. There is no explanation, at least not one that can be put into words. Hoop Phi is the thing that people search for in their lives. It is the thing that we have found to which we belong, contribute and love. I am no longer searching for my 'Real Love.' When I began the process of looking at colleges and teams I had a very unrealistic approach. I found that I began searching for a team like ours. The more I looked the more I began to realize that what I have experienced in this winter season is unique and simply unrepeatable (if that is a word). What I remember most is not the wins or the losses (except for Hamp) but it is the bus rides, team cheers, locker-room antics and of course Friendly's. The weirdest thing about being a senior is that you realize things don't last forever and at the same time they do. The games will stop, the practices will end but what will remain? Two words will remain—Hoop Phi."

In addition to team tributes like this one and team dinners at Jamila's house, there were team scrunchies (cloth-covered elastic bands for ponytails), team necklaces with their names and nicknames on little beads, team rings (plastic but fanciful, bought for ten cents apiece by Patri), little bottles of team lotion (from Kim), and there was also team pressure:

"Please, Lucia, you have to."

Lucia's eyes widened, her lip curled slightly, she looked away.

"But, Lucia, this is for the seniors."

"It's too embarrassing . . . in front of so many people . . . What if I make a mistake."

"*Pu-leeeze*, Lucia. It will pump us up."

Lucia had a classic look; the hoop earrings she favored furthered the sense of a face that was round and inviting and opulent. On three separate occasions people had voluntarily informed her that she reminded them of Mona Lisa. She gave an impression that no matter what else she was doing and/or what was happening around her, she was, on some level, quietly, deep down, taking notes.

She surveyed the faces of her teammates, the eagerness in Patri's and Rita's, the sudden seriousness of Jen's and Jamila's, the sweet placidity in Kim's and Kathleen's expressions, the drive in Kristin's, all fourth gear or nothing. A couple of the other girls had their hands folded, church-style, as if to beseech her.

Jamila's private call to Hoop Phi required a public showing.

Lucia's teammates had created the functional equivalent of a pressure offense to see if she would sing the national anthem before this last home game of the regular season. Here she was, not especially patriotic, and they were leaning on her to sing a government song.

Jen said, "I'd do it myself, but with my voice. . . . Hey, if you want, I'll sing a Beatles song: 'All the lonely people, where do they all come from?' The reason we want you to do it is then people will actually stay and watch us play."

"Oh, okay, I guess so."

Lucia had a natural vibrato, which created in her listeners their own inner tremor. Slowly the fear of singing diminished as the fear of disappointing any of her teammates loomed larger.

Lucia cleared her throat and bit down on her lower lip. She wanted to look like a musician she'd once read about who sang in such a way that all expression left her face and entered her voice. She tried to give herself over to the experience, fully, silently invoking one of her favorite lines in all of literature, the last sentence of Toni Morrison's *Song of Solomon*: "If you surrender to the air you can ride it."

At first, Lucia's parents had both been taken aback by her pursuit of sports, not so much the passion itself as its object. But lately, whenever she went to a game, Gigi Kaeser enjoyed looking at her daughter and her teammates with her photographer's eye, appreciating the ease in their motion, the cadence of it: "Just think what it must be like to go through puberty and have your body on your side."

As Lucia stood in one corner, facing the flag, her father slipped into the gym at the opposite corner, next to where John Wideman stood. Lucia's father, Jim Maraniss, is a classically absentminded professor, capable of translating Antonio Benitez-Rojo's novel *Sea of Lentils* but not necessarily of remembering his wallet at the same time. Once the previous year he'd arrived at a game for which there'd been a nominal charge with empty pockets. Coach Moyer had motioned him in: "Come on in, Jim, we need all the bodies we can get."

In what Lucia considered one of the most embarrassing pieces of writing in the history of prose, he'd submitted an article to the *Daily Hampshire Gazette*.

It was all about his wonderment at watching her play basketball or practice her pitching in softball: "To me, she was the virgin goddess Atalante, her arm held out with Venus' golden apple in her palm displayed to all the rivals who would fall before her."

He wrote that his daughter's talents surprised him: "I teeter forth heartbreakingly on tinker-toy legs. My wife, Virginia, whose subtle and commanding grace cannot be dealt with appropriately here, was never, in our youth, an athlete. She was a shrine to the athletic world, as I recall."

It bothered him, he wrote, that Lucia did not want him to attend her games. She gave him explicit orders. If he did, he should please sidle in silently and to be sure to protect her from the knowledge of his presence.

With his red hair, which gave the appearance of a hat donned without thought, shambling gait, and glasses, he seemed not just removed from the world of sport, but sometimes removed from the world entirely. His favorite item of clothing

was a leather jacket he'd ordered from a catalogue that said BEA-
TLES. WORLD TOUR. 1964. When asked, he always said yes, he had
been on it. On occasion people who did not know better
thought perhaps he was a boarder in his own house.

In his marriage, Lucia's mother, Gigi, did everything—the
lawn, the cars, the driveway in winter, the books—in exchange
for his cooking the evening meal. She marveled at his ineffi-
ciency. "He shops as if he lives in Europe. He goes to Bread &
Circus every day."

"And," she added, "he never makes enough for leftovers."

A professor of Romance languages at Amherst College, he
enjoyed the benefaction of that institution, Amherst's secret
country club if there is one. As a member of the faculty, he and
his family got to live in a rambling house that used to be an inn
for a rent of only six hundred dollars a month. It was an even
better deal before the federal government started to count dis-
counts on faculty housing as income. On his campus he was
sometimes known as "Nighttrain." Most people thought it was
for his habit of whistling ditties so that people were used to hearing him before they actually saw him. In fact, the name was
generated during a faculty intramural football game in the mid-
seventies in which Lucia's father intercepted a pass with a grace
so thoroughly opposite his normal capacities that he was nicknamed after Dick "Nighttrain" Lane, a defensive back for the
Detroit Lions. On his campus Professor Maraniss was celebrated for his intellect and his wit, and no one there required
him to have all that and a wallet too. When it had come time to
put a hoop in his driveway, he'd dug the hole with a trowel,
much to the amazement of a neighbor who taught classics and so
was herself not attuned to modernity in its more tawdry mani-
festations, but even she had heard of a posthole digger.

He loved his daughter's name. "Any pronunciation is
okay, really. Loo-sha. Loo-chee-a. Loo-see-a. They're all beauti-

ful." Lucia is named after a great-great-aunt. The name comes from the Spanish word for light, and it is used in the Spanish expression for giving birth, *dar a luz*, "to give to the light." As she sang, he contemplated her features: classical, generous, and evenly spaced. He always thought she had a lush quattrocentro appearance. She'd started drawing recognizable scribbles before the age of two and had begun her study of the piano when she was four, often sitting at the piano in the dining room, filling the house with her music. When she was nine, she'd decided she wanted to play *Für Elise*, which she had heard on a McDonald's commercial. She put a lot of space in it, a lot of rubato. As she grew older, she became adept at Mozart's D Minor Piano Concerto and Debussy's *Suite Bergamasque*. She would do the first section, more difficult and beautiful than what he thought of as the less entrancing *Clair de Lune* section.

When he got a CD of Beethoven's *Appassionata*, Lucia had learned it and played it with rumble and with joy. To him, "No matter how unsophisticated children are, they become Beethoven or Debussy or Chopin when they play. They become complicated, and that's the case of anyone's child who plays the piano. They do all this stuff without any big fuss. They don't act like Franz Liszt."

And now that she was older, his Lucia, who had once loved the mathematical purity of sound, embraced instead the purity of moving through space. It made him feel disoriented, light-headed, discombobulated, that this child, when he wasn't looking, had changed, had metamorphosed into a jock.

"And the rockets red glare . . ."

She was straining to reach the high notes; for her they are always the hardest.

"The bombs bursting in air . . ."

Her father contemplated the mystique of what it meant to be on this team, to kick butt week after week, the feeling of belonging. It must be, he thought, a really powerful drug.

She neither veered into a screech nor faded into an echo.

She had climbed the mountain. The song would be over soon. It would be easy from now on; everything would be easy.

"Gave proof through the night that our flag was still there . . ."

With the final syllables reverberating in the air of the gym, John Wideman turned to Jim Maraniss and said something that, when she heard it later, taxed Lucia's patience. It was a nice thing to say; it's just that so much of what grown-ups of that generation say sounds so old-fashioned, as if the very observations are wearing peace symbols and bell-bottoms.

"She sounds," said the one man to the other, "a lot like Joan Baez."

Later the team celebrated the victory (57–44) with a food fight in the locker room, and after cleaning the frosting from their faces, the seniors took John Wideman up on his offer for a late lunch to celebrate the end of the regular season. While waiting for the pizza, the girls complained about Amherst and how little there is to do in a town favored by grown-ups as a place to bring up children for precisely that reason.

"It's not that there's absolutely nothing to do," the seniors said in what amounted to a chorus.

"Yeah. You can hike on the Robert Frost trail."

"Or bike on the new bike path. The pavement is made from—guess what?—glass recycled from our community!"

"You can go to the mall."

"Which one? Live or dead?"

The Hadley Mall, known as the live mall, is right next to the Mountain Farms Mall, known as the dead mall. The live mall has a video arcade, a food court, and a roller rink, and is anchored by Kmart and J. C. Penney. The dead mall is a ghostly structure, gray and looming. It has a rug store called the Rug Store, the Warehouse Depot, Dave's Soda, and Pet Food City, and on Sundays Jackson's flea market, in which merchants sell out-of-season gift wrap, World's Fair souvenir spoons, and Desert Storm sweatshirts and memorabilia. These are not the glitzy upscale malls of extremely affluent communities; they are the stripped-down version, the mall equivalents of cars without air-conditioning and with only two doors. There's not a Gap or Banana Republic at either one, no floors with fancy inlay or Italian tiled walls or magnificent fountains.

"There's nothing to do except go to the mall, and once you get there, there's still nothing to do."

"We could tip cows."

"Tip cows?"

"You know how they sleep standing up. We could go and knock them over."

Patri looked chagrined. "Do you really know anyone who's done that?"

It was Kristin who found the perfect way to sum up the peculiar, almost consoling, lack of outward drama in Amherst.

She recounted a dream of the night before.

"In my dream, my mom and I, we went to Stop & Shop, and while we were there, we went down, you know, all our usual aisles in the regular order, picking out all the things we usually buy, and after that we got in line to check out."

"That's it?" asked the other girls.

Jamila's father thought maybe the dream had another dimension, and so he tried a gentle psychoanalytic probe. Layers, he often reflected, were an indigenous New England phenomenon. People wear them; they respect them. Perhaps this dream had some undiscovered thickness. He had a quicksilver face, his expression changing in a flicker from stormy to melancholy to soft and forgiving. Now it was contemplative.

"Did you run into any unusual people?"

"No."

"How about money? Did you run out of money or anything?"

"No."

"Kristin," said her teammates, "that's so sad."

Kathleen, who was in the top 10 academically in her class of 250, told Jamila's father that she had tried reading a collection of his short stories, "the one called *Jungle Fever.*"

"I'm not Spike Lee. It was just *Fever.*"

"Mr. Wideman, I tried reading it," said Jen Pariseau, also in the top 10 academically. "I found the shortest story I could, and you know what? I think I understood it. I can't guarantee it, but I think I did."

He looked at his guests at the table, a blur of happy faces and ponytails. Their teasing was a joy. Girls' basketball is not boys' basketball being played by girls. It's a whole new game. There's no dunking. They can't jump as high. They can't play above the rim. But they can play with every bit as much style. And there's that added purity, that sense of excellence for its own sake. It's not a career option for girls; after college the game is over, so there is none of the desperate jockeying for professional favor.

As a black man, Wideman knows only too well the shallow triumph of token progress. He had told Kathleen's father, "This is just one team in one season." It alone cannot change the discrimination against girls and their bodies throughout history. But here in these girls, hope is a muscle.

"Here's to the senior girls," he said, looking at them.

They hoisted their ritual glasses of water.

"This is," he said, "as good as it gets."

* * *

The seniors were children of the mid-seventies. They were born in 1975, a year distinguished by leisure suits fashioned from pastel doubleknits for men and skintight jeans accessorized with high narrow boots for women.

"Mandy," "You Are So Beautiful," and "Breaking Up Is Hard to Do" were the popular songs. *Gunsmoke* was televised for the last time. *A Chorus Line* opened on Broadway; Bruce Springsteen's *Born to Run* was released.

One of those year-end list-oriented volumes available at the library noted that *Ragtime* was a bestseller, Anne Sexton's *Awful Rowing Toward God* was published, and *One Flew Over the Cuckoo's Nest* won an Oscar for the best film.

Mood rings, pet rocks, and skateboards were popular. The words *fireperson* and *chairperson* were introduced into usage. Individuals were permitted to buy gold for the first time since 1933, and word processors were manufactured. Tampons were advertised on television.

Harvard University changed its five–two admissions policy to equal admissions for both genders. A black woman named Joanne Little was declared "not guilty" of stabbing with an ice pick a white prison guard who had tried to rape her.

An obscure Georgia governor named Jimmy Carter was running for president.

In sports, Catfish Hunter signed a $2.85 million contract with the Yankees, Cincinnati beat Boston in the World Series before a record TV audience of 75.9 million viewers, and Jack Nicklaus won the Masters. The New York Cosmos soccer team signed Brazilian star Pele to a $1 million contract. Philadelphia won the Stanley Cup, and Arthur Ashe won Wimbledon. Pittsburgh defeated Minnesota in the Superbowl. In horse racing an unbeaten three-year-old Ruffian broke an ankle and had to be destroyed.

Golden State beat Washington in the NBA championship, UCLA was the college winner, Foolish Pleasure won the Kentucky Derby, and Muhammad Ali beat Joe Frazier in the Thrilla in Manila.

Chris Evert won the women's U.S. Tennis Open. The first women's Kodak all-American basketball team was named, and the first women's collegiate basketball game was played at Madison Square Garden, Queens versus Immaculata.

They grew up watching *Love Boat* and *Fantasy Island*. The movies they liked were *E.T.*, *Tootsie*, *Endless Love*, *Flashdance*, *Foul Play*, *The Jerk*, and *Rocky*. They read *Are You There, God? It's Me, Margaret*, *Tales of a Fourth Grade Nothing*, *The Phantom Tollbooth*, *Freaky Friday*, and Beverly Cleary's Ramona books. Their toys included Legos, *Star Wars* figures, Atari, Rubik's Cube, Snoopy Sno-Cone Machines, Donny and Marie dolls, Silly Putty. When they were growing up, their trademark expressions were:

"Book it" (for running fast)
"In your face"
"Wicked"
"Massive"
"Awesome"
"Gag me with a spoon"
"Gaylord"
"Queerling"
"Bogus"
"Tubular"
"Grody"

The seniors were in nursery school when their global consciousness was first stirred by the hostage crisis in Iran: The captivity dates and simple addition were conflated in their minds.

Despite their good educations, they still thought of Pearl Harbor as the day, in Gumby's words, "some big military thing happened." To them *president* meant either Ronald Reagan or George Bush. When they were really little, someone tried to shoot President Reagan, and way before they were born he played a dying football player in a movie that people liked to make fun of. In high school whenever one of their teachers, Joe Jacobs (who taught Bible as Literature), found them intellectually deficient, he would say, "Oh, sorry, I forgot. You're children of the Reagan era."

When they were in the sixth grade they saw Christa McAuliffe and the space shuttle *Challenger* explode, over and over and over.

They were sophomores during the Gulf War. It was vivid to them in part because of a sign that the man who owns the bike shop across from Emily Dickinson's house put on his window:

NOT MY SON.

NOT FOR OIL.

NOT FOR BUSH.

NOT FOR KUWAIT.

They were sickened when a former student, one of those gentle souls who come to the Valley to study and then never leave, set himself on fire on the common as a protest against the war. For several weeks afterward, people who knew him and people who had only heard of him placed flowers in the charred circle where he had died and held a round-the-clock vigil. Sometimes on Pleasant Street cars would roar by, with someone, always anonymous in a shadowed vehicle, shouting an actual obscenity or shouting what was, under the circumstances, functionally just as harsh—"Get a life!"—punctuated by a guffaw and the squeal of tires.

They were juniors in high school during the riots in Los Angeles. Jamila's father was one of the people recruited by the networks to make talking sense of an event in which, among other acts, people not only shot one another but also looted stores for hot dogs and paper towels. At the time Jamila wrote:

I am lost in the night
Unseen until the fires are lighted

There were tragedies in Amherst. Farmers are sometimes killed in the backfire during field burnings. Every year a few students overdose or have bizarre accidents, such as plunging to their death while "elevator-surfing," a late-night, generally debauched dorm activity in which kids jump from one elevator roof to another, sometimes missing. The Hurricanes knew kids who had dropped out of school and were living on the streets; sometimes they hung out in the courtyard between the Unitarian Church and Bart's Ice Cream—rollerblading, smoking, and engaged in endless games of hacky sack, in which a small beanbag is kicked in the air. The setting was more fetching, but the emptiness was as real as on an urban street corner. Kristin remembered the boy who had killed his stepfather because of beatings so severe that the walls of their apartment had shaken enough for neighbors to make formal complaints. Since 1989, they had heard from their parents how important it was to be careful after "what happened at the mall," referring to the murder of the U Mass psychology major on that winter night. In Amherst, the particularity of each tragedy made each one especially real, and lamentable. Amherst was not a place awash in loss, like so many of the cities in America, not a place in which the sacrifice of humans seemed a necessary propitiation, a cruel toll exacted in exchange for a more exciting place to live, in some awful way, part of what made those places exciting.

To look at the seniors, they all appeared lit from within. One would assume their lives have been, so far, seamless journeys. But most of them had a before and after. Their lives, like the map of Massachusetts in which the center had been seized to create the Quabbin Reservoir, had been punched in the middle.

Jen was the most outspoken about the trauma of divorce and its aftermath.

She observed that "in a lot of cases, kids whose parents get divorced are forced to grow up earlier. When your parents don't get along, you have to be a mediator. There's this delicate balance about what you can say and how you can act. This whole awareness has to be developed. It's tough. The things that gnaw at you are the everyday things, little situations that other people take for granted, like when a game is over, which parent do you hug first? It can add a lot of stress to a childhood, a lot of pain and avoidable worry. Some kids don't make it out of it. They don't have the strength and the heart, and they let the situation consume them. In a strange distorted way it can help. What you lack in the nurturing department you learn to provide yourself. But you can go overboard and build a shell up around yourself and become callous. You're always looking for normalcy, for something consistent, that strength that doesn't leave, that family you hope is there and is not there. That one constant."

There were other sadnesses not openly discussed, even among the closest of friends.

"Most of us," said Jen, "do not come from a Dan Quayle type of family."

Yet, whatever doses of disruption they'd been dealt, an opposite force followed them onto the court.

"Ladies, it's showtime."

Coach Moyer never could resist the built-in excitement of a

packed gym, all of it, even the row of hecklers from Hamp whose very insults seemed tailor-made to pump the Hurricanes to even greater feats.

Feiker Gymnasium. February 19. Friday night. Hamp at Hamp.

The local press fanned the ardor of the crowds with stories like Marty Dobrow's HAMP-AMHERST TO PACK GYM TONIGHT in the *Daily Hampshire Gazette*:

Here we go again.

It's Showdown II at Feiker Gym tonight between the Northampton and Amherst Regional girls basketball teams (7:30, WHMP AM). When they met for the first time last month—a matchup of undefeated powers—the Hurricanes posted a frenetic 45–40 victory on their home court.

Since then both teams have lost at Agawam, setting the stage for tonight's regular-season finale that—depending on your viewpoint—means everything, or hardly anything.

An Amherst win would give the Canes a 19–1 record, the championship of the Valley Wheel for the second consecutive year, and the No. 1 seed in the Western Mass. tournament.

A victory by Hamp would forge a three-way tie for the league title (with Agawam). The three 18–2 squads would then get their WM seeding with the flip of a coin.

"You always want to win what you can," said Hamp coach Tom Parent. "We want to win this one."

Amherst coach Ron Moyer added, "We have a piece of the rock. The worst we can do is be tri-champs."

Neither coach was willing to admit it, but the conclusion was clear: the Valley Wheel title, though desirable, was not the ultimate goal. Both teams have their hopes pinned to larger booty, a Western Mass. crown at least, and perhaps a state title.

Moyer well knows that the top seed is not necessarily a blessing.

"Last year we were the No. 1 seed," he recalled. "We won the league, and went to the tournament, and we didn't do anything (losing in the semifinals to a Blue Devil squad the Canes already had beaten twice). Hamp came in with five losses, they were the fourth seed, and they won the whole banana."

Regardless of its eventual meaning, this game has had as much hoop hype as any local contest in a long time. A brisk pre-sale of tickets has all but guaranteed a jam-packed gym tonight. Hamp athletic director Jeff Boudway said there will be tickets available at the door, but he advises fans to get there early to make sure they get a seat.

Hamp certainly has a few things working in its favor tonight. The Blue Devils are undefeated and unchallenged on their home court. Standout guard Liz Moulton has recuperated from the ankle injury that took her out of action in the opening minutes of the first Amherst game.

Still, Hamp is mightily concerned about another ankle, the one Beth Kuzmeski sprained in Monday's loss at Agawam. Kuzmeski, headed to UMass on a full ride in the fall, was on crutches for part of the week and only practiced at half-speed yesterday, according to Parent.

"We really haven't had her 100 percent all year, and we don't now," Parent said. "But she's still probably the best shooter around. She's a real key for us."

Parent says that an important factor for Hamp is applying constant defensive pressure.

"We need to make them work very hard to score," he said. "Jamila (Wideman) is going to get hers, and Jen (Pariseau) is going to get hers, but the harder we can make them work, the more we can take the other kids out of the game."

Parent also hopes that his team will respond in a more relaxed fashion to the intense atmosphere surrounding the game this time around.

"Getting through all the hype and the crowd, and just playing basketball is important," he said. "The first game was 100 miles per hour, and no one could be in control of anything. We like to go quick, but we only want to go as fast as we can."

On the other side, Moyer has his players primed for the game. The Amherst coach knows that his glittering back court of Wideman (headed for defending national champ Stanford on a full ride) and Pariseau (bound for Dartmouth) will not be enough to carry the team. Hamp can defend as well as anyone with tenacious guards Johanna Clark and Betsy Gonski. Amherst will also need strong inside play on both ends of the court.

"We're not 100 percent there," he admits. "And frankly, if we don't get there, we're probably not going to win the whole thing."

Still, the front court has made great strides since the beginning of the year. Kathleen Poe (termed "our silent assassin" by Moyer) has become a powerful inside scoring force in recent games. Junior Emily Shore and the center platoon of Kristin Marvin and Emily Jones have also picked up their play considerably. Jones, battling the flu, is questionable for tonight.

Moyer says he likes the mental toughness of his team.

"We're going to go right at Hamp," he promises.

In terms of the Blue Devil personnel, Moyer says that he is particularly concerned about containing Moulton and Addie Stiles.

"You expect Beth Kuzmeski to hurt you, and you expect Kim Frost to do her thing," he said. "But those are two key players. If you see those kids having a big game, you figure they're going to win, no matter what else we do."

"Let's go, Devils; let's go, Hamp."

That night, once again, as in Amherst, hundreds of fans were turned away at the door but the ones lucky enough to be inside displayed their gratitude with chants scribbling the air like graffiti.

The Hurricanes poured out onto the court for their warm-ups.

Jamila Wideman carried her boom box and placed in on the floor near the Hurricanes' warm-up hoop. This large noisy contrivance was an integral ritual for her team.

They loved "When Doves Cry" by Prince and "What's on Your Mind" by Eric B. and Rakim and "360 Degrees" by Gran Pubba. Prince's "Seven" used to spook them out: What seven special things were doomed to disappear? They liked "Hip Hop Hooray" by Naughty by Nature for its beat; they liked "You Can't Play with My Yo Yo" by Yo Yo for its sass.

For the frank chauvinist fun of it, the plain old pelvic appeal, they liked lyrics from Wreckx-N-Effect:

I like the way you comb your hair
I like the stylish clothes you wear

It's just the little things you do
That make me want to get with you.

When they wanted to feel down or sad, they listened to Boyz II Men's "End of the Road" and "It's So Hard to Say Good-bye to Yesterday."

There was one song that in the right mood could send them rocketing, Mary J. Blige's "Real Love":

We are lovers through and through
And though we've made it through the storm
I really want to put you on
I've been searching for someone to satisfy my every need
Won't you be my inspiration
Give the real love that I need

Chorus:

Real love
I'm searching for a real love
Someone to set my heart free
Real love

Meanwhile, in a show of support that was historic, at least for Amherst, the all-girl cheerleading squad, led by Sarah Gagnon, a small dark-haired senior headed to Skidmore in the fall, leant their voices and their gymnastics to the excitement. For some of the mothers of the Hurricanes, who remembered when to be a cheerleader was the only way to feel connected to a sport and physical beauty was the first criterion, the moment was a vindication. A circle had been closed. It was as if the Hurricanes colluding with the cheerleaders and the cheerleaders colluding with the Hurricanes were sending a message of reconciliation.

Taunts always exist on the floor, trash talk between the players baiting each other with disparaging references to the opposing team's style of play. Among the girls in the Valley Wheel League it was not uncommon under pressure to refer to opponents with muttered slings and arrows. Had Coach Moyer heard certain street terms, he would have benched his athlete. He believed there was language and there was language, and the second kind could get you into trouble.

On this evening a small group of teenaged boys started a scornful chant, directed at Jen and Jamila: "You're overrated. You're overrated." To the younger players they shouted, "Useless!"

They also tried to demoralize the Hurricanes with comments about the defects they perceived in their appearances.

They made fun of Jade's hair extensions; they shouted "Weight Watchers!" at Kim's broad shoulders, "Acne!" at Jen.

They lampooned Emily's size-fourteen shoes and called them "skis."

They snickered and they jabbed each other in the ribs, muttering about each girl and her body.

There were two elements to the victory that night.

First, the junior varsity played a legitimately exciting game.

Amherst, down 5 with just a minute left in overtime, ended up with a 46–44 win.

Jan Klenowski, who garnered a team-high 11 points that night, tied the game on a long jumper.

And then Rita Powell scored the winning deuce on an offensive rebound at the buzzer. A basket at the buzzer! It's the candy in the box you thought was empty, the wad of cash you forgot about, the extra hour when daylight saving time changes in the fall. For Rita, the basket was all that and more, it was her first-class ticket to the varsity in the postseason. She had achieved her personal milestone.

All the hours sitting for those kids, the onions she had

chopped, the papers she sold those cold mornings, the endless drills at Dave Cowens's camp, all were an investment that had paid off in the one moment of that shot. The best part of basketball was that it was filled with forgiveness; one minute you're losing, and a few seconds later you've not only won, you've conquered.

The slaps on her back and on Jan's, those clunky good-natured swings from her teammates, were pure caress.

"Thanks, Rita, and thanks, Jan, for pumping us up," said the older girls as they poured on the floor. They didn't know it at the time, but Coach Moyer and junior varsity coach Trish Lea had already decided who would be moved up for the postseason: Jan, of course; Jessi Denis, a dark-haired girl who loved all sports (including wrestling, which she had watched on TV as a kid); her best friend, Carrie Tharp, the shortest Hurricane ("Five feet three inches with my shoes on"), whose ambition was to own her own health club and who remembered being the only girl willing to play tackle football at recess during grade school; and the player who had pleasantly surprised both her coaches this season, Rita Powell.

The air still pulsed with cheers and excitement as the two varsity teams squared off against each other in the opening tip-off.

The epithets against the Hurricanes evaporated seconds into the game when one of the Northampton players lined up to take a three-point shot from the wing, and Jen Pariseau, sensing the momentum that that shot might give Hamp, went airborne and blocked the ball, six rows deep into the stands, directly at the Hamp boys who had been taunting them. *Whack!* "Ah!" said one fan, in a regional Yankee accent. "Now that showed moxie."

And then came the infamous spatula pick.

Why spatula?

Easy: You don't avoid it, you're a pancake.

Hamp went into a full-court press, hoping to rattle either of the two Js bringing the ball up the court. Coach Moyer's solution was to run one of the forwards, Gumby, from the front court back into the back court and to stand like a statue on the left-hand side. Jamila would angle sharply, aiming at her teammate's hip. The idea was to create enough space so the defender had to duck around the pick, creating a window for Jamila to bring the ball up the court. On this occasion, none of Hamp's players called out a warning to the girl trying to guard Jamila. Eyes focused on Jamila, unaware of Gumby's rocklike presence. The Hamp player crashed into Gumby and fell to the floor, dazed. The game was halted for fifteen minutes to allow rescue personnel to come, put her in a neck brace, and take her to nearby Cooley Dickinson Hospital. If there had been any fire in Hamp beforehand, Gumby had extinguished it with one solid shoulder. Even Coach Moyer, speaking later, said he hadn't seen a pick like that since his days on his college team. Fortunately, the player suffered only a mild headache and no major injury.

As the game progressed, the connectedness between Jen and Jamila, the unspoken but constant contact, their radar, was as electrifying as their play.

At one point Kim Warner missed an open shot, releasing a flaccid looper that had as much hope of making the basket as asparagus shooting up in January. She ran to the back court with her head hanging down.

There was a synchronization to Jen and Jamila's perception of that moment; they seemed to signal each other in some extrasensory way. "Kim," they shouted, "you can't do that."

The two captains arrived at the same sudden conviction:
Enough is enough!

Kim had to do better, had to think better of herself.

They came at her, two ponytails with a cause, Jen from one side and Jamila from the other in a V formation so perfect as to invite the envy of a flock of Canadian geese; as they moved toward her, they shouted: "Keep your head up!"

She looked at them, stunned. She had just missed yet another shot, and she had automatically lowered her head, thinking, *I'm not helping.*

Jen and Jamila, talking to her this way?

They were her pals. They didn't yell.

They raised the volume, rivaling the roar of the fans.

They shouted.

"We said keep your head up!"

Never before had they addressed her that way, never that loudly, never with such force. As they all raced back with the rebound, Jamila passed the ball to Jen who passed it back to Jamila who passed it to Kim who, in the paint, stopped, stared at the rim, thought fleetingly of all those summer nights at Crocker Farm and the aging hoop where she had practiced by herself, took the round weight, and tossed it up:

Two points.

There would be 8 points in all that night for Kim, and in her memory that moment when her two friends, her two captains, double-teamed her and told her what they actually expected of her remained the emblematic high of the season. Bob Pariseau turned to his wife and said, "These kids are confident. They're taking no prisoners. They're not looking back."

The score was 72–53.

The word was out in Western Massachusetts. The Hurricanes had arrived at a new style of play. They showed no hesitancy. They were bulldozers. Area fans were urged by Marty Dobrow of the *Gazette* to "Skip dinner, blow off the date, cancel the vacation, drop everything." Catch those Canes!

Coach Moyer thought of it as simply the best game his team had ever played.

The Hurricanes wasted no time leaving Feiker, aware that their win could stir the fistfights that sometimes occur after the boys from Amherst and Hamp play each other.

Coach Moyer savored a couple of moments. The first was when Jamila brought the ball up against Hamp pressure, stared at Kathleen, stared at Kristin, started to move toward Gumby, and then suddenly, after looking at everyone else, threw the ball like a laser straight through a mass of players to Jen for an easy layup. Then, seconds later, she threw a blind pass to Kathleen, who caught the ball in stride and laid it up. This series of gestures encapsulated Jamila's style: They were, he thought, graceful, extraordinary, unselfish, and unique. Basketball at its best.

The flip side of what Jamila did on offense was what Jen did on defense. It always bothered him slightly that people didn't recognize the feats that Jen performed against the other teams. She was creative, she was dogged, she was always a step or two ahead.

Amherst played a man-to-man, but in each game Coach Moyer would select what he called a "designated shooter," which was the opponent's weakest offensive player. This would be Jen's person. This was one of his favorite bits of coaching strategy. Jen was known as the best defender, so it would have been usual for her to match up against the other team's strongest player. Instead she played the weakest, which is to say, she really didn't play her at all. "Cover," he would tell Jen, "but don't cover."

In his mind, Jen then acted like a football free safety. Her job was to diagnose the play, and find the right spot to disrupt it. She could, at any moment, be almost anywhere on the defense. In particular, she roamed the passing lanes. Other teams would look up, expecting to be able to make the pass they made at prac-

tices a thousand times in their own gym, only to find Jen Pariseau in the way, all elbows, arms, incredible leaping skills, and
riverboat gambler's hands. If Jamila was his captain on offense,
this responsibility shifted to Jen in the defensive zone. That was
what made the Hamp-at-home game so remarkable, when Jen
took over both ends while Jamila went to the bench, and what
made them on this night so, well, so breathtaking.

Coach Moyer boarded the bus last.

"Okay," he asked, "who's missing?"

At least three Hurricanes raised their hands. "I am."

He'd better watch it: Their humor was getting as bad as his.

"Captains, have you done a head count?"

"Everyone's here, Mr. Moyer," said Jen and Jamila.

Coach Moyer stood, crouching slightly, as the bus, swaying
in the snow-packed parking lot, made its way out onto Route 9,
past Smith, over the Coolidge Bridge, toward Amherst.

"I have," he said, "just one thing to say."

Raising a fist, looking as demonic as Skippy at her worst, he
shouted:

"Yes!"

The bus ride home was, if not the best ever, close to it.

They had jumped on the bus, grinning and laughing, breaking into a joyous cacophony of song and slogan. "We are the
champions," sang Patri, quoting Queen's famous anthem. They
sang Muppets songs from *Sesame Street*, they sang the *Brady
Bunch* theme song. They sang "Every Day People" and "Revolu-
tion," changed to "Revolucia," both by Arrested Development.
They sang a selection from Naughty by Nature to which they
swayed as they crooned: "Hey . . . ho . . . hey . . . ho." They sang
Patri's favorite tune:

> This is the song that never ends
> It just goes on and on, my friends.

Some people started singing it
Not knowing what it was.
And they kept on singing it
Forever just because . . .

The Hurricanes slapped the ceiling of the bus, and as they pulled through the center of town, with the Common on their right, they opened the windows and they shouted:

Who rocks the house?
The Hurricanes rock the house.
And when the Hurricanes rock the house,
They rock it all the way down.

Obliging knots of college students, not actually certain of what they were cheering, cheered nonetheless.

As the bus pulled into the parking lot, they gave their ritual cheer: "Give me an *A*."

"*A*."

"Give me an *M*."

"*M*."

"Give me an *H*."

"*H*."

"Give me an *E*."

"*E*."

"Give me an *R*."

"*R*."

"Give me an *S*."

"*S*."

"Give me a *T*."

"*T*."

"What have we got?"

"Amherst!"

And then they went to Friendly's on Route 9 to, as Kristin put it, "dork out"—which Kathleen kindly translated, "That means act giggly and stupid"—where they ate huge mouthfuls of ice cream and built a bridge of interconnecting straws from one booth to another.

Basketball was invented by James Naismith in 1891 only a few miles away in the city of Springfield, the site of the Basketball Hall of Fame, where for a small admission price you can see, among other artifacts, Bob Lanier's size twenty-two shoes. In many other parts of the country—Iowa and Tennessee and California and Philadelphia—particularly in the Catholic schools, there has been a long rich tradition of girls playing basketball. The history of the game as it involves women is just over one hundred years old, the same as men. Yet the game as it has been played by men has gotten billing as the real game. And even though the game was appealing to women from the start, there were efforts to restrict their participation. Girls were often not allowed to play at night because it would be "too stressful." At the turn of the century, girls were not allowed to play during the first three days of their periods, and female coaches were hired especially as the enforcers of this policy.

The girls on the Hurricanes did not discuss their periods with Ron Moyer, but in the locker room they often made teasing references to what they called "Teatime," the punch line of a menstruation joke that Kathleen Poe said was too vulgar to relate, but that Skippy was only too eager to tell: "See, there's this guy and he goes into a bar . . ."

"That was our way of being boisterous," said Jen.

"But not the only way," Kristin quickly amended.

Periods were sometimes referred to in that age-old girl code as visits from Aunt So-and-so or "My cousin is here from Connecticut." One opinion was shared by all: the hope that no one would have hers on the day of a big game. And one fact was universally acknowledged: Someone always did.

A few nights after the win against Hamp, Bernadette Jones decided to cross the river from Amherst into Northampton to attend a lecture and slide presentation entitled "The Ladies of the Club" at Smith College by Stevada Chepko, a professor at Springfield College. The school was celebrating "women's basketball, the first one hundred years."

Bernadette Jones was the oldest in a family of eleven children, and she had devoted herself to rearing her own, by comparison, modest four offspring, three daughters and one son. Her husband, as the most prominent local pediatrician, occasionally played the role of team physician.

Bernadette Jones was soft-spoken and somewhat abstemious. Amherst is an area known for dressing down; the more worn-out and holey or patched a garment, the more it is prized in frugal New England, yet she *really* dressed down in jeans and sweats. She worried about the environment and was known to insist on only a certain level of bath water. After composting, her family barely produced a bag of garbage a week. Her oldest daughter became a farmer after graduating from Yale, and her organic mix of obscure and gathered greens, called mesclun, with its beet tops and chard and radicchio, was featured in the summer at Bread & Circus. The family traditionally consumed the final offering from their backyard garden, sweet crunchy carrots, at Thanksgiving. At least once a month she prepared a lunch for a soup kitchen in Holyoke, several huge trays of a set recipe of meat and potatoes and vegetables. "Hunger really gets to me. I don't know. The thought of that." With her black hair laced with gray and unremitting blue eyes, Bernadette Jones surprised the other mothers with her occasional ferocity. She was the one who always fought for lower-priced tickets to the sports banquets at the end of every season, saying that anything above five dollars a person was a hardship for most people.

It's hard on winter nights to leave the house, to extract oneself from the web of warmth and need and artificial light. She tried to get Emily to go with her, but her daughter had too much homework, and so Bernadette headed out by herself in the old Chevy wagon. She left her family with their usual fare, a pot of soup, lentil tonight, which they could eat plain or gussy up with slivers of cheese or slices of meat. She passed the banks of filthy snow that lined both sides of Route 9, reminiscent of a Robert Frost poem in which he compares a dirt-splashed drift with an old scrap of newspaper:

> It is speckled with grime as if
> Small print overspread it,
> The news of a day I've forgotten—
> If I ever read it.

She herself had saved several old clips from her days as Bernadette Baecher of Saint Mary's High School, girls' division, in Manhasset, New York, the news of days she'd almost forgotten. From the *Magnificat*, her school newspaper, 1962:

ST. MARY'S POSTS EASY VICTORY

Bernadette Baecher scored twenty points to spark St. Mary's of Manhasset to a 44–23 victory over Our Lady of Wisdom of Ozone Park last night in a Catholic Girls High School Basketball game at St. Mary's.

BERNADETTE BAECHER NETS 22 IN VICTORY

Bernadette Baecher scored 22 points—six fewer than the entire Carle Place team—as St. Mary's of Manhasset came from behind to win 37 to 28.

She could see herself, young again, in those annoying thick glasses, before the era of contacts, in that knee-length uniform with its sharp angles and stiff material, making the sign of the cross before every foul shot. She could even picture the old nun who was the team's "monitor"; at Catholic schools every group had a monitor. What was her name?

She thought about how the girls from Saint Mary's used to practice once a week; there had been none of this everyday thing back then. There were six players on the team, three forwards and three guards, and you weren't allowed to leave your side of the court. After a while, they changed the rules and allowed one forward to shoot. You could dribble only three times.

She recalled the long arguments she'd had with her brothers. They told her she was playing a Mickey Mouse game.

As she sat in the library at Smith, waiting for the lecture to begin, she went over her own history: Her brothers had been right; you didn't need the stamina. It had been a much less physical game. But her brothers had also been wrong. Under the old rules, you had to think: Strategy became extremely important. Her favorite thing had been to fake. You could be sly and sneaky, and it was okay.

The lecturer flicked the switch on a slide machine. Her soft Southern voice was a perfect fit with the low-key quietude of Neilson Library.

"Tonight we have gathered to celebrate the 'Ladies of the Club.' Membership to this social club is rather exclusive, rules are very stringent, and a strict code of conduct must be adhered to at all times. You can't buy a membership to this club or even bargain your way in with fast talk or a smooth line. No, you must be born into this club called women. Often we compare and contrast membership of this club with that of another club called *men*, but we don't often celebrate the unique experiences of the members of this club. Tonight I hope you will join me in celebration. A celebration of one hundred years of women's participation in basketball.

"We won't be celebrating with a slam dunk, but we will be playing with a real ball."

Professor Chepko lamented the introduction of the smaller-sized ball in 1984. She believed that "our hands have always been smaller. We played the game for ninety years with these hands. Changes like that one, based on our differences, are used to discredit us."

Her research into the games at Smith in the latter part of the nineteenth century and early part of this one revealed that basketball competitions were second in excitement only to graduation. The only men likely to attend were college officials and relatives. A newspaper at the time called them the "favored few Adams in Eden." She found that many accounts emphasized the "hysteria" of the event, "a key term." Sometimes, said Professor Chepko, boys weren't even allowed in the gym in order to preserve the genteel nature of the gathering.

She showed a slide of the two teams enjoying a postgame social hour:

"Afterwards there was a custom in which the two teams joined each other for milk and cookies. Back when I was in college, we still had that custom, and I can't tell you how many cookies and glasses of milk I gagged on after a game."

Two more slides showed a young black boy and a young white one. "The first cheerleaders were little boys."

"Why," she asked, "did women embrace the game of basketball?"

The next slide showed some women in billowing outfits holding or attached to what appeared to be torture devices.

"The alternative was pretty bleak. Women's collegiate experience in physical training classes consisted of a strict regimen of Swedish exercise done en masse. Given the choice of exercise by the numbers with wands and clubs or a competitive game, women quickly chose the game. Not even an attractive, young instructor such as Berenson (seen here modeling the latest fashion in uniforms for instructors of physical training) could maintain any long-term enthusiasm for the repetitive and monotonous drills in the Swedish system. So she incorporated basketball into her classes as part of the training. Swedish drill and corrective exercise continued to be the major focus in class, but out of class, basketball became the students' favorite activity.

"Like most of her generation, Smith College Coach Senda Berenson believed with every fiber in her being that women were intrinsically different than men. These differences mandated a different sporting model. The interclass games may have not been Harvard-Yale, but they were important and valuable experiences for the women who participated in them. Senda Berenson knew that the women at Smith, the ladies in her club, were having the time of their lives playing basketball. It didn't really matter that the decorations and mascots got more ink than the actual game. It wasn't about just the game. It was about being in the company of educated women and sharing a joyful experience. A game needs only to be important to the people involved, Miss Berenson understood."

Those games back at her high school on Long Island had been important to Bernadette Baecher Jones. The shaft of light from the projector that illuminated the black-and-white slides also caught Emily's mother from the side, the pure lines of her face made fierce. As she observed the pictures of the women of Smith College dressed in billowing bloomers while huge lines of girls waited in the snow for tickets to what often got twin billing as girls' basketball and ribbon display, she compared her own experience of the game with that of her daughter, already a brilliant rebounder and scorer as a sophomore, and her young friends.

Sometimes, she wished that she had had the same thing when she was young: "Not the status, I'm not sure I like that word, but the recognition."

The lecturer had shown her last slide. Speaking in that calm steady voice, she offered her closing remarks.

"It seems only fitting tonight that I leave you with some advice that Senda Berenson gave to the young women at Smith. It seems to me to be appropriate for the time, the place, and the person. While lecturing on aesthetic, she offered her charges this advice:

" 'It is the duty of each one of you to be as beautiful as possible.

" 'It is not given to all of us to be born beautiful young girls—but it is our fault if we do not become beautiful old ladies.'

"Tonight my hope for you is to become beautiful old ladies."

Over the years, Betsy Moyer had made herself something of an expert on Title IX, the federal legislation signed into law on June 23, 1972, by President Richard Nixon:

"No person in the United States shall, on the basis of sex, be excluded from participation in, be denied the benefits of, or be subjected to discrimination under any education program or activity receiving federal financial assistance."

Betsy Moyer chose to discuss this legislation, intended to grant women equal opportunity to excel in sports, when it came time to give her talk as a member of the Tuesday Club. This Amherst organization, started by the wives of Amherst College professors, met once a month on Tuesday afternoons to explore a variety of subjects of intellectual and social significance.

She was nervous beforehand: "I hate public speaking. I leave that to Ron." But the grateful attention of her audience and her own convictions quickly dispelled the quiver in her voice.

"Although it applies to all areas of education, over time the law has come to be associated primarily with sports. It means that high schools, colleges, and universities must offer men *and* women equal access to sports. Gender equity is the ethical and moral ideal of Title IX. It is the intent of the law that if the male/female ratio of a school is 60/40, then there should be participation in athletics to match that ratio. It also means that the awarding of athletic scholarships should fit into that ratio as well. Another component is that women should have equitable practice times, uniforms, accommodations, transportation to away competition, money for meals, and money spent on recruitment."

She told the women, who ranged in age from late forties to over eighty years old, that at first the law was more confusing than it was effective.

"Opponents of the legislation kept not getting it. They said that women would never be as good in sports as men, so why should they get equal financial support? This was also the era, the early seventies, when women sometimes resorted to grandstand tactics to bring attention to their plight as athletes whose gifts were often ignored or disparaged; this was when the culture delivered televised tennis matches between Billy Jean King, God bless her, and Bobby Riggs, and when the news was filled with stories about girls suing to play on Little League teams.

"The law didn't actually become effective until 1975, when the first federal regulations enforcing it occurred, and even then the schools were given until 1978 to comply. One of the greatest changes in girls' basketball happened in 1976 as a result of Title IX. Victoria Ann Cape was a guard on her high school basketball team. Because of the girls' rules at the time, she was never allowed to develop her shooting game. The guards had to stay in their own zone and never had a shot at the basket. She sued the High School Athletic Association of Tennessee and won. This suit led to boys' rules (five on a team playing full court) in girls' basketball. It took almost eighty years for girls to showcase their athleticism, and the game has become increasingly more enjoyable to watch ever since.

"During the early eighties Title IX began impacting greatly on girls' basketball. Coaches were given better salaries. Schedules became more competitive, equipment upgraded, practice time more equitable, and more college scholarships were made available. Women no longer had to travel in broken-down vans with no heat, sleep four to six to a room, and eat bag lunches while men's teams travel on luxury buses, sleep two to a room, and eat vast training meals at fancy restaurants! In 1983 there was a major setback for women's athletics. Title IX was temporarily disemboweled by the U.S. Supreme Court, whose decision in *Grove City College* v. *Bell* effectively ruled that the law's provisions did not apply to athletics. For five years the *Grove City* decision had a chilling effect. Scores of complaints were suspended or dropped. No further progress was made; in fact the participation ratio disparity widened again. Then Congress, after being bombarded by lobbyists from many different groups, passed (over President Reagan's veto) the Civil Rights Restoration Act of 1988, which made clear that Title IX did in fact apply to athletics. So in essence the law has only been enforced about half of its twenty-year life.

"Since 1988 there have been hundreds, or more likely,

thousands of law cases filed relative to gender equity in athletics. Now most court rulings reflect that Title IX is supremely reasonable, and they have ruled overwhelmingly in favor of gender equity. As a result intercollegiate and interscholastic basketball will continue to change and improve.

"Overall great strides have been made in women's basketball since the passage of Title IX. Despite the willingness of the schools to take Title IX seriously, the law has its limitations. It can't address the issue of public interest or media coverage. Even though a school like Stanford has a model program and gets national TV coverage, the games are often aired in the middle of the night. Thank goodness for VCRs!

"Through basketball women can learn what it is like to make a commitment to themselves as well as a team, they can experience pushing themselves to the limit physically as well as mentally. As women move on into professional life, they have had some experience being a team player, being comfortable playing a role, and they will know they can be a leader without being a star. Women who play basketball have more self-confidence and self-esteem, and they know there is more than just their physical appearance. But for the most part the media is not giving recognition to women's accomplishments. Young women can't read about their sports role models or learn what might be available for them. How can they aspire to something they have no information about?"

Then she quoted from an article written in 1974, just after Title IX, in which a male reporter wrote about Marianne Crawford of Immaculata College in Pennsylvania:

"Men, you're not going to believe this, but Immaculata College's Marianne Crawford, a girl, scooped up this loose ball, dribbled between her legs to get past one East Stroudsburg defender, then took off on a three-on-two fast break. She dribbled a while left-handed, then right-handed, a few stutter steps here and there, then looked left and threw right to the lovely Rene Muth for two points."

The word *lovely*, normally light and liquid, lodged on her tongue, sluggish and heavy: *llllooovvveeelllyyy*.

"In summary, I find it very interesting that most young women today do not know what Title IX is all about, including my own two daughters. They know they have opportunities to pursue the sport of their choice, they know that if they work hard to improve, there might be an athletic scholarship available. Girls today, especially in Amherst, are no longer just spectators of the games, and they no longer care about the milk and cookies."

"That Mr. Moyer!" Kristin Marvin, never a wallflower with her feelings, was seething. "He can be such a jerk."

It was the beginning of the postseason, Amherst had just beaten Longmeadow for the third and final time this season, and the Hurricanes were in an uproar. This was the last time their team would ever play in the home gym, and Coach Moyer had deliberately, calculatedly, with full consciousness of his actions, let Patri sit the game out on the bench: Patri, who—as the last player out—customarily attracted the loudest and longest and most heartfelt chants:

"Patri! Patri! Patri!"

Her presence on the court was the signal that the game was under control, all the instruments had been played, and now they would just keep playing, only louder.

How could he just let her sit there?

At first Patri thought he must have simply forgotten: "It hadn't clicked into me what was happening." She kept looking at him as all her other teammates were being rotated back onto the floor and she remained on the bench.

Afterward, Kathleen advised her, "Ask him. Ask him what happened."

Kathleen was glistening with sweat. The phalanx of bangs on Patri's face were soft and fluffy as new snow.

So she strode up to him, one of the shortest players on the team confronting the tallest person in the room.

"Mr. Moyer, why didn't you put me in?"

"You were on the late list for school today, and it doesn't set a good example."

"But I was there. I got to school at nine thirty-six, and you're not counted as absent until nine-forty."

"The list I saw said you weren't here even at nine-forty."

Patri did not appear satisfied with this explanation.

That evening Patri had come to the game in a borrowed van with a huge contingent of family—her mother, her brothers, including Reggie (the baby, aged three), her cousins, and her step-father—a fact that inflamed her sense of indignation. Often, because of work schedules or faulty carburetors or a combination of the two, her family could not come to watch her. But tonight they were there.

"Besides, I feel that you've been clowning around and not giving one hundred percent at practices."

Patri walked off the floor, where dazed and happy fans, thrilled at yet another victory, milled about, reluctant to leave.

She stormed into the locker room. She ignored the consoling gestures of both Emilys. She pushed Kim away when she tried to give her a hug. She kicked a door, overturned a trash can, and said, "Forget it. I quit."

On the way home, in the crowded vehicle, Patri's family, led by her mother, sang to Patri.

Ilene Madison was not sure how to interpret what had happened, and at this moment she was more concerned that her daughter recover emotionally and go forward.

It had been a long day, a long winter. The family did not like where they were living in the basement of a raised ranch house for which they were paying $750 a month in rent. The windows, such as they were, were situated up near the ceiling. The family awakened on a strict schedule in order to parcel out the bathroom time.

Ilene Abad Madison had left her Cuban husband when Jose, now eleven, was still a baby: "Silently I planned my getting out. He would say in his culture, the slapping and the mistresses were permissible, and I told him I did not permit it in mine." She always had the inclination to further her education, and she picked Amherst because "I wanted to study at the University of Massachusetts, but never in my life had I lived in a cold place."

She got her degree, remarried, and had Reggie.

In the mornings she left the house at seven-thirty to drop her son at day care at eight to be in Springfield by eight forty-five for a job as a bilingual teacher in the first grade. She stood in front of her students all day, teaching them the names of objects in the room: door *(puerta)*, clock *(reloj)*, sink *(fregadero)*, paper *(papeles)*, books *(libros)*, blackboard *(pizarrón)*.

Every day a different child was chosen to be *estudiante del día*. Her goal was to see their eyes shine.

Money was short, the car kept conking out, the job was draining, the house with its one bath and no room for a dining room table would have been even more frustrating if she didn't keep in mind that at least the landlord had rented to them when others had declined to do so for the obvious reason. There had been one house they'd liked, but the landlord kept saying he couldn't show it to her because the family living in it was away at the Cape. As Ilene Madison told Lucia's mother, "My sister-in-law called in her white voice and he said, 'Yes. Come on and see the house at three o'clock tomorrow.' It's so hard. We know we are professionals and educated people, but they smash your pride. This guy was a hillbilly. So we had to pay a fee to a company to find us a place. We paid fifteen hundred dollars to get the place we got."

She sometimes compared Amherst to a beautiful woman who is rotten on the inside, or to a lotus flower, a fruit famous for its ability to produce indolence and dreamy contentment. But the time in Chicago had not been a solution to anything except perhaps the predicament of her oldest son, who had seemed without purpose, but who was now in college and who worked part-time at Kinko's Copy Center. For Jose's birthday Tony bought him a new bike and a helmet and a lock. Patri had been accepted at U Mass as a premed student. "I always dreamed to have a daughter like her, so beautiful and so smart."

Reggie was healthy: "My children have all bloomed into super flowers." In a life where time and money were both at a premium, she was most obsessed with only one real arithmetic, the sum of her children's well-being.

And so, on the way home, "We started singing, and that put her up and up and up. We sang, 'We love you, Patri, oh yes we do,' and we sang the song from Barney:

I love you.
You love me.
We're a happy family.
With a great hug and a kiss from me to you,
Won't you say you love me too?

* * *

Lucia went home and puzzled about the incident.

She talked to her mother about it late that night, and again in the morning. Like most mothers of teenagers, Gigi Kaeser secretly welcomed the garrulity.

"Mom," Lucia kept saying, "it isn't fair. If Patri wasn't taken seriously enough as a player to be criticized in practice, why would Coach Moyer take the time now to criticize her tonight in front of so many people?"

Jen was also troubled.

Sure, Patri could have been more serious in practice sometimes, but the timing was "pitiful." At first it made Jen feel almost lonely, as if she couldn't completely trust Coach Moyer's leadership, and then a different realization took hold. The Hurricanes would have to count on themselves, have to be their own leaders.

After the game, Coach Moyer went out with Bob Pariseau and Tracy Osbahr and had a quick bite of pizza.

He had no misgivings: "Patri rolled into school late. She's been goofing off at practice. She had to skip out one day because some form was missing from her application to U Mass. I don't have a deep doghouse or a long memory. All she has to do is come back tomorrow and work hard, and she'll be the first kid off the bench at the Cage."

The Cage! Despite the snarling menace of the name, this was a revered facility at U Mass, built specifically for basketball in the large barnlike style of East Coast gyms with, originally, a dirt floor and a glass ceiling. The Western Mass semi against Wahconah was scheduled to take place on the U Mass campus at the Cage, the same facility where Julius Erving (Dr. J) had mesmerized the masses in the seventies. This was a site that combined sentiment and prestige.

Coach Moyer finished his pizza in a hurry. He had promised a couple of kids that he would go to the boys' hockey game at Orr Rink at Amherst College, and he arrived just in time to see Amherst make two goals.

It was Kathleen who talked her best friend back onto the team.

She spoke to her on the phone late at night with whispered urgency. "I know you're mad now, but I don't think this is what you want to do. Mr. Moyer was wrong. But the team isn't him. The team is us. He can have his fist and flag, but as Jenny always says, we have our heart and our legs. There's only one way to prove him wrong: Go back in and work that much harder. Show him he made a mistake."

The next day at practice Patri walked in wearing sunglasses. She didn't look at Coach Moyer, but she followed his drills and she worked her hardest.

In the contest five days later with Wahconah Patri was put in the game early and quickly.

She took a shot that defied not only her expectations but those of her teammates and of the fans. It was not one of those wild junk shots tossed up as an afterthought. It was brave and knowledgeable. It went so high up that for a moment it was as if she had borrowed Jen's nickname of Cloudy. It was perfect. Coach Moyer was pleased: Patri was back on board the Hoop Phi express.

If keeping Patri on the bench during the last home game of the regular season was Coach Moyer's idea of a gambit, this shot was her idea of the perfect repartee. Or as Coach might say, punning, she had been "repatriated."

Patri's shot was not the only memorable one that evening. On a fast break Jen fed Jamila a behind-the-back pass for a layup that astounded the entire assembly. The skill of it! The unselfishness! The depth of friendship it revealed.

The final score: 55–39.

For two hours after the game, while Hamp and Agawam warmed up, and then later while they played, the whole team was swamped by children, boys and girls, seeking autographs. It had happened before, this wish for a signature or some other concrete remembrance from a fan, but never before for this long, on this scale, in front of so many witnesses.

Jen for one could not say which was more intoxicating: the victory or its aftermath.

10

The Long Shadow

Everyone agreed. It was the worst winter in recent memory. It was real winter. You'd go to *Kiss Me, Kate* at the high school under clear skies at seven-thirty, and three hours later the powder was so thick that even Volvos, clunky and wistful in their promise of immortality, littered the perimeters of country roads. The most common greeting was not "Hello" but "I saw your car on Station Road, and you weren't in it."

The momentum of the season had a salubrious effect on the entire town, however. Strangers stopped the Hurricanes on the street to wish them luck. Middle-aged women would touch them on the arm and say, simply, "Thanks." The Camera Shops, a store on North Pleasant, did a booming business in rush orders for photos. At a restaurant in North Amherst called Daisy's, featuring abstruse omelets and frequented by men in ponytails doing the *Times* crossword puzzle, Jen was recognized and treated to a free glass of fruit juice. At Hastings customers grilled Kim on the most recent games; little girls asked if her ankle was okay (they'd seen it being taped by the trainer) and asked her to tell Jen that her behind-the-back pass was awesome. At Jen's former elementary school, teachers were scrounging up old papers and photos (from class trips or the time she dissected a rat) to honor her at season's end with "Jen Pariseau Day," no matter what the outcome of the Hurricanes' game(s) in the regional and state finals.

By the time the Western Mass Regional Finals were held on March 5 at the Civic Center in Springfield, hundreds of Amherst fans proceeded down Interstate 91 in weather-weary vehicles, paralleling the progress of the Hurricanes' thin metal bus past dark clumps of mountains and the Soldiers' Home with its named spelled out in big letters on a hillside.

Coach Moyer sat in front on the aisle so that his legs could extend out. This was it, the long shadow on the lawn that haunted every season, the game at season's end that Amherst had lost five years in a row.

Instead of saying hello to Kathleen, her teammates asked, "How's the ankle?"

During the Wahconah game at the Cage earlier in the week, Kathleen had fallen and someone had run over her foot. Dr. Jones examined it the next day and suggested she go to Cooley Dickinson for X rays. In the same way that supportive fans sometimes wave their hands upward to help a free shot go in, the Hurricanes were collectively telepathing healing thoughts to Kathleen's foot.

She marched onto the bus without any hesitancy. Coach Moyer couldn't help worrying. Was this a sign that the ankle was all right, or was she secretly wincing?

As the wheels spun southward, the Hurricanes all appeared to be in a private pregame trance, listening to their Walkmen or, like Jen, curled up under a parka crusted with winter.

Jen hated bus rides, especially long ones like tonight. When she and her brother, Chris, were little they were always the first ones on the bus to school, and they rode forever through their little town before finally arriving at their destination. The anxiety was always there but in January it became sharper and heavier when she read a *Sports Illustrated* article by Leigh Montville about the accident that had claimed the lives of two members of the Notre Dame Women's Swim Team in the previous year. She tried not to think about it, but the subject kept intruding:

> For the Notre Dame women, the events of Jan. 24, 1992, always will be a part of whatever they do. Two of their friends and teammates, freshmen Margaret (Meghan) Beeler and Colleen Hipp, died. Almost everyone else was injured physically, the injuries ranging from simple scrapes to a broken back with the devastating prognosis of paralysis. The emotional injuries were as wide-ranging and serious, the insulated joys of college interrupted by sad reality. Forget it? How is this possible?

The details from the article would not leave Jen's mind ("[The] accident occurred on the return from a meet at Northwestern in Evanston, Illinois"). She was powerless to silence the internal harangue:

> Normally the men's and women's teams of Notre Dame travel together to meets at the same school, but on this one night the women traveled alone. The Northwestern swimming programs are separate, and the Notre Dame men had already swum against the Northwestern men. The men joked that it would be nice to be freed from the women for an afternoon workout.

Jen knew the score of the meet: Evanston had won, 183–117.

She knew the weather was not alarming in Chicago, that "the trip was not considered long. . . . Ninety miles away, Chicago sometimes seems like a South Bend suburb."

She'd read about the pizza and Gatorade served on the bus, about the movie shown on three television sets. The title of the movie was *Dying Young*.

The accident occurred so close to the Notre Dame campus that when the swimmers' bus started to slide, some of the women thought they simply had arrived at the exit.

Help started arriving from assorted directions. Ten ambulances and fire fighters from two departments hurried injured swimmers to three different hospitals in the South Bend area.

Jen shut her eyes tight against the drafty vehicle and its southward journey. The bus almost made her sick. Buses are treacherous, unstable, ready to tip at any second. It was torture being on one. She willed herself to think about brighter topics. She had two new contenders for a niche on her "strong women" wall: Hillary Clinton and maybe this woman Janet Reno from Florida, who lived in a house in a swamp that her mother had built by hand and who was being considered for attorney general.

The bus deposited them at the entrance for players and performers. It was a short walk in the slush and over the mounds of snow.

The Hurricanes usually counted on Jen and Jamila for the pregame invocation, those talismanic words that would goad them to victory. It was important that they say something special beyond whatever remarks Coach had to offer.

Tonight in the tense private moments as a team just before the game in the washed-out light of the locker room, it was Kristin Marvin who stepped forward. Both Ron Moyer and Trish Lea, the junior varsity coach who had moved up in the postseason to lend her skills, waited outside in a dingy corridor. This was the team's time to commune with itself. Kristin, who sometimes liked to act as if life were just a party, one huge Big Mac fully loaded with pickles and ketchup and onions, had the look this evening of zeal as she commandeered the floor. The intensity of Kristin's expression was mirrored in the way she gripped a scroll of thin white computer paper; her face glowed from the inside out. The words spilled out, quick and interlocking, like pieces of a jigsaw puzzle still stuck together, as she read from a document she had composed during a bout of insomnia two nights before:

"I'm sitting here on Thursday night, thinking that the possibility of sleep is about four hours away. Watching our hockey team lose by one point tonight got me so pumped and hyper for Saturday's game that I've been pacing my house and hyperventilating. I've watched so many of our teams become 'almosts.' Almost win Western Mass, almost be good enough, almost have it. And as I stood there and watched the tears roll down Kunk's face, I swore I would not let that kind of sorrow hurt any one of us right here.

"I know that the one obstacle that stands in the path of a Western Mass Championship is inside us. Kathleen said to me tonight she felt she wasn't pumped enough. She didn't feel the "fire." I feel it now, and I want to record the intensity that it's causing. I don't need to whine about losing to Hamp two years in a row, or mention Lauren Demski, or remind you of what total bitches the team is now. You all know that. And that gets your mind pumped, and it makes you want to be angry and intense, but it doesn't provide that indescribable rush of adrenaline and emotion that makes us go out and kick ass.

"I'm not gonna ask any of you to win the game, or try to win the game tonight. That's Coach's job. What I ask of you is, every time you see a loose ball, lunge for it. Every rebound, reach for it as if it were rightfully yours—'cause it is. Concentrate on every shot like it's your last. Push and hurt your player a little harder each time. Everyone box out like you're Lucia. And most of all, feel the love of the game and the love for each other every second you're on the floor or on the bench. That kind of passion, which I know we have, if we play with it tonight, Hamp is gonna be out in the first four minutes. They know it too—they know as well as us what we have is unstoppable, and they're scared. They should be. I want Hamp blood, we all do. I want to see their cowardly, prejudiced, pathetic, selfish pride squirming and dying on the floor by the end of the game."

The Hurricanes were ensnared; the very language of Kristin's speech was a kind of contraband, especially to the younger girls, who were at the point of trying on vocabulary as if it were a daring garment. It resounded in the dank utilitarian room, a renegade trumpet.

"Okay, I've gone on enough. I just couldn't do this without putting my two cents in. I was gonna write a petition, but I was afraid Jen wouldn't sign it."

There was a brief pause, a momentary inward gasp as everyone wondered how Jen would react to this acknowledgment of the tensions that sometimes existed between the two friends. Jen hated petitions, the way they preened with the often false promise of due process. Under most circumstances, she believed it was better to "suck it up," teenage slang for "grin and bear it." Would Jen flinch or smile, look askance or raise a fist? Jen gave Kristin an approving look: "You go, girl."

"Let me just say, this could very well be the last time in my life that I put on a uniform and play in a real game of basketball. Last time. It could also be the last time we all play together as a team. Just think about that. It's a pretty intimidating thought. So I just ask that you all pretend tonight as if this were the last game of basketball that you could ever play, and put that much heart into it. But I don't really need to. I know you'll all do it. I hope you all feel that fire, because tonight we all need each other to be here. You are my sisters, and I honestly love every one of you that much. Thank you for providing the most rewarding, special experience of my life. I will never forget any of you. No matter what happens tonight, I want you to remember Hoop Phi and know we're the best.

"We have more heart than the whole fucking town of Northampton, so let's prove it."

And then Kristin paused, and with all the dignity of a priest who recites a sacred phrase and all the feistiness of a drill sergeant who expects the troops to hop to, she shouted her most rousing rendition ever of "Hoop," to which the crowd of girls huddled in their circle, arms entwined, fired back, as in a fusillade:

"Phi!"

Coach Moyer knew they would win.

Two of Northampton's strongest players plowed down Kathleen just as she took the first shot of the game, a successful two-pointer on a fearless drive down the middle. He was terrified she'd landed on her ankle. But she scurried up from her momentary spread-eagled pose on the floor, and at the foul line where she had the chance to make another point for a three-point play, she situated herself square to the basket.

As the tension grew, and the contradictory cries from fans on both sides filled the air, she hoisted the ball with strong arms and, using her entire body, propelled it upward in a clean curve.

Another nifty point.

Even though there were twelve minutes left in the first half, it was at that moment that Coach Moyer decided the game was over: If we have Skippy, we have everybody, and Skippy was one for one from the floor, three for three from the line. And of course he was right.

The Hurricanes were also able to employ a play they'd been working on all week called the Emily.

The plan was this: Bring Jonesbones off a double screen from the top of the key at the three-point line, and get the pass to her so she could shoot it up for three over the double screen. Everything went perfectly. Jonesbones got the ball, and she put it up, pure *swish*.

Jen wanted to stop the action for applause: What she admired most about her teammate was the way she accepted her role on the team.

Jen stood there, thinking:

Jonesbones's job was to come off the bench and grab rebounds, and dang, if that girl didn't grab rebounds. All season she'd played with an injury, a bum elbow she'd gotten during softball when she'd slid right over her arm. She had never complained. She wouldn't even mention it unless you asked her. She was a pro.

The story in the next day's paper captured a portion of the emotion:

CANES FINALLY REIGN AFTER BLASTING HAMP
by Marty Dobrow, staff writer

SPRINGFIELD—When the friendly, but ferocious rivalry was over, Jamila Wideman and Beth Kuzmeski hugged each other in an emotional press of consolation and congratulation.

Wideman's Amherst Regional Hurricanes had just dethroned Kuzmeski's Northampton Blue Devils as Western Mass Div. 1 champs, 63–41 Saturday evening at the Springfield Civic Center. It was a one-sided game, devoid of drama. The poignancy waited until afterwards, the farewell between stars who had lifted the local interest in girls' basketball to unprecedented levels.

"Last year was our year," said a still teary-eyed Kuzmeski. "This year Jamila was so determined to win it, and I'm happy for her."

Kuzmeski's glittering high school career comes to an end. Wideman will lead her crew into tomorrow night's state semi-finals against Central Mass champ Wachusett.

Even before Saturday's showdown a sense of finality hung in the air. In the introductions Hamp coach Tom Parent, who has had to contend with Wideman since she was in the seventh grade, gently grasped the all-American's forearm and spoke to her for several seconds.

"It feels like I've been playing against her since she was ten," Parent later reflected. "I said [to her], 'Is this finally the last time?' "

Thankfully for Parent, this was, indeed, the end.

Wideman lived up to every bit of her considerable billing, scoring 25 points, grabbing 11 rebounds, nabbing 7 steals. And in the end, she had the Western Mass crown, a prize that had somehow eluded her throughout her career. For all the individual accolades she had received, this was the prize she wanted most.

"This is it," she said, beaming. "Since seventh grade this is what I've been pushing for. It's the greatest feeling in the world."

The story caught the broad outlines perfectly.

But to an "affectionado," as Coach Moyer liked to call himself, the narrative that had unfolded was even richer, filled with the history of place (Cathedral had for years been the frequent site of Amherst's doom) and also all those side stories easily overlooked in the sweep of Jamila's accomplishments.

Bob Pariseau was struck by the difference between Kathleen a year ago and Kathleen on this evening. In all his time of watching sporting events, he could not name another transformation, amateur or professional, on such a sweeping scale.

Kathleen herself could hardly believe that it had been at the exact same point in the season a year ago that she'd collapsed in a sniveling heap outside the gym at Cathedral. She had bottomed out, and that plunge downward had triggered a transition in her head, a psychological transformation as slow and subtle as water and air and light on the smallest seed.

She thought about last year's final game:

After such embarrassment, you kick yourself. You kick hard and it hurts. But after that, you get pissed. You realize that in all the Mr.-Nice-Guy, "Nah, I'm not good" games, you've been pushed around. You start to feel used and manipulated. All this time, not taking what you should have, always being polite. Not anymore—look where it got us. Sorry, but it's time we got what we worked for; we simply didn't realize that after you put in the work, you don't automatically get the reward. You've got to be greedy, you've got to push, you've got to do impolite things like taking the trophy.

Politeness is nice, and niceness is, well . . . nice. But when do you stop kicking yourself for being nice in the past and start smacking yourself into waking up to the present, pushing yourself to prepare for the future? Enough regrets, enough "I should haves," because pretty soon there are no more chances.

That's what happened. We got proud. We got pissed. We got a little scared of losing time. I learned self-confidence is not only acceptable, it is indispensable.

Be nice when it's time to be nice and when others are nice to you. But niceness has no place on the court because the other team wants you to lose. *The court is where you can be all those things we're not supposed to be: aggressive, cocky, strong. It's okay; it's alright.*

There's this feeling that you get. Once you get it, you can get it back again and again, just thinking about the game. It's when you can't distinguish between the emotions that are driving you, but you know that they're all there and they all want the same thing. It makes you grit your teeth, bite down on your back teeth so that your jaw is tight. Unsure if you're about to cry or about to attack, your nose flares and every muscle in your body tightens up. It happens when you take every last feeling of indignation and resentment, love and confidence, onto the court. When the court is your outlet for this feeling, you can't lose. For every time I felt I'd been manipulated or that I hadn't stood up for myself, hadn't proven that I deserve credit and respect, I pushed that much harder with my legs and wanted that much more. The cause of that feeling was different for each of us on the team, but we all had it and we quietly respected where it came from in everyone else. I don't need to know what or who has pushed Kristin around in her life or why it made her push twice as hard against Kim Frost. She just needs to know that I understand and that I can relate. Each time she grabs a rebound, I see the look. I see how she grits her teeth, how her upper lip curls just a little bit. The only sound that could possibly come from such a face would be a low growl. She has inside her what I have inside me. The fact that we all recognized tonight that each one of us is fighting against something different allowed us to fight for one common goal with all our hearts.

We weren't conceited, we were proud. And in between those two seasons, we wanted to be the best and we wanted everyone to know it. That's not selfish or cocky; that's the mentality of an athlete, and that's what I found!

And so, twelve months later, Kathleen Poe faced the opponent who had caused her to curl into herself on the floor, and this time, head high, she walked off the court.

The score: 63–41.

From the *Daily Hampshire Gazette*, March 8, 1993:

FANS ARE THE BIG WINNERS

SPRINGFIELD—Basketball mania was alive and well Saturday as thousands of fans poured into the Springfield Civic Center to watch arch rivals Northampton and Amherst vie for the girls regional tournament title.

Many also came to watch the female athletes who have elevated girls basketball to a popularity unknown in recent years in Hampshire county.

However, the Western Massachusetts Division I final was hardly the "battle of Titans" as many had hoped. The easy Amherst win, 63–41, was its third straight over Northampton this year.

But despite the lopsided victory, many people said they were glad they came to see why Amherst Regional High School point guard Jamila Wideman has garnered national publicity. As master of the court, Wideman wasn't a disappointment.

An estimated 4,000 to 5,000 people watched the girls game, including entire families from each community, contingents of proud relatives of the players, and entourages from each school.

By far the noisiest crowd was on the Amherst side, which had the advantage of cheerleaders whipping up the fans. The Hurricanes also gave them something to cheer about—big leads.

And to underscore the serious attention given to the Hurricanes was a program like those typically found at professional games.

The program—printed on neon pink paper—contained a complete scorecard as well as individual statistics for each Amherst player.

The program was distributed courtesy of Richard M. Howland, an Amherst lawyer and big booster for the team.

Howland said he follows girls basketball partly because he has two daughters.

Jackie Quirk of Northampton said of the rivalry, "I think it's fabulous. It's about time girls got to compete with honor and respect."

Quirk organized a group from Northampton that included two fathers, three 8-year-old girls and a 7-year-old boy.

"I thought it would be good to bring the girls," noted Michael Southerland, who was part of Quirk's group.

He said the female athletes were good role models for young children, including boys.

Douglas Cropper, an assistant boys basketball coach in South Hadley, came because he "heard it's a great matchup." He believes girls basketball can be just as exciting as boys.

Daniel Banks, a basketball fan from Amherst with no ties to the school or players, said the girls "have done a lot for basketball in Amherst."

Amherst Regional High football coach Thomas Cullen hobbled to the Civic Center on crutches after undergoing knee surgery Tuesday.

"I can't miss this game," he said, adding, "I think girls athletics have come a long way. It's great."

Barbara Boudway, the mother of senior Northampton player Heather Boudway, said that sports brings people together.

"It's a whole community thing. The community here is supporting the girls and it's a real positive thing," Boudway said.

With a little sigh she noted, "I only wish the score was a little closer."

Bob Pariseau and Tracy Osbahr had issued a win-or-lose invitation to come to their house after the game for a party.

The bus back to Amherst buttered the highway home, a contrast to the sullen choppy journey of a year ago.

On this night the men slapped each other on the back, raised their drinks, and tried, with only some success, to avoid preening.

Milling about in the small combination dining and living room, munching on cheese and celery, sipping wine or soda, the women were equally touched by the events of the evening, of the season really, almost beyond words, telegraphing by the look in their eyes how proud they were to be related to these girls by blood or by circumstance, and when they did talk, among each other, it was with an intimacy that took itself for granted. No one bothered to lecture anyone about the touch-and-go trepidation that afflicts all mothers and stepmothers of daughters, that knots their hearts and sabotages sleep, the posse of doubts and fears. *Grant me*, the girl at the Bat Mitzvah had said, *the confidence to raise my voice that I might be heard.* On this night in Springfield at the Civic Center the team had raised a collective voice, on behalf of their fathers and stepfathers and uncles and brothers, but especially on behalf of the women in their lives. Buried amid the dip and the Doritos, the high fives and the hugs, was a silent recognition that at long last that annoying interrogatory so beloved of the pundits, "What do women want?" had found an answer here in the heat of this room.

A lot of things.

And this is part of it.

11

An Untouchable Breed

Perhaps this is true of every place in the country, but it seems particularly true of Massachusetts that the construction of big buildings is fraught with problems. Ideally, there should be a predictable and pleasing rhythm to these ventures, first the excitement, then the excavation, and then the slow coloring in of floors and roofs and walls and at last the triumphant unveiling. But the Bay State may well be the world capital of construction glitches. The designers of the world's tallest library at U Mass discovered there is a good reason why at twenty-eight stories high they have the world's record.

Books are heavy.

So heavy that for a while the area outside the building was cordoned off so that bricks popping out of the exterior walls of the twenty-eight-story building would not bean anybody.

Not that U Mass is alone in its construction woes. In the early seventies the John Hancock Tower in Boston used to have a problem with splintering windows, for which the polite term "defenestration" was sometimes used.

Around the same time, a sports and entertainment center called the Centrum was proposed with the usual flurry of euphoria for the city of Worcester, about forty miles west of Boston. CIVIC CENTER WOULD 'ACCENTUATE THE POSITIVE' was a typical headline of the time.

A decade later, just as the facility neared completion, the opening was delayed, and then delayed again. The pipes in the drainage system kept bursting and the usual culprits of "substandard construction and numerous imperfections in the steel fabrication" were held responsible.

At last, on September 2, 1982, its premier act was Frank Sinatra; since then the Centrum had featured Aerosmith, Barry Manilow, Tina Turner, Pavarotti, Billy Joel, Kenny Rogers, Genesis, Hulk Hogan, and Madonna, in a presentation that a city father witnessed and later pronounced offensive, "the details of which cannot be enunciated in a family newspaper."

And now the Amherst Hurricanes.

They were filled with fear and awe, but when someone suggested they might be intimidated by the prospect of following Madonna, however belatedly, it was Rita who set the record straight.

"Madonna is not my hero. She wanted attention, she wanted money, she wanted glory, she wanted the microphone, and she did it just by taking off her clothes. I treat my body three hundred degrees different. I lift weights not so I'll look strong to other people, but so I'll *be* strong. I take care of my body. I make sure I sleep. I sleep a lot more than my friends. I eat well . . . too much sugar, but other than that I'm fine. If I get an injury like a pull, I listen to it. I don't drink, I don't smoke. I ask enough of my body without asking it to deal with random substances. Once she got hold of the microphone, she just took off more clothes. She never did anything except be sexy. I resent the message that if you are sexy, you are powerful. That's what I think Madonna stands for. As an athlete, it kills me."

Coach Moyer kept calling the Centrum "Disney World North."

The nervousness was pervasive.

Okay, so they beat Hamp in the Western Mass Regional Finals, they weren't really champions—not yet. Did they have what it takes, these sweet-looking girls reared in maple syrup country? Playing before a few thousand fans in what is almost your own backyard is nothing compared with a stadium that seats 13,800, where real pros play.

Rocking Feiker is one thing, but the Centrum?

"Hey, Charlie, how you doing, old buddy?"

It was Betsy Moyer on the phone with Captain Charlie Scherpa. The two knew each other from hot summer days on the fields where their daughters had both been members of the Lassie League softball teams.

"No complaints here. How can I help you, Betsy?"

"You know how Ron's kids are going to Worcester for the state finals?"

"Is there anyone in town who doesn't?"

"I'd like a little help with an idea I have . . ."

The police officer did not hesitate. This is a small town. This wasn't really even a favor, more along the lines of a professional courtesy.

"No problem, Betsy. You tell Ron to consider it done. By the way, congratulations. I hear that younger girl of yours is breaking records on the swim team."

Jen and Jamila had a new ritual greeting for each other in the corridors of the high school. From the wan acknowledgments of a year ago in which, as Jen had once said, "we barely said hi-hi to each other," they now gave each long looks and smiled broadly.

Schoolmates who observed the silent exchange stood to the side.

They parted so that each girl could plunge forward toward the other, with her characteristic stride: Jen's no-nonsense and efficient, Jamila's on the balls of her feet (a local writer once said she moved in a slight sway, like oil in a can).

When they got close enough, they stopped for a second and agreed, in voices loud enough to carry down the long corridors, low enough to vibrate with conviction:

"We're not losing."

The championship game was scheduled for Saturday, March 13.

No one thought to worry about the weather. It was the kind of winter that had surely exhausted its quota of rotten days.

Friday, the day before the game was to be played, was sunny, cool and clear. A pep rally was held in the gym at the high school. George Graiff, the janitor who prepped the gym before each game, sweeping, pulling down the bleachers, dry-mopping the floor, who had worked at one time for Jen's father and who had attended the school when Kim's mother was enrolled, gave each girl on the varsity and junior varsity as well as their coaches and trainers a red and white carnation (he deliberately chose the school colors) in appreciation for the way they had treated him. "There will always be," as he put it, "some apples in the barrel, but these kids were nice. They said 'hi' and 'thanks.' The guy upstairs gave them arms and legs, and they don't mind using them to lift a tray."

Friday smiled.

But the newscasters told a different story:

The UMass Minutemen have scored their second Atlantic 10 win in the title championship against Temple, 69–61. . . . Pablo Escobar, Colombia's most powerful drug

leader, may be willing to surrender to authorities and return to prison. . . . In Waco, Texas, David Koresh of the
Branch Davidians said they would give up next week, but
God spoke to him, so he changed his mind. Negotiators
are still optimistic that the standoff can be resolved
peacefully. The government has brought in tanks that are
not armed. These will be used only defensively. . . . In
other news, major Northeaster coming through the area
on Saturday . . . very windy . . . snow mixed with sleet
and rain at times. Chances of precipitation: one hundred
percent. This is a storm of historic proportions.

Pippin Ross at WFCR, a National Public Radio affiliate,
went so far as to call it "the mother of all storms," although an
Amherst listener later filed a complaint about the "blatant sex-
ism" of that expression.

The lines for gasoline and at the liquor and the video stores
would have been even worse if the college students weren't away
on spring break. As it was, Video to Go was open that Saturday
for only six hours and came close to doing its best volume ever;
for some reason it never occurs to patrons what it would be like
if the power did go off and you tried to watch a video by candle-
light.

SCHOOL PLAYERS PUTTING EXCITEMENT ON HOLD
By B. J. Schecter
Special to the Globe

. . . Because of the anticipated storm, the three
boys' and three girls' state basketball championship
games scheduled at the Centrum today have been postponed until tomorrow at the same times. . . .

The Amherst girls didn't find out about the change until two minutes before their pep rally. "We were all set to go, and then we heard about this," said Coach Ron Moyer. "It's tough for the kids and for the school. We don't know when we are playing. If the storm is as bad as they say it is, we may not play until next week."

On Saturday the snow came down, and because of the winds it also went sideways and up. The snow was general throughout New England. Horizons and boundaries, lines and edges vanished.

Rita finally had a little extra time to devote to her journal:

I am writing in the middle of the biggest storm of decades—we have about 2 feet of snow, hurricane force winds in some parts of New England and flooding from the tides. The power is expected to go out any time. Today after watching *Hoosiers*, we went out skiing (in the luminous dark of a night white with snow) it was so wonderful. First it was athletically exhilarating. I could feel my quads pushing and sweat dripping down my back, my face being stung with gusts of icy snow/sleet—so fun. And I was thinking about basketball and Hoop Phi, and how thankful I am to be playing with them and how psyched I am to go to camp this summer and how much I love the game and it is my dream to play in college.

I kept imagining myself a Norwegian princess in the time of fairy tales, stories of saving people on skis and fighting bears and fishing in a blizzard kept flickering through my head like firelight from a huge hearth at a ski lodge in the Alps. When we got home of course this idea was broken by the cars in the driveway and the electrical wires above.

Then my dad and I shoveled ten feet of the driveway

and played basketball for half an hour. There was a huge bank by that time bordering the driveway so I ran and jumped in it like it was a wave in the ocean. So fun.

The game was rescheduled for Sunday night at six.

And then it was postponed, again: The roads were a disaster and even working overtime, the plows couldn't clear them.

There is a way in which an athlete prepares for a contest that has nothing to do with the obvious skill-building and calisthenics. It is quiet and invisible, an elaborate and subtle psychosomatic preparation, all those signals from the brain that orchestrate the sleep rhythms and the eating rhythms and the mind rhythms that speed up healing of tissue and slow down the response to pain, that prep a player in a way that no mere drill ever could. To build in this way toward a game once and then to have to back off because of a postponement is frustrating; to have it happen twice is excruciating to a whole different degree.

On Monday, Coach Moyer was able to arrange for a practice at the Cage. He relished the idea that he could take a small town and make it even smaller, that he knew someone who knew someone who would open the door so his kids could practice in a big-time gym.

They practiced solemnly.

Their eyes were veiled.

It was hard to tell if the Hurricanes were in their game or out of it, if the bland imperviousness of their expressions was a good sign or not.

Coach Moyer warned them that Haverhill was a team that knew all the tricks and that Amherst might need to employ some of its special strategies, the "Shoelace" or the "Murphy."

"There's no Chuck and Chase on Haverhill," he said, employing the term he had used since the start of the season to describe teams who let fate run them.

Patri raised a tentative hand.

"Coach, I've been wondering all season, who is this guy Chuckie Chase?"

The remark was greeted first with silence, then awe, then cries of "Patri?" by way of disbelief, then "Patri!" by way of affection. Had Patri really assumed Chuckie Chase was a person, someone she apparently missed meeting because of her junior year in Chicago? The lightness of the moment helped cut some of the anxiety.

Coach Moyer signaled to Trish Lea, the coach of the junior varsity and his assistant in the postseason: Would she say a word or two?

A likable, serious young woman studying at the university, she frequently voiced the opinion that she wished her own high school basketball team had been more like the Hurricanes. She admired the way the Hurricanes had been coached: Coach Moyer kept the girls progressing mentally and physically. It was not as if the final game were a cliff he was asking them to climb; it was a ladder. She admired the way he got the girls to discipline themselves. Sometimes after practice they'd head over to the U Mass football stadium, all of them, not just Kathleen, and they'd run up and down the stairs all on their own. Jen and Jonesbones liked to do sit-ups before they went to bed because they liked drifting off with a sore stomach. The trouble was the Haverhill girls had in all likelihood been doing the same since September.

She cleared her throat and even looked a touch fearful herself as she explained what it had been like back when she played in the Merrimack League against the mighty Hillies from Haverhill in their brown and yellow uniform with the short shorts. What she had to say was not what anyone wanted to hear at the moment, but the team listened attentively anyway.

"First of all, they're big. I don't know what they eat up there. They're confident. When you go out on that floor, they'll rattle you. They're known for their aggressive ball, nothing dirty

or David Robinson, pictures of their fathers and their grandfathers in their hockey uniforms or playing lacrosse or on a school team. You're used to them getting *Sports Illustrated for Kids* and owning a sports encyclopedia and a sports dictionary, and when it comes time to bring in a fact about the Middle Ages for a school project, they come up with something about how soccer began in China as a game where soldiers played with a dead enemy head and then moved to England in the fourteenth century.

You're used to seeing their rooms and the garage and the various hallways in the house overtaken by athletic equipment—knee pads and whistles strewn about with the graphite baseball bats and the assortment of gloves (one for catching, one for infielding, and one for their father) and a batting helmet and a dozen balls and uncountable baseball hats. There are basketballs, plus shoes, usually a minimum of two pairs, this year's and last, and sometimes there are soccer balls and of course a pair of cleats. Depending on whether your son goes for the quieter father-son stuff, there might be some lightweight L. L. Bean waders and a Patagonia fly vest and a Bean's six-weight fly rod with a Martin single-action reel. He might also have a wet suit and boogie board, skis and a trail bike. It's common to have a basketball hoop or at least access to one. It's less common but not unheard of to have a batting cage; at least one family on Southeast Street floods its yard in the winter so their boys can skate on their own private hockey rink.

In Amherst, the social life of a lot of boys consists of going from tryouts to scrimmages to games of teams sponsored by places such as Pinocchio's Pizza, Paige's Chevrolet, Matuszko Trucking. At the end of the season there is a celebration called, with false ennoblement, a banquet, in which a buffet of food presented in tin bins is served, and at which the players wear their only tie and earn awards like the "Mr. Hustle" certificate.

They spend their summers at sports camps being assessed in cat-egories ranging from ball control to dribbling and shooting and passing and creativity with ball and creativity without ball and vision and rebounding and crossover steps and one on one and T-slides (a drill in which a player practices moving from side to side and backwards and forward) and zigzags and tap-rebound drills and pivot drills and superman drills and spin dribbles. There are boys in Amherst who have so many trophies that they have actually given some to their sisters.

You hear the men talk, those fathers and sons, and it is not always possible to distinguish who is saying what, because they all agree with one another so totally.

"Some people belittle sports," says one.

"Dismiss games as a series of silly maneuvers."

"Life is maneuvers," says one.

"And life's not silly."

For years Diane Stanton had been on the sidelines, watch-ing and listening. Over the years, she had observed hundreds of kids, and Jen and Jamila stood out; it takes tremendous courage to play as a girl in an all-male Little League and as a girl in an all-male basketball league.

In the weak early light, she thought about them and of course made inevitable comparisons to herself:

Jenny and Jamila didn't fall victim to "girl" things—like ex-treme flirting, acting dumb around boys when, in fact, they are intelli-gent, being less than they could be in sports. I was somewhat like them when I was their age. I didn't play head games with the boys; I was their friend. In fact, the guys in high school used to call me "one of the guys." I never acted dumb in class—at least not any dumber than any other teenager! I did some flirting, of course, but that's natural. The only thing different that I found was that I wore a lot of miniskirts—girls these days don't wear dresses as much.

I never, never compromised my physical ability. I remember once going on a double date with my (then) best friend and we went bowling. It was a first date for me with this particular guy. Her date was fairly new as well. I happened to be bowling really well. I bowled a 224—the highest score I had ever gotten even when I bowled in a league! But it was during this game that I realized that I was different than her. She came up to me at one point during the game when I had gotten a few strikes in a row, and she asked me not to bowl so well. I was stunned. I'm sure my mouth was probably open!! She went on to explain that I was not being a good date since I was beating everyone there (meaning the two guys). I simply said something like "So what?" and continued to bowl my way. I noticed that she was throwing a few more gutter balls than she would normally get. I didn't let it bother our friendship, but I never forgot what that meant either. She had temporarily forgotten about self-respect.

As I watch Jen and Jamila play, I realize that a part of me was like them. A part of me that I hadn't been in contact with for a long time. I began to question where my courage had gone, the tenacity to be my best, the desire to do things just for myself.

I don't know why some women lose this part of themselves. I don't know if we just shelve it to take care of our families because we think that's the sacrifice we need to make or if circumstances just force us to leave it behind or what the reason is. I do know that many, many women did and still do leave a part of themselves behind when marriage and children come along. I grew up in a very equality-minded family. My parents just did the work, it didn't matter if my father mopped the floor or ironed the clothes, or my mother mowed the lawn or vice versa. So my role models were what any feminist would want for a young female.

No matter how many people stand up on a soapbox and try to knock the importance of sports, I believe sports added to Jen's and Jamila's development in a very positive way. It gave them more confidence, more self-awareness, more pride. Sports were not responsible for these traits, it just enhanced these existing traits.

And so the thoughts washed over her and crystallized into phrases and then sentences and paragraphs as she composed her near-silent music at the keyboard, *click, click, click.*

At four that afternoon, the voice of Coach Moyer rose above the din of shuffling footsteps, loud greetings, the slamming of metal, the thud of books. "Listen up. I want you to check right now. Do you have your uniforms? Your shoes and your socks? Do you have any other items of clothing that might be needed?"

Instead of asking them to pack the usual intangibles, their "intensity" and their "game face" and their "consistency" and their "defense," he looked at all of them, the multitalented Lucia, the two Emilys, Gumby and Jonesbones, one dark, one light, both formidable, at coltish Rita, serious Jan, reserved Sophie, quiet Jessi, Kristin the Firecracker. He glanced at Jade and thought about her famous imitation of Aretha Franklin's song "Respect." There was little Carrie, who had moved up from the junior varsity; at five feet two she was a spark plug of energy. And there was Julie, a quiet but competent practice player. He thought of Skippy, his silent assassin (Kathleen wasn't able to make it), and of kindhearted Kim, Patri the beloved, Jen and Jamila, and he said, "Today, I want you to pack your courage."

What Coach Moyer knew about Haverhill was that the one thing it and Amherst had in common was the silent *h* in the middle of their names. He also knew they had an excellent basketball program with strong support from the town. They'd been in the state finals four times in the last five years and they had won all four times.

He had never been there, never seen its proud hills filled with old factories, had not driven down the main drag where so many of the stores and restaurants are named after people and where there are two hardware stores, one right next to the other, and a huge meat store smack in the center of town. In the twenties the town had been a major manufacturer of women's shoes, known as Queen Shoe City. The Merrimack River flows twelve miles along the borders of the city and through its center.

To the people of Amherst, Haverhill was just a name, about two hours away, north of Boston in the eastern part of the state, the bullying part that steals small towns to create water for itself.

This afternoon, the Hurricanes could not stand still. The Hurricanes made a point of touching one or the other of their captains, as if Jen and Jamila could transmit the power of their playing. They were, all of them, frisky, giving each other piggybacks, lifting each other on backs that should be preserved for the task at hand.

Coach paused. Was this excessive roughhousing or just a natural drainage system for all those excessive spirits?

He looked as if he might rebuke them for all the squirming, but he shrugged and flashed his trademark grin. "Let's go." Then, perhaps more to himself than to them: "While we're still young."

Shortly after five in the evening, the sky was thick and gray and hooded, the cloud cover a welcome hedge against the bitterness.

The bus, festooned with a colorful banner bearing the words Hoop Phi Express, was different from the usual yellow ones.

"Hooked up and smooth!" said Jen Pariseau, as she moved confidently down the aisle, taking in all the special features, including upholstered seats, a toilet, four television sets, and a VCR mounted on the ceiling.

Already, three "pep" buses had left for the game, unprecedented support for an atheletic event, boys' or girls'.

247

"Fasten your seatbelts," said Coach. "Beverage service will commence shortly after takeoff. There'll be turbulence coming into Haverhill when the Hurricanes hit Worcester." Then he announced the people to whom he would like them to dedicate the entire season. "And that's to the 140 girls who are now playing youth basketball in Amherst for the first time this year."

Jen Pariseau stood up and said she wanted to read a letter from Diane Stanton, Chris Stanton's mom.

All chatter ceased as the girls looked up and listened.

"Jenny and Jamila, I am addressing my comments to you because I know you best, but this letter is for the whole team," the letter began.

> Your existence as a team represents a lot of things to a lot of women like me. . . . As a young girl I remember standing outside the Little League fence and watching the boys and knowing that I could hit and catch better than at least a third of them. When our high school intramural field hockey team and softball team asked for leagues, we were told flatly—NO, because there was no money. When this group of girl athletes got together to form an intramural basketball team, we were subjected to ridicule and anger from some of the student body. I lost courage, I'm embarrassed to admit, in my junior year and would no longer play intramural sports. Part of it was a protest against the failure of my school to recognize that we needed to play as much as boys. I know the struggle.

Coach Moyer gave the driver a signal and the vehicle started to roll.

A police car just ahead suddenly activated its lights and in a slow ceremony led the vehicle to the corner of Main and Triangle Streets, where another officer had been summoned to stop traffic. Coach Moyer was beaming: "Thank you, Charlie."

The bus proceeded down Main, past the house of Emily to the corner of Northeast, where they got to run a red light, turning in front of Fort River Elementary School, then heading out to Route 9, where the escort lasted all the way to the town line. Then, that odd juncture where in an instant the sign appears that says ENTERING PELHAM and in another instant a new one looms ahead that says ENTERING BELCHERTOWN.

The girls watched the film they had chosen unanimously to pump them up for the game, A League of Their Own. Coach Moyer always found it significant that even though they liked the characters played by Geena Davis and Madonna, they seemed more connected to the homely character of Marla. Sure, they hooted with superior delight when she made a gawky fool of herself during the charm school sequences and they could see that her face, which lacked beauty, was also devoured by shyness, but they also, during the game sequences, saw that she had the strongest arm and the surest pace, and they always gave her the biggest cheers.

They respected her. They could see that she was good. They understood she had it.

What would he say to them tonight? For once he felt that perhaps he had brought a team to the limits of self-knowledge. They had listened eagerly, and they knew what they had to know, both about the sport and about themselves. The cliché was true, well, almost: Even if they did not win tonight, they had won, simply by allowing themselves to get this far.

As he sat, comfortable at last, on that palace of a bus, the closer Coach Moyer got to Worcester, the closer he also traveled back to his own childhood in Philly in the early fifties. Tonight it was all coming to a grand finale. Here he was, coach and counselor of this little high school in Western Massachusetts, and in one of those elections as mysterious as it is thrilling, the Great Gods of Hoops had delivered to him an all-American, and what's more they had delivered Jen Pariseau, who was acting more and more like an all-American every time she hit the floor, as well as all those other kids who at this moment on this bus had no idea, couldn't have one because of the very nature of youth, its fickle addiction to an ever-present present, that Jamila's father was right: This is as good as it gets.

Had his mood been different, he might have, as the bus swerved off the highway into the brightly lit side streets and pulled up in front of the arena with its monolithic grayness, felt jittery.

But instead he felt contentment. It was a honor to be here, all six foot six of him, that former little kid who grew up in a house with only one rule ("What's the matter? Are your parents against bowling?") and no real space of his own dedicated in adulthood to a pursuit filled with rules, a game in which space itself is the ultimate quarry, under, over, on, beneath, and above, all of it, every invisible inch.

When the bus finally pulled in front of the Centrum and it was time to leap off, the expressions on the faces of the girls were tight and determined. The words from the movie they had just seen resonated: "Someone will walk out of here the champion, and someone will just walk out." To the world, they were a bunch of teenage girls; inside their heads, they were commandos. To the world, they had pretty names: Patri, Kristin, Jen, Kathleen, Kim, Jamila, Sophie, Jade, Emily J., Emily S., Jan, Lucia, Carrie, Rita, Jessi, Julie. But as far as they were concerned, they were the codes that encapsulated their rare and superb skills, their specialty plays, their personal styles. They were Cloudy and Snowplow and Jonesbones and Gumby and Grace and Skippy. They were *Em* squared. They were warriors.

In the arena their parents nodded at one another, touched a

back, squeezed a hand. Judging from their expressions, both distracted and attentive at the same time, they all appeared to be caught in the past as much as in the present, as if running old family movies in their heads, scraps of footage from the days long gone: Jamila, in the lights of the preemie ward, Jen telling her grade school teacher she did everything herself, thank you, Kathleen, in her one renegade moment ringing the sacred bells at Hampshire, Kim, steeped in quiet in Ms. Bouley's Resource Room, shyly handing her a photo of herself, Kristin learning the Constitution and visiting her birthrights on her parents and stepparents, Patri ("I'm not a nun") pacing outside that apartment in Chicago, praying for a return to Amherst, Emily "Gumby" Shore driving home from the hospital with her father, for whom the memory of the illness fades away but never completely, Emily "Jonesbones" Jones hoping to be a doctor like her father, little Rita ("*cupcupcup* all day long"), Jade, whose mother didn't want her to be the second black in a school system with 527 children, Sophie, her mother haunted by two separate sounds, bookends to an era, the tires of the truck screeching and then years later the ballet teacher informing her daughter, "You're too tall and your head is too big," and Lucia, whose father wanted her to play the piano, who loved to listen to her as she became Beethoven or Debussy or Chopin, became, in his opinion, "complicated, and that's the case of anyone's child who plays the piano."

Complicated: the case of anyone's child who plays.

Complicated: anyone's child.

The girls crowded into a locker room. Solemnly, with very little commotion, they dressed in their capacious uniforms. They slapped hands and stood tall. Meanwhile, the stadium was redolent of hot dogs, popcorn, sweat, and anticipation, one side of the bleachers filled with their people and the other side with the fans from Haverhill. You could hear their fight song:

1, *We are the Hillies*
2, *A little bit louder*
3, *I still can't hear you*
4, More, *more, more, more, more*

The girls walked out wordlessly. They looked up.

You have to live in a small town for a while before you can read a crowd, especially in New England, where reticence and fences are deep in the soil. But if you've been in a town like Amherst for a while, you can go to an out-of-town game, even to one in as imposing and cavernous a facility as the Centrum, and you can feel this sudden lurch of well-being that comes from the soothing familiarity of faces that are as much a part of your landscape as falling leaves, as forsythia in season, as rhubarb in June. You scan the rows, and for better, sometimes for worse, you know who's who. You know whose parents don't talk to whom else and you know why. You know who has troubles that never get discussed.

You see the lawyer that represented your folks or one of their friends in a land dispute or a custody case. You see the realtor who tried to sell a house next to the landfill to the new kids in town. You see the doctor who was no help for your asthma and the one who was. You see the teacher who declared your brother a complete mystery and the teacher who always stops to ask what your remarkable brother is up to now. You know which man is the beloved elementary-school principal, now retired. You recognize the plump-cheeked ladies from the cafeteria who specialize in homemade cinnamon buns for sixty-five cents. You see your family and you see the fathers and mothers and stepfathers and stepmothers of your teammates. You know whose brother flew in from Chicago for the game, whose stepgrandparents came from Minnesota.

But what is most important about all this is how mute it is.

The communality is something that is understood, as tacit as the progression of the summer to the fall to winter to spring, and just as comforting.

Usually there is a buzz of cheering at the start of a game, but this time the Amherst crowd was nearly silent as the referee tossed the ball.

The Haverhill center tapped the ball backward to her point guard on the left side of the court, who drove through the lane, uncontested, past Jen. Easy layup. Amherst blinked first. Two-nothing. In the Haverhill stands, the crowd cheered. It was the only pure cheer they got.

Within a few seconds, the score was 6–4 Amherst, and something remarkable took place. The Hurricanes entered into a zone where all of them were all-Americans. It's a kind of con-trolled frenzy that can overtake a group of athletes under only the most elusive of circumstances. It's not certain what triggered it, perhaps it was Jamila's gentle three-pointer from the wing, or more likely, when Jen drove the baseline and she swooped be-neath the basket like a bird of prey, then released the ball back over her head, placing it like an egg against the backboard and through the hoop. It might have been ten seconds later when Jamila stole the ball, pushing it down court in a three-on-one break, made a no-look pass to Jen, who just as quickly fired the ball across the lane to Kathleen for an uncontested layup. What-ever it is that started it, there was nothing Haverhill could do to stop it, and time-outs repeatedly called for by their frustrated coach only fueled Amherst's frenzy further.

Jen was amazed:

It was a struggle to get up to the tempo in the first couple of min-utes. We were playing even. But then as soon as we got in our rhythm, we stayed on that level. Coach always says basketball is a game of shifting momentum. It's like a car speeding up a hill and braking on the way down. You rev it up, you slow it down. But with us, right now,

253

we hit cruise control and it is well above the speed limit. Everyone on the court is playing as close to their best every moment. It is unconscious, but it's not like sinking. Look: There's Jamila with four steals in a row, and the whole team just looking as if we won't try to catch up with her, thank you, because we just know she'll get there first. And the passing, from Jamila to me, me whipping it across the key to Kathleen, and Kathleen making the bucket. Everyone is in the right spot. Everything is clicking.

Two plays during the first half sealed it for Jen.

They both involved Kathleen.

Jen looked at her teammates and realized that often she measured the Hurricanes' success by how well Kathleen played in the forward position. When she started off well, the team played well.

Jen was coming down the court at a fast break and knew Kathleen was on her right and without looking passed the ball backward. Usually passes like that get kicked out of bounds or missed because the receiver doesn't expect them to come, but Kathleen knew it was coming. She caught it, perfectly, and laid it in.

The other great moment that demonstrated to Jen Kathleen's evolution was when she stepped out, got the ball to the foul line, and without a moment's hesitation, not a flicker of a second thought, went up and shot.

Nothing but net.

That basket summed it up.

Right before the half, when all the starters were on the bench, they got to cheer for the subs, for Jan, for Jade, and for Sophie, who all got to the foul line and scored.

Even Kristin, never an inside power, made a layup from beneath the basket for which she felt entitled to indulge in that now-nearly-universal expression of the well-served gloat, a slash-ing pumping gesture with her right arm.

When Patri entered the game, ensuring that Amherst had sounded all its cymbals, she couldn't resist a quick skip across the floor. The crowd responded with a chant:

"Patri! Patri! Patri!"

The Hurricanes could not be stopped. They made basket after basket after basket, in, in, and in again.

The sportscasters were stunned.

The disparity between the performances of the two teams was not supposed to happen. The Hillies and the Hurricanes had been groomed, carefully, each at their own end of the state, to meet as equals. If anyone had been favored as Goliath, it was surely Haverhill.

On and on and on it went, this streak, this fabulous finish to a remarkable season: a 37–0 run.

No one could remember anything like it, at this level in the competition, at this point in the season, at a state championship.

The halftime score was 51–6. The effect was surreal.

An astonished Amherst could hardly even cheer. One Amherst fan shouted: "Where's Dr. Kevorkian?" Another made the very un-Amherst comment: "They should bring on the Haverhill boys for the second half."

Among the spectators was Kathleen's father, Donald Poe, who saw how her defense, along with that of Kristin and Gumby and Jonesbones, kept Haverhill's score so low.

When his son, Chris, was an infant, he had tried to teach him to say "ball" as his first word, until he was told that *b* is a hard sound for a baby. He'd expected a son to be an athlete, but when Kathleen came along, he had no such expectation. Yet whenever they went into the yard and she pitched a ball to him, it took only five minutes before his hand hurt. She threw a heavy ball.

To him, what was important was not that Amherst had this great lead, but that the spirit of girls' sports endured. Next year, it wouldn't have to be Amherst; it might be West Side in Springfield. Its junior varsity was undefeated. When he'd been a student at W. T. Woodson High School in Fairfax, Virginia, the girls were not allowed to use the boys' gym, which was fancy and varnished with the logo in the middle of the floor; the girls had a little back gym, without any bleachers. Now, after a game, whenever he saw the little kids asking his daughter for autographs, he was glad to see the girls, pleased that they had models. But he was just as pleased to see the boys asking; to him their respect for the girls' team was just as important.

For Jen, as she trooped with her team back to the locker room, the game was over at halftime.

The second half was just a technicality.

Coach Moyer and Trish Lea exchanged glances on the way into the locker room for the halftime talks.

Coach Moyer, Mr. Joke, Mr. Pun, Mr. Emcee, was speechless.

Everything went right.

All season he'd kept a piece of chalk in his pocket to throw up in the air at the wall when things went wrong or if he wished to make a strong statement.

This was probably the only coach trick he had not used all season.

What do you say to a group of kids who were playing beyond their best, as individuals and as a team?

He took the chalk, and with a smile, tossed it into the shower area.

Jamila and Jen also exchanged puzzled looks: *What do we do? The team is so pumped; what can you say?*

Jen thought fast.

Usually at halftime one of them would say, "If we're up by

ten, we have to play like we're down by ten. You can't let up because if you let up, you let the other team back in."

But that night she realized they couldn't say: "Let's pretend we're down by forty-five."

That wasn't what Jen believed her team needed to hear.

So Jen said, "Basically we have a comfortable lead now, and I don't think the question is whether we're going to win or not. We played an incredible first half, and we are right now where we should be. We've proven to everybody out here that we're good athletes and that we're a great team. Now let's go out and show the crowd that we're good sports and finish the game with class."

During the break, in the stands, Fran Deets, Kathleen's mother, turned to Bernadette Jones and asked, "Have you stopped being nervous yet?"

"I don't know," she laughed. "The roof could fall down."

John and Judy Wideman and all the other parents, groping their way to the concession stand for a soft drink, could not move more than two feet without being swamped by people filled with congratulations, more of the usual hugs and high fives.

Everyone tried to be seemly; too garish a display might be indelicate until the final moment of the contest had been played out.

When the final seconds were running down on the clock, all the starters were on the bench, and they grabbed each other's hands and they all sat on the edge of their seats and then when the clock ran out they raised their hands as if they were a single unit and they ran out onto the floor.

The final score was 74–36.

After they'd received the trophies and collapsed in one

huge hysterical teenage heap, they all stood up. First they sang "Happy Birthday" to Kristin Marvin, who turned eighteen that day. Then they extended their arms toward their parents, teachers, brothers, sisters, even to some of those 140 little girls whose parents allowed them a school night of unprecedented lateness, and in one final act as a team, these girls shouted, in the perfect unison that served them so well on the court, *"Thank you!"*

One among them made a move away from the group to where parents and fans were being blocked off by Centrum functionaries in their gray blazers with the C on the breast pockets. No one from the stands was allowed to walk on the floor; it hadn't occurred to the officials that someone from the floor might wish to join the stands. You could see her mouthing something: "Dad. Dad."

Taking advantage of the goodwilled confusion and her own flexibility, Jen Pariseau swung herself up over the barricades. She hesitated for a moment, as if to get her bearings, and then pushed forward, faster and faster, not frantic, but almost. Blinded in part by the crowd that kept blocking her path, she lunged upward until she reached the level at which her father stood, and finding him at last, she fell into his arms. And while many in the crowd of Amherst fans saw the tall man with his curly hair, with his eyes pressed shut, being hugged by the girl with the dark ponytail, only Tracy Osbahr, standing next to them, caught her stepdaughter's exact words, and so later when Bob Pariseau asked, "What did Jenny say? . . . Exactly?" as if he couldn't remember, his wife would tell him: "We did it, Daddy. We did it. I love you."

But for now, back in the locker room, Kristin Marvin sucked on orange slices and sloshed water on her face. She then stood on a back bench, raised her right fist, turned to her comrades, and shouted. "Holy shit! We're the fucking champions!" And then she lost it, not in the prim sense of dropping a needle on a carpet, but in a grand historic explosive way, heaving herself into the waiting arms of one teammate after another as they all sobbed and convulsed.

There was one injury. Someone's elbow had caught Emily Shore on the face during the game, and a tooth had penetrated her cheek, leaving a jagged hole.

Emily Jones's father, with his tall sloping frame and mild-mannered expression, stood in the corridor outside the locker room performing a quick consult.

"I'm going to butterfly-bandage it for the time being, but I think it needs a stitch or two. You can't put it off till the morning because after four or five hours the wound will start to close up."

"Where should we go?" asked Sally Shore, standing at her daughter's side.

"Probably Holyoke," said the doctor. In that way that hospitals and medical centers triage themselves, it was known that if you got stabbed or shot (or elbowed, if you're a basketball player), you'd go to Holyoke Hospital.

"If there's a scar, it won't be much of anything," he added.

"It doesn't bother me if there's a scar," said Emily, who looked as if she might actually welcome the badge in it.

Emily's mother sighed, "Well, at least it's for a good cause."

Inside the locker room, the Hurricanes were refusing to leave. Coach Moyer kept knocking on the door, trying to roust the stragglers. Finally, he announced he was coming in, and what greeted him was a roomful of girls who returned his level gaze with eyes that were rheumy and red as they sputtered, "Last . . . final . . . never again."

He looked at them as directly as he ever had in all those moments of coaching when they'd needed a solid unforgiving gaze, and he said: "You're wrong. This isn't the last. There will be more basketball." His tone was conversational, almost adult to adult.

"But . . . ," they started to say.

"I promise you. There will be lots more basketball."

Still they regarded him with disbelief. They couldn't decipher his real message, at least not at that moment. They couldn't fathom how the word basketball might have more than one meaning.

Over. The game was over. On the way home, they watched a videotape of the game and drank Martinelli's sparkling cider supplied by Jan Klenowski's mother. Coach Moyer was already envisioning a swank community banquet at the campus center at U Mass, something classy and memorable, not just lukewarm lasagna and chicken thingies but sliced roast beef, lukewarm lasagna, and chicken thingies.

Someone had already asked him, did he plan to retire Jamila's uniform? At Amherst she had ended her six years with 1,728 points, 569 rebounds, 511 assists, and 433 steals. It was impressive, but you didn't retire a uniform until after there had been a whole career of such achievement. Besides, there might be a few hundred points left in it; one of the younger players might wish to choose number eleven next fall, though he doubted anyone would take on that mantle lightly.

He wondered how long it would take Jen and Jamila to become captains at Dartmouth and Stanford.

He had already picked the leaders of next year's Hurricanes: the two Emilys, Jonesbones and Gumby. It was a title Gumby had been craving ever since the sixth grade.

As he settled back in his seat, outside it was still, of course, winter, but to him summer had arrived again, at last.

Kim began mentally composing a letter to her father: "Dear Dad, At long last a lot of hard work finally paid off."

Jen was stunned at how it had fallen into place: *We were so fluid, it was scary.* And then she too, like Kristin, began to sob.

From the seat in front of her, without turning around, someone thrust her hand back to Jen to hold: Jonesbones, goddess of kindness.

While they watched themselves, television viewers all over the state were witnessing recaps of the highlights and hearing the verdicts of professional commentators who claimed these girls had wandered into the wrong league: They shoulda been playing Calipari's men at U Mass; they coulda taught the Celtics a thing or two.

The girls would hear all that in days to come, but at this moment they were mostly thinking about the present—when truth itself had become a dream. The bus was going backward, retracing its earlier path, down the Pike back through Palmer, where the only sense of abundance is in the fast-food stores, then through Bondsville, with its gin mill and the sunken rusty metal playground with a metal fence, back through the center of Belchertown, a singularly flat stretch in a town with a singularly unfortunate name, and back in and out of Pelham—thanks to Jen, on the map at last.

Kathleen Poe wished that the whole team could sleep that night in the gym at the high school, the coziest, most homey, softest place she could now imagine, that they could all sink into its floor, become part of it forever. She kept trying out rhymes in her head, phrases popping into her head like sudden rebounds: *top* and *stop*, *pride* and *ride*, *forever* and *sever*, *heart*, *smart*, *true*, *you*.

> *Hoop Phi is of an intangible, untouchable breed,*
> *It satisfies the soul and a life-long need.*
> *We represented our school, represented our sex,*
> *Now maybe both will get some well-earned respect.*

No one really wanted the ride to end. The bare trees, the velvety night air, the cocoon of the bus itself.

At the town line there awaited another police escort, this time back into town. The cruiser was once again full of proud, slow ceremony. At the corner of Main and Triangle, the cruiser seemed to lurch right to take the shortcut back to the school, but then as if that were only a feint, it continued to move forward so that the girls would be brought through town the long way.

The bus, boisterous in its very bigness, moved past the red-bricked Dickinson homestead with its top-heavy trees, tall and thin with a crown of green: We're Somebody! Who are you? The college kids who could afford it were all in Florida for spring break, and so downtown was almost empty save for a couple of pizza eaters in the front window of Antonio's and a lone worker sweeping in the back shadows of Bart's Ice Cream. As the strobe lights from the police cruiser bounced off the storefronts, the bus wheezed past Saint Brigid's and the bagel place, turning right, then left. They gave their ritual cheer one last time:

"Give me an A . . ."

And then, finally, the bus pulled into the school parking lot a few minutes shy of midnight. All of a sudden one of the players shouted: "There are people there, waiting for us!" And, indeed, in the distance was a small crowd standing in the cold and in the dark, clapping.

When the bus came to a stop, Coach stood up. "I promise it won't be mushy. There's just one thing you should know. When you're the state champions, the season never ever ends. I love you. Great job. And now, I'd like everybody else on the bus to please wait so that the team can get off first."

How often in the past the Hurricanes had bounded off the bus in a joyous squealing clump! But on this night the pace of their leave-taking was different, almost regal. They rose from their seats, slowly, in silence. State champs! For the final time this season, with great care bordering on tenderness, the teammates gathered their stuff, their uniforms, their shoes, their socks, their game faces, and their courage. And then in a decision that was never actually articulated but seemed to have evolved as naturally as the parabola of a perfect three-pointer, the Hurricanes waited for Captain Jen Pariseau to lead the way, which she did, and one by one the rest of the women followed, with Captain Jamila Wideman the last of the Hurricanes to step off the bus into the swirling sea of well-wishers and winter coats.

Overhead the sky was as low-hanging and as opaque as it had been earlier in the evening, but it didn't need stars to make it shine.